Sophie Lasne is a history and geography instructor who has worked at the National Archives of France.

André Pascal Gaultier, a film editor, has written for television and theatre.

A DICTIONARY OF
Superstitions

Sophie Lasne
André Pascal Gaultier

Translated by Amy Reynolds

A SPECTRUM BOOK

Prentice-Hall, Inc.
Englewood Cliffs, New Jersey 07632

Library of Congress Cataloging in Publication Data

Lasne, Sophie
  Dictionary of superstitions.

  Translation of: Dictionnaire des superstitions.
  "A Spectrum Book"—T.p. verso.
  Includes index.
  1. Superstition—Dictionaries. I. Gaultier,
André Pascal. II. Title.
BF1775.L3713 1984   001.9'6   84-11717
ISBN 0–13–210881–X
ISBN 0–13–210873–9 (pbk.)

This book is available at a special discount when ordered in bulk quantities. Contact Prentice-Hall, Inc., General Publishing Division, Special Sales, Englewood Cliffs, N.J. 07632.

ISBN 0-13-2-0881-X

ISBN 0-13-210873-9 {PBK.}

Prentice-Hall International, Inc., *London*
Prentice-Hall of Australia Pty. Limited, *Sydney*
Prentice-Hall of Canada, Inc., *Toronto*
Prentice-Hall of India Private Limited, *New Delhi*
Prentice-Hall of Japan, Inc., *Tokyo*
Prentice-Hall of Southeast Asia Pte. Ltd., *Singapore*
Whitehall Books Limited, *Wellington, New Zealand*
Editora Prentice-Hall do Brasil Ltda., *Rio de Janeiro*

Contents

Intoduction

"In order to laugh at the occult—at all magical effects—one must believe that he or she possesses the explanation for this world and all that happens here. That is only encountered in men who cast a superficial glance at the world and do not even suspect that we have been plunged into a sea of enigmas and incomprehensibilities, for, in an immediate manner, we understand neither things nor ourselves." Arthur Schopenhauer.

At one time or another we all have laughed at strange beliefs and half-heartedly used the word "superstitious" to hide a lack of comprehension. We are, after all, aware that laughs or insults are spontaneous manifestations of fear or uneasiness. Looking at the world around us, we can find evidence of the superstitions scoffed at by rationalists, theologians and scientists. Such superstitions make their appearances in so-called primitive civilizations as well as in Western societies. (Perhaps they are the only common cultural ground that all societies have.)

To define a superstitious phenomenon is a difficult exercise, because we attach the term "superstition" to all thoughts or behaviors whose origin, logic, or even purpose we do not understand. Thus, magic and "irrational" beliefs define themselves in terms of a single truth believed in by an individual.

In addition, this individual carries an external judgment of a universe from which he or she has extracted an isolated practice from its context. (Couldn't Mass appear to be a ridiculous ceremony to someone who doesn't understand its logic and symbolism?) In his journal Paul

Leautaud pointed out what those individuals and the "primitives" have in common; on January 13, 1931, he wrote: "The funeral ceremonies for Marshal Joffre . . . this glorification, this apotheosis, this solemn transport of a dead body, this sort of deification of that which is no more, are, in essence, a throwback to old superstitions, very similar to the idolatries of uncivilized clans. There is absolutely nothing lofty about them. Napoleon's tomb, Lenin's body preserved in a glass coffin and exposed to the people's veneration, the lying-in-state of Marshal Joffre, the preservation of this man's sword or that man's hat—all these are extremely primitive mysticisms that survive."

Superstition must be placed in the domain of beliefs and customs in the same way it is affirmed and accepted in the domain of physical sciences. In effect, the primary territory of superstition proves to be magico-religious, a space in human thought where the criterion of truth and error remains indefinite and fluctuating. But for all that, religions are not conceived as superstitions; they constitute a coherent, controlled system explaining the world. Whereas religion defines itself as a belief and tries to establish itself, superstition affirms its own truth, but does not seek to justify itself: It is as good as its effectiveness. The analysis of a phenomenon can be incorrect, but the custom that concerns it can be totally effective—thus a farmer can be ignorant of the origin of lightning, but can interpret the attitude of the animals who foretell a storm. Illness can be misunderstood, but a superstitious person, convinced by well-founded custom, can cure through some magical practice. What is of special importance to this apprehensive way of the universe that is superstition is an internalization of contact established between man and nature and man and society. Thus, phenomena of religious superstition, very popular in the Middle Ages, could result from a tendency to ally oneself with forces that are abstract and make them familiar, everyday, and immediate. Some famous Christian "diversion," such as excessive worship of saints or holy relics, integrate divinity into the home—the supernatural spirit makes itself a friend and neighbor. Likewise, divination, knowledge of hidden things, present, past, and future, by the intermediary of a very old, true science is at the origin of numerous superstitious forms such as omens, vows, the meaning of sneezes, sighs, and so forth.

Defining what is or is not superstitious brings a belief or custom back to the level of the civilization of a society, for superstition is always situated at this level, if not below it. Although the so-called primitive religions don't concern us in any way, we can see that if all believe that a man's soul is absorbed by the mirror in front of him, it is logical to fear the breaking of this mirror.

A Westerner who maintains a belief despite any evidence to the contrary will be considered superstitious. But why does he or she insist on doing this? Such a mentality seems a combination of a "sacrilezation" of the ordinary and daily world on one hand and an anthropomorphic "humanization" of extraordinary, incomprehensible, or sacred phenomena on the other. The sacred world is organized into a human society peopled with inauspicious beings or tender friends. Thus, a person must conciliate some and maintain the good will of others. Through this mechanism of superstitious thought appears the profound reason for a person's existence and permanence, such as T. S. Knowlson described it: "The true origin of superstition is to be found in early man's effort to explain Nature and his own existence; in the desire to propitiate Fate and invite Fortune; in the wish to avoid evils he could not understand . . ."

Fear and the desire to master the universe are the two motives of man's superstition. The number of beliefs and customs concerning atmospheric phenomena, the great stages of life (birth and death in particular), health, and illness are explained by the control that societies attempt to bring to bear on themselves and the surrounding universe. In reality, "sacrilezation" and vulgarization are nothing but two facets of the same attitude.

Superstitions fall into two distinct groups: survivals and innovations. The former concerns set customs stripped of meaning, such as inactivity on Friday the 13th, as well as practices or customs that have new significance. The Christmas feast, formerly celebrating the winter solstice, became the feast of the Nativity, and exists today without our knowing why gifts should be offered to children on behalf of Father Christmas or Saint Nicholas. Traditional taboo days of ancient societies were relayed, under the pretext of work and leisure time organization, into long weekends or national holidays.

Modern civilization, especially urban society, gave birth to its new superstitious traditions and dropped many of the old traditions that had arisen from a more rural way of life. Undoubtedly, the extraordinary development of horoscopes in magazines and daily papers is a better example of the renewal of the credulous mentality than all sociological analysis. The vogue of fortunetellers who, like medieval magicians or African sorcerers, predict the future, the success of games of chance like off-track betting, lotto, and the lottery, is part of the same mental background.

Superstition is situated on two levels. On the first level an individual can adapt to a surviving ancient custom or belief, confer a totally personal meaning on it, and create a magical universe, particularly at essential moments in life. When something important is at risk, when the instant is prophetic or irreversable, he or she can make ancient gestures and re-create conjuratory words. A person can make absurd wagers and invent decisive possibilities and constraints—in brief, seek to know, if not master, the future.

On a second level, superstition wedges itself into a regional, cultural, familial, or communal knowledge that also often includes an original language and particular mythological references—in brief, a conception of

life. Superstition then comes under three general forms that can be uncovered in all countries and cultures:

1. It is a matter of presenting the future, the unknown monster,
   through the patient reading of natural or provoked omens. (A shooting star at a certain time of year announces a certain event, no
   matter what the desire of the person being informed. But a young
   girl, soon to be wed, questions destiny by some ritual invocation.)
2. On the other hand, specific rites that refer in general to a rather
   simple, common ground are performed in order to obtain a certain
   result. Whether this result is scientifically obtained or not is of little
   importance; what is important is man's faith in the value of the act or
   ritual words.
3. Finally, everyday acts are invested with a power that surpasses their
   practical or automatic, simple reality. Bound to a temporal and
   spatial system, the most benign act conceals a complex meaning that
   then needs to be deciphered: According to the rules that govern it,
   in effect it influences the destiny of whoever performs it. Thus,
   whoever gets up on the left foot will have a bad day; whoever faces
   night without the necessary talismans is exposed to punishment by
   devils. Good and bad luck most often flow from these seemingly
   innocent initiatives.

Therefore, whether superstition is an omen, rite, or prejudice, it
expresses itself in a tentative reading and deciphering of both the human
organism's world and established relations between the levels of universal
life: celestial, terrestrial, human, and underground.

This basic orientation determines the cohesion of the language of
superstition that is set up either in a maxim ("to obtain this, it is necessary
to do that"), a probability ("if you do this, or if this happens, that will
happen"), or in evidence ("if this occurs, it is a sign of . . ."). To neglect
these structures and formulations would without a doubt be to alter the
meaning of these beliefs. The hypothetical "if" introduces a condition (the
rite or omen), an eventuality, or a wish; thus, it belongs to the domain of
desire and the future, to the domain of the possible, of magic. The "it is
necessary" formula lays down a necessity linked to a loyal adhesion to
superstition: Rites and customs revealed by tradition cannot be believed
in halfway or in word only. On the other hand, "scientific" character is
affirmed here, extremely precise ancestral magic whose effectiveness
rested on the strict application of rules that were unalterable in appearance. Popular sayings take up the same grammatical construction. We
have taken into account those that, in one way or another, contain or
illustrate a superstitious belief. We have skimmed the surfaces of witchcraft as an historic phenomenon, and astrology, cartomancy, and alchemy

as "science" when they can explain certain superstitious happenings. But the beliefs and practices sprung from these domains, liberated in a way from the iron collars of scholarly knowledge, will be recorded and examined.

In order to emphasize the themes of the superstitious mentality and to underline its many ideas and central interests, we have grouped beliefs and practices in thematic chapters preceded by brief synoptic introductions. The opening chapter discusses the most common of these thousands of recipes, thoughts, and affirmations. Thus the reader will easily find the general "logic" masked under a complex or lightly absurd formula. Without pretending to reveal the origin of superstitions (for the most part, they come to us from the obscure night of time past or minor events), we have attempted to show by cutting through the maze of prejudices and flowery formulas, the astonishingly structured frame of a world too often scorned.

Alchemical allegory by Basile Valentin. Engraving from the 18th c. (Bibl. de l'Anc. Faculté de Médecine de Paris).

The Keys
of Superstitions

Throughout centuries and civilizations, permanent themes have dominated the variety of languages and beliefs; they form a common, immutable foundation, in a way the KEYS of superstitions. The superstitious universe is magical, sexed, oriented in time and space, and finally, endowed with a rather simple symbolism where forms, colors, and numbers correspond.

Magical thought rests on a belief in souls and spirits. A soul, distinct from an individual, can separate itself from the body in certain circumstances such as death or sleep and penetrate other human beings, animals, or objects. Numerous superstitions refer explicitly to the Devil and to all kinds of demons. The Devil is but a "Christianized" variant of ancient evil spirits. Spells and their conjuration, the importance accorded to vows, wishes, and predictions, whether they concern what the weather will be like or the future of an individual, belief in particular properties of certain places, and the role of the dream in superstitions are all reminiscences of this fundamental certainty.

The universe presented to us by superstitions is profoundly sexed. All cosmogonies have a feminine element and a masculine element that contend with and complete each other. In the West, the male element is most often linked with the positive, the female element being impure and evil. Grand Albert in his "Admirable Secrets" teaches us that "woman by nature is cold and humid; and that man, on the contrary, is warm and dry." Medieval magic followed the biblical tradition of the corrupting woman allied with the serpent. There are many references to sterility in superstitions—sterility-fertility is in reality only one of the innumerable forms that the battle between Pure and Impure or Good and Evil can take.

Time and space are not neutral: They are *oriented*. Left and right continue the battle, the latter beneficent, the former hostile.

The cardinal points themselves have a meaning: East, West, South and North all put their powers in opposition. Before being divided into months, days, hours, and years, Time is above all a succession of lucky and unlucky periods. Soothsayers and diviners who defined the succession of lucky and unlucky days for the community were succeeded by little signs and horoscopes that again defined the character of each epoch. Friday the 13th and certain other specific dates still have this aspect today.

Engraving extracted from the "Musée Hermétic," 1625 (Bibl. Nat.)

Finally, a constant symbolism governs the domain of superstitions. With varying or even opposing significance, some symbols are found throughout all ages and civilization: the perfect forms, circle, triangle, square, the world divided into four elements, numbers, colors, horns, the cross . . .

Before studying the various points we have just outlined, let us salute the psychoanalyst Jung, who, with the notion of an archetype, enabled us to better approach these constants of the human mind.

Circle

Image of completeness and perfection, it is, without a doubt, of all the symbolic shapes, the most important. When concentric, circles symbolize the universe; a full moon and the sun, both round, are the two fundamental poles around which various cosmogonies were built. Hell itself is made up of concentric circles that encircle that which is absolute Evil.

The wheel is the image of time, infinity, and eternal recommencement. Within the zodiac circle is inscribed a man's destiny. Radiating, it incarnates chance: a Pythagoras' wheel (or the wheel of fortune) pursues its work today in carnivals as much as in casinos.

The magic circle drawn by sorcerers marks the bounds of an impassable, sacred space. Whoever is on the inside must not come out without taking great risks; whoever is on the outside cannot cross the boundries of this fundamental taboo. Going around a sacred space or object is one of the most popular practices for honoring it—and for protecting yourself from it. Moslems must, at least once in their life, walk around the Kaaba which, let us not forget, is a cube inscribed in a circle. You must go around a Saint John fire three times and cross yourself if you want to be protected from headaches and kidney ailments for one year. Turning around three times exorcises evil spells.

People gathered in a circle around a given spot form the bounds of a sacred space: a circle preceded temples. One of the early forms of the arts and of theater can be seen here. A crowd in a circle surrounded priests, dancers, and even criminals about to be executed. In the "Bible" man danced around the Ark; musicians arrange themselves in a circle to play. Children who dance in a circle around a tree are only repeating exactly the old German rite of adoration.

"Religious Dance of the Negroes," 19th c. (Bibl. Nat.)

Perfect and infinite, the circle symbolizes power and protection: A crown was the attribute of emperors and kings, a tiara that of popes. All jewels, bracelets, and rings indicate possession. A symbol of authority in Egypt as much as in Christian countries, a ring binds he who wears it to the world of gods or forces of the occult. Gyges' ring, worn on the middle finger of the right hand, makes whoever turns the stone toward the interior of the palm invisible. Jade rings have great curative powers in the Orient.

In the form of a wedding band, a ring has symbolized an engagement or a marriage since the most distant antiquity. The superstition that a husband who, in putting the ring on his wife's finger, is not able to get it past the second joint, will be dominated by his wife, shows that a ring continues to symbolize authority yet today. A broken or lost wedding band foretells the death of the husband or wife or at least the approaching breakup of the marriage. A ring is worn on the ring finger because, according to ancient belief, a vein runs directly from this finger to the heart.

Women often refuse to admit their age, but a method exists for learning the truth! Tie a hair from the woman to a gold ring and suspend it over a crystal glass. The ring will touch the edge of the glass as many times as there are years in the woman's life.

A wedding band is endowed with its own power of divination: Suspended by a hair of its owner, it constitutes the best of pendulums.

In Christianity, the consecrated wafer, round and white, took the place of bread for the representation of Christ's body. A Twelfth Night cake remains as one of the survivors of this protected, sacred bread.

Two concentric circles of different colors that form an *ocellus*, found on certain butterflies' wings and peacock feathers, have lost their positive value as a circle to a more ambivalent one; that of the eye, most often, the evil eye.

Colors

> *White paper reproaches ink with the blackness that soils it.*
> Leonardo de Vinci, Notes

Only the color green is itself an object of supersitition: Green is forbidden in theaters! Many actors, even in their private lives, refuse to wear green or to possess the slightest object of this color.

The other colors change value and power according to the objects that they cover. The combination of black and white remains the most important, incarnating the fundamental opposition between Evil and Good. In everyday language, that which is criminal is attributed with dark, wicked intentions, whereas anything innocent is presented in the form of a white dove. The law itself protects seagulls and seamews, but authorizes the hunting of their relatives, ravens and crows.

WHITE

Being absent of color or stain, white is first of all the sign of purity and virginity. Lilies and other white flowers find themselves linked to baptisms and weddings. White is also exempt from all maleficent attacks due to sin; it is the dominant holy color, that of the Druids, popes, and kings. From birth to death, it is linked to the great stages of life.

To this white, considered as an absence of stain, is added the symbolism of the "color" white, that presents itself in two opposing aspects:

"Evocation of the Spirits," 19th c. (Bibl. Nat.)

- The white of paleness and the moon, linked with death, is that of winding-cloths and ghosts. White Ladies and phantoms are livid and "incarnate," if this word can be used—evil forces from beyond. A vampire is pale until he drinks blood and again finds the red color of life.
- The bright white of light and of the sun is that of God and Apollo's horses. Being solar, it is in opposition to the preceding and rejoins the white of innocence and purity. It is in a way the radiating white of the Holy Ghost that appears in the form of a dove.

BLACK

The negative of white, it is perhaps regarded as an absence of color, but in the sense of extinction or as the specific color that is then that of night, evil, and the unknown. Being indifferent, it is the mark not only of humility, but also the mark of respectability and respect—it is the dress of priests and magistrates.

Often linked to red, black is the distinctive character of the demonic and of death. In a prophetic or divinatory animal species, the black animal is chosen over the others for sacrifices—a black rooster or cat incarnate the absolute of their species.

Black can, however, be associated with fertility: Many black virgins in churches are still the object of worship and greatly followed pilgrimages.

BLUE

Color of the sky and the sea, blue is the image of depth and of a certain immaterial purity. It even symbolizes the inaccessible in the form of the Blue Bird of Happiness. More human than bright white, in general it is positive and in opposition to evil forces. In the Orient, it is very beneficent and effectively protects against the evil eye. It is, however, linked to occult forces; for Orientals blue eyes are a mark of magical powers. Precious stones of this color draw their power from this double postulate.

Christianity made blue the color of the Virgin Mary. Blue protects a child from illness in infancy.

YELLOW

Very ambivalent, yellow has very little symbolic value in itself. It draws its value from the stronger symbols with which it is linked. In its golden form, it is linked to the sun and wealth; pale, it is allied with illness. Yellow is the color of fear, the color that the Nazis chose for the star the Jews had to wear.

RED

Red is in a way the very image of color. Being greatly varied, its symbolic value is complex. Linked to blood and fire, red incarnates life and passion. The color of fire, it is linked to the demonic and Hell. Somber, in the form of purple, it envelops the terrestial majesty reserved for monarchs and cardinals. When bright, it is a negative as well as positive image of war. Above all, linked to blood, it is ambivalent, both the sacred blood of life and the impure blood of menstruation.

Red is very positive in the Far East, particularly in Japan.

GREEN

"I sought to express the terrible human passions with red and green."

Vincent Van Gogh.

Halfway between hot and cold, a complementary color of yellow and blue, green is the color of the earth. It is the color of vegetation in spring and in this way has symbolized the hope and immortality of things beyond the cycle of the seasons—the eternal return. It has been chosen as the color of emblems by herbalists, apothicaries, and today pharmacists. Green is very positive in Islam.

In the West, particularly in the Middle Ages, it was the color of the Devil and criminals. Green light was a sort of negative fire for alchemists. For sorcerers, it was propitious in evoking forces of the night. In Scotland, rifle bullets were said to prefer going through the green squares of tartans. It was undoubtedly from this negative aspect that the total prohibition of green from theater stages was born.

BLONDS, BRUNETTES, AND REDHEADS

Oriental, Mediterranean, and even Celtic people attributed blonds, especially if they had blue eyes, with divinitory powers or even the evil eye. Brunettes were either neutral or propicious. In Scotland, tradition has it that the first person to cross the threshold of a house should be either a brunette man or boy with a piece of charcoal in his hand. Redheads, whose hair evokes the red of Hell, are demonic and malevolent. In certain Mediterranean regions, you are supposed to turn aside or at least spit on the ground when you encounter a redhead.

Cross

Two heterogenous origins preside over the symbolism of the cross. First there is the cross as a form, linked to the circle, square, and triangle, then there is the Christianized cross in the form of a crucifix, which adopted many aspects of ancient tree worship.

A cross, as a form, functions as a link—it joins the four cardinal points. Like a square it is linked with the number 4. Two lines that cross create an intersection where forces concentrate. A crossroads where two paths meet is the preferred place of spirits with evil intentions (for this reason crucifixes, that should keep evil spirits away, are found there).

A crucifix as an essential symbol came rather late in Christianity. It enabled a religion to adapt, in its own way, numerous pagan rites that refused to die—a bell and a cross were substituted for the poles, erect stakes, and raised stones that continued to be objects of devotion. Originally, the condemned were crucified on trees: The tree and cross found themselves linked by a common symbolism. Touching wood is to touch the god tree, the source of life, but also the sacred wood upon which

*Illustration of Philippoteaus for a Breton Count, 19th c.
(Bibl. Nat.)*

Christ was executed. Worship of a crucifix replaced tree worship, particularly with the Germans. It also took over certain supersititions. A cross became the tree of life whose roots touched the underworld, whose summit reached the sky, and whose two boughs encircled the world.

Among the forms of the cross that had a great symbolic value, let us cite the Celtic cross that links together a circle and a cross and thus represents the universality of the world and the swastika, found in the Indies as well as on Druidical monuments. It was a dynamic cross and an emblem of life. When inversed, it became the swastika, or dead cross, chosen by the Nazis. The sign of the cross, made with the hand, brings happiness and enables evil spells to be exorcized. Thus you make a sign over and bless newborn children, cattle, houses, boats, and so forth in order to protect them. The sign of the cross remains the best tool of exorcists. It permits vampires, sorcerers, and demons to be recognized and chased away. Crossed fingers, the ring finger and little finger, also ward off the evil eye (let us note that in England, these same crossed fingers make lying permissible). A cross, like the Bible, remains the best guarantee of an oath. "Wooden cross, iron cross, if I lie, I'll go to Hell" is still in common use. In England also, when you make a vow or want a conjuration to succeed, you must cross both your arms and legs.

Objects *intentionally* placed in a cross also have a great exorcizing force. In the Roussillon region of France, two bouquets of flowers placed in a cross at the doors and windows of a house on the morning of Saint John prohibit access by evil fairies. Straw crosses placed over bee hives increase their production.

All crosses formed unintentionally bring misfortune. Beware of crossed forks and knives! You must not step on a cross formed by two sticks of straw. If a sick person's bed is perpendicular to ceiling beams it will prevent his recovery. Four friends who meet or separate must absolutely avoid crossing each other's arms.

People who squint have often been considered evil because their eyes appear to be crossed. Encountering such a person leads to no good. Elsewhere, "crossing" a man who squints is said to be a good omen, a woman who squints, unlucky.

Two straws set in a cross are reputed to make the blood from a wound stop flowing. If a sick person wants to get well, he must drink a glass of water "in a cross" (drink successively from the four "corners" of the glass).

In Germany, in the case of exorcism, the heart of a bewitched animal is stuck with pins placed in a cross. The heart of the person who cast the spell is stuck in the same way and thus, he is made to die.

God rewarded the donkey that warmed the baby Jesus in the manger by drawing a cross on its back (also it is the only animal in which the Devil cannot incarnate himself).

Divination

Divination is the art of predicting the future. Extremely important in antiquity, it decided the lucky and unlucky days and determined one's social and private lives. Gwen Le Scouezec, in her *Encyclopedie de la Divination* enumerates nearly 250 forms of divination. Diviners studied bird intestines, particularly the liver, but all animals, plants, the sky, and various objects could be tools of divination. Astrology, palmistry, cartomancy, and geomancy (divination using points drawn on the ground) were the most elaborate forms: We will not deal with them in this book since they form complex and coherent entities, removed from what we believe to be the spirit of superstition.

But it is possible to try to understand the role of certain animals like hoopoes or cuckoos or of certain objects like mirrors or crystal balls without calling on their role in ancient means of divination. A young virgin girl or a child were the best mediums. In France today, it is still the innocent child in the family who is asked to divide up the Twelfth Night Cake. Before delivering oracles, diviners and chamans sometimes took hallucinogenic plants that prepared them for their functions. All plants "that assist in learning the future" belong to this category. Finally, let us cite oneiromancy or divination by dreams, which interpreted dreams as omens of coming events.

Dreams and Nightmares

Sleep would be like death if it didn't lead us to a wonderland, the world of dreams—the other side of a mirror. The images that a soul brings back from the world of dreams (North American Indians specify that it leaves and re-enters through the nose of the sleeper) have always intrigued man. From the dreams of the ancients to present-day psychoanalysis, oneiromancy has always fascinated humans. Codification, however, remains dangerous—each dreamer combines and arranges symbolic images that often only draw their value from inextricable entanglements. Many people today recognize the existence of prophetic or forboding dreams.

In general, it is believed that it is best to forget dreams.

Like a mirror, dreams reverse the value of things, but when you have the same dream three nights in a row, that dream will be fulfilled.

Nightmares come directly from Satan. It is best to protect yourself from them

- by folding your hands on your chest,
- by placing a rock crystal under your pillow,
- by hanging a diamond or other talisman on your left arm,
- by putting a purslain branch over the bed and a knife or other metal object at the foot of the bed,
- by placing two sticks of straw cut on the night of Saint John, on each of the four corners of the bed,
- by pinning your socks to the foot of the bed, as they do in the British Isles,
- or by previously having hammered some coffin nails into the bedroom door.

(All these precautions will be ineffective for the person that stayed in bed during midnight Mass.)

The Four Elements

First let us note that for the Chinese there are five elements instead of four: water, fire, wood, metal, and earth. We will, however, go by the Western tradition of four elements: air, earth, water, and fire.

AIR

This humid, warm element is linked to the masculine sex. Generally it is associated with the zodiac signs of Gemini, Libra, and Aquarius. This subtle, purifying element is found in superstitions only in the form of ether that rises from the evaporation of perfumes. It is linked to meteorology in the form of wind or atmosphere.

EARTH

Feminine, dry and cold, earth is associated with the signs of Taurus, Virgo, and Capricorn. Often qualified as maternal, the earth is linked to the source of fertility and the life cycle—a plant dies and returns to the earth, but its seeds and roots give birth to other plants. The act of burying bodies is linked to this principle of immortality and resurrection.

When the foundation of a building was being laid in ancient times, a human or animal victim was buried in it as an offering to the gods. Still today, objects such as papers or coins are often included in the laying of the cornerstone of a new building.

In the Far East, earthquakes were considered to be the jumping of a dragon claiming sacrifices.

The earth of certain privileged places, such as the Holy Land, was protected from sorcery and could even cure illnesses. The earth of Sardinia was reputed to heal snake bites, because Sardinia, like Ireland (and islands in general), does not harbor these animals.

Earth as a material is linked more to magical practices than to superstitious ones. Burying an object, most often by the light of a full moon, is done by anyone who wants to cast or exorcize a spell. Burying a jar containing twelve crayfish in river water is said to protect crops from late frosts. Another frequent example illustrating the relationship between the nourishing earth and life is the planting of a tree when a child is born—the growth of the tree and the child should be parallel.

WATER

Feminine, cold and humid, it is associated with the signs of Cancer, Scorpio, and Pisces. Of divine origin, it is the strength of life, linked to fertility, both purifying and regenerating. By this it is linked to the earth, which is also feminine, and in opposition to devastating fire. The Devil, like cats and fire, does not like water. He sees it as an enemy that purifies and washes away impurities and illnesses (thermal waters). Corpses are cleansed to keep away evil spirits (in some rites this is substituted for by washing the feet). A rather generalized superstition says that water must

11

not be thrown outside after nightfall—this divine substance must not be mixed with the world of shadows. It is also said that two people should never wash in the same water, because the second person risks acquiring the impurities abandoned by the first person. In ancient Greece it was even believed that a man should never bathe with water used by a woman—he ran the risk of losing his virility.

Let us note that a distinction must be made between *rainwater*, linked to the sky and air, *spring water*, linked to the fertile earth, source of life, and seawater, considered sterile.

Water has always been considered divine, from sacred fountains, still found today in Ireland and the Brittany area of France, to sacred rivers such as the Ganges where immersion rites are practiced. Everyone knows the Trevi Fountain in Rome where custom has it that if you want to return to the Eternal City again, you must turn your back to the fountain and toss a coin over your left shoulder. Water still has its power as a tool of divination: in Brittany, a child's shirt is thrown into water in order to know his or her fate. If the shirt floats, the child will survive; if it sinks, he or she will die. Magical, hidden beneath the earth, water does however reveal its presence to sorcerers who use a hazelwood rod.

The myth of Narcissus, who disdained the nymphs' love to devote himself to the worship of his own image, also brings to light the relationship between water and a mirror, another divinitory object. Hydromancy and catoptromancy intermingle when the surface of water contained in a glass is used as a support.

Water, divine by nature, can become sacred after certain rites. Druids made *lustral water* by extinguishing a flaming coal from a sacrificial fire in spring water. The *holy water* of the Christians, consecrated during certain ceremonies, has the power to chase away evil forces and keep devils and sorcerers away. Holy water from the Pentecost has the power to keep storms away.

Finally, let us cite two rather unusual superstitions: the first comes directly from the marriage of Cana. In Provence, water kept in jars is said to change into wine at midnight on Christmas Day. Finally, in England, it is said that a girl who splashes water on her clothes while bathing will marry a drunkard.

FIRE

Masculine, hot and dry, it corresponds to the signs of Aries, Leo, and Sagittarius. Ambivalent, fire is both the sun that warms and gives life and the lightning bolt that destroys.

Fire is an element of hell and lust. Lucifer and his acolytes prosper in the middle of flames. Fires are of his labor. Holy water and the sign of the cross can combat them, unless you prefer to put them out by throwing on the flames an egg laid on Good Friday or a black cat. This diabolic origin is proven by the fact that fire gives off no light in sunlight. In Scotland, children are not allowed to play with a fire before going to bed because they will wet their beds.

Although at times it is destructive and diabolic, fire can, however, be just as positive as water on earth. Cremation is a form of rebirth—it allows the passage from the material and incarnated being to immaterial ether. It forms a connection with the world of gods. The smoke of burnt offerings, incense, or pyres is pleasing to their noses. Also, torches used at wakes and burials are substitutes for cremation.

Like its enemy water, fire is purifying. The Druids, who worshipped fire, made their herds pass between fires at Fire Festivals to purify

"Hell" (detail), Memling's workshop, 15th c.
(Strasbourg, Musée des Beaux-Arts)

them. Saint John Fires are a Christian form of these ceremonies. These fires have the ability to purify and sanctify rosaries, and it brings good luck to jump over the flames. This last custom comes from an ancient ordeal that held that only the innocent could cross the fire without being burned. The guilty and sorcerers, black cats included, perished there. The Celts celebrated equinoxes and solstices by making immense fires. Saint John's feast day corresponds exactly to the summer solstice. The first day of the year was marked by the feast of the New Fire—no particle or spark could come out of a house that day or else its inhabitants would have to face terrible catastrophes during the new year.

All that is necessary to keep storms away and chase off evil spirits is to throw salt in the fireplace.

Purifying and even sacred, fire symbolized God in the form of the Holy Ghost. The tongues of flame that visited the apostles on the day of the Pentecost represented both God and knowledge. Jupiter, like Yahweh, was master of fire and did not hesitate to use it in the form of lightning bolts to punish man.

From the complexity of this element comes the necessity to respect it; it is particularly inadvisable to spit on it. Most superstitions dealing with fire were born of ancient divinations that found signs of destiny in its flames as well as in its embers and smoke. A' true language of fire even exists: sparks announce new kin, falling soot, important news; when a fire sizzles there is going to be a heated discussion or a storm; when it revives

"The Sabbath," by Claude Gillot, 17th c. (Bouvet coll.)

itself or gets lively for no apparent reason, it foretells a visit; tall flames and flaring are a sign that a loved one far away is thinking of you. A fire that refuses to catch on Christmas morning presages a bad year; if, on the contrary, it catches on its own and immediately begins to crackle, it foretells an excellent year.

Fertility–Sterility

For primitive peoples, often farmers or breeders, (and later on for Christianity that always encouraged procreation), the sterility of the earth, cattle, or man is absolute evil. There are numerous conjurations, rites, and superstitions that combat sterility. The directions for tying and untying a codpiece convey this primitive, quasi-archetypical illusion of castration. Freud was the first to demonstrate its importance. Also the general fear of menstruation, considered a mark of the demon and impurity, leads to this paradox that a menstruating or even pregnant woman (fertile) makes all she approaches, touches, or looks at, sterile. All these superstitions go back to a time before birth control was commonly accepted or at least tolerated. Superstitions concerning virility and virginity remain much more long-lived.

Left–Right

Throughout the ages everywhere in the world, except in China and Japan, the left or sinister has been linked to the idea of evil, impurity, and bad luck. God places the righteous on his right and the damned on his left. Adam, according to certain biblical traditions, was originally hermaphroditic—his left side was female and his right side was male. The left was linked to the moon, the North, and lying; the right was linked to the sun, the South, and fidelity. Still today, a person is asked to take an oath by raising his right hand, the fighting hand, the one that brandishes a sword. Some have looked for the origin of this phenomenon in the apparent movement of the sun; this is hardly likely since in the southern hemisphere the symbolism should be reversed. The rationalistic explanation comes from the fact that right-handed people are much more numerous than left-handed people and therefore constitute the norm or what is normal. In the Far East, where people are less Manichean, the left sometimes even predominates over the right. The right, feminine, is above all linked to the earth; the left, masculine, is linked to the sky, wisdom, and faith.

In all omens coming from ancient divinations, the left is unlucky

"The Tree of Good and Evil," French school, 16th c. (Musée de Blois)

without exception; it only has a "positive" role in certain conjurations, but we will not go into the domain of magic.

Lucky–Unlucky

That is what this book is all about. A superstitious mind believes that certain objects, places, animals, or deeds are lucky (good omens or charms) and that others are unlucky (bad omens or signs of misfortune). In French, the words "faste" (lucky) and "nefaste" (unlucky) come from the

"Witches' Dance," Polish engraving from the beginning of the century.

Latin "fas," meaning divine will or destiny. Superstitious people believe in determinism and predestination: Each man has his destiny, his star, but certain facts allow this destiny to be foreseen or even deviated from. This is where the contradiction lies. Divination and omens allowed a previously fixed future to be known and the function of soothsayers was to reveal which days were favorable for action. Temptation was great to go against this destiny; that was the domain of magic and religions. Religions have always run up against this problem of free will versus predestination. In their own way, superstitions have resolved this problem by simply accepting this contradiction: Omens of destiny can themselves be conjured up or exorcized.

Numbers and Figures

> *The thirteenth comes back . . . It is still the first.*
> *Gérard de Nerval*

In antiquity, linked to music, architecture, and knowledge, numbers were the key to harmony and wisdom. Although abstract, numbers were endowed with an unknown soul and strength—Pythagoreans even equalled them to God. Counting had a magical value. The fourth book of the Pentateuch, or Book of Numbers, is a long census. Counting brings misfortune: Still today, you should not say the number of your children, animals, or even age. Counting your sheep would be doing the work of a wolf. This belief is found in Islam as well as in Christianized Europe.

Numbers and figures are linked to secrets; people even speak of a "code number." Arithmomancy, practiced by Jews, Greeks, and Arabs, was one of the most esteemed forms of divination; in Rome it had taken on such importance that Vitellius had a death penalty decreed for all mathematicians.

The superstition "Never two without three!" became a proverb through evidence. It doesn't apply to fortunate events and signifies that one misfortune never happens at a time. It condenses all beliefs that deal with a series of events. This principle of seriality, that gamblers improperly call the "law of big numbers," has been studied by individuals as diverse as Camille, Flammarion, Jung, Kammerer and Arthur Koestler ("Chance and Infinity"). Here we leave the realm of superstition to enter that of science and philosophy. Beyond chance, the universe reaches toward a quasi-platonic unity that transcends the world of causality. So this famous "never two without three" is one of the crossroads where science and superstition can meet.

All figures and numbers have a symbolic value. Before studying a few of them in particular, let us cite this well-known belief: "Odd numbers please the gods." In fact, even numbers, which are perfect, are reserved for the gods; man, through humility, must be content with the odd numbers—3, 7, and 13 are well known to gamblers. Bretons say there are 365 islands in the Morbihan Gulf and an Arab storyteller doesn't stop talking for a thousand and one nights. If a Kabyle who has killed a man wants to avoid vengence, he must jump on his victim's tomb seven times, three days in a row. Three and seven appear over and over in treatises on magic. They are both odd numbers and primary numbers (13 and 17 are also often used).

ONE

The symbolism of the abstract sign "1," the number of God or of a prince, fades when compared to the symbolism of "first"—January 1st is the day of wishes, and it is the first person you meet or who crosses the threshold who determines the character of the coming year. Likewise, a wish can be made when a cuckoo is heard for the first time in the year or when the first fruit of a given kind is bitten into.

TWO

The number "two" is masked by the idea of a couple, both a mark of balance (the astrological sign of Libra, the scales) and of conflict (God vs. Evil). Having taken the form of Manicheism in the West, this fundamental dualism is more subtle in the Orient in the form of Yin and Yang.

Twins incarnate this idea of doubling. They have always been found both fascinating and disquieting. Finding a twinned fruit is in general a good omen unless it foretells the birth of twins, but an egg with two yolks is a death omen. There is still a long-lived French tradition of the "philippine": Two persons, after having shared twinned almonds or hazlenuts, agreed that when they met again, whoever said "Good day, Philippine!" would receive a gift from the other. The word "philippine" supposedly comes from a deformation of the German "vielliebchen," the loved one.

THREE

Odd, linked to the triangle and a primary number, the figure "3" is fundamental in magic. For Christianity, it is the Holy Ghost; for Celts, it is the figure for the universe. As a general rule, it represents the family— father, mother, and child. It also represents rivalry and conflict to be overcome. Some have even symbolized dialectics by the formula

$1 + 1 = 3$. The number three is essentially positive. Spitting or spinning around three times exorcizes evil spells. Remedies do not work effectively unless they have been taken three times. Finally, it was from a three-legged stand that Pythia delivered her oracles.

To avoid attacks by demons at night, besides having a lighted lantern, you should go out in threesomes. In casinos in Great Britain, it is a good idea to walk around the table three times before beginning to play. In the theater, three light bulbs are never turned on at the same time in an actor's dressing room.

It is well known that three cigarettes must never be lit with the same match; whoever holds the last cigarette (or, for others, whoever is the youngest) will die within the year. This belief dates from the Boer

Pythagoras and Boèce calculating, according to "Margarita Philosophica." Engraving from the 15th c.

Wars: at night, when the enemy saw the first light he raised his rifle, at the second light he aimed, and he fired when he saw the third. As is often the case, this explanation is itself part of a legend and conceals a more ancient origin linked to the very magic of the number three. Traditionally, for the orthodox, only a priest has the right to light three candles.

FOUR

The four cardinal points, a cross, a square . . ., "four" is a number of completeness, well liked by mystics and initiates. A four leaf clover refers more to a cross than to the number itself.

In Japan, the word for four signifies both the number and death. Uttering it is avoided.

FIVE

Five fingers, five senses, a pentagon, a five-pointed star, a "quintessence"—five is a sign of union, the "nuptial" for Pythagoras. It is situated in the center of the decimal base. Lucky in general, it is even the sacred number of the Mayans. For Moslems an outstretched hand with fingers spread keeps evil away. However, the Greeks avoided saying the word "five."

SIX

The six-pointed star called the "Star of David" is formed from two inverted triangles (see Triangle). Let us note that the most complex symbolic shape, a pentagram, a five-pointed star, is divided into six elements. Both odd and even, six is made of three couples or two triangles. God created the world in six days and rested on the seventh. The "magic" number seven exists only as a function of the completeness of its predecessor six (likewise, the magic of thirteen comes from twelve).

SEVEN

God created the world in seven days, there are seven mortal sins, seven planets for the ancients, and seven colors in a rainbow. This number is an expression of a perfect cycle and is universally sacred. It is also cosmic and of great importance in superstitions.

It is the very duration of the human cycle: Every seven years man is entirely regenerated. No good marriage goes without crisis and quarrels every seven years (others who are more optimistic say every nine years). In Doctor Faust's homeland it was known that a pact signed with the Devil lasted seven years. Whoever breaks a mirror will be subject to evil influences for seven years.

In Portugal a woman who wears seven petticoats at one time is assured of happiness. In the Brittany section of France,, in order to avoid death by drowning or to find a husband from the Middle East, it is necessary to let seven waves pass over your head when swimming. In Morocco, to protect herself from sterility, a woman must leave her belt wrapped around a tree seven times for seven days.

The seventh son in a family will always be a protegé of the gods. For the Scottish, the seventh son of a seventh son will have the gift of second sight.

In ancient Greece it was necessary to roll your tongue over seven times before speaking, undoubtedly because seven was the number associated with sages.

NINE

Nine evokes the idea of a cycle and of beginning anew. It is also a sign of fertility: Human gestation lasts nine months. In addition, being odd and a square of the fundamental number three, nine has certain magical characteristics: Multiplied by another number, the sum of the numbers composing the product always equals nine; this is called the proof by nine. In sacred or esoteric texts, its compounds, 999 or 999,999, represent that which is infinitely great. In China, nine is a sacred sign.

For the superstitious, nine often has the same conjuratory power as the number seven. If you want to get married within the year, you must jump over a Saint John fire nine times or else jump over nine different fires. Nine grains of salt exorcize an evil spell. Finally, tradition has it that a drowned person comes back to the surface of the water after nine days.

TEN

The base of the metric system and adored by Pythagorians, ten is the sum of the first four numbers ($10 = 1 + 2 + 3 + 4$), and an accumulation of all their symbolism. Presented in the form of a triangle,

```
      *
     * *
    * * *
   * * * *
```

it is represented on numerous talismans.

TWELVE

The twelve signs of the zodiac, the twelve months in a year, the two times twelve hours that make up a day, the twelve tribes of Israel—twelve is also a number of completeness. Let us note that for mathematicians twelve, divisible by two, three, four, and six, would have been a much better base for calculation than the decimal system, since ten is only divisible by five and two.

We have cited this non-superstitious number only because all the symbolism of the number thirteen comes from its relation to twelve.

THIRTEEN

Of all the numbers, thirteen is the one that still today has the greatest aura of superstition. Lucky or unlucky, it is omnipresent in daily life, sometimes in advertisements for certain games or in its negative form when it hides behind the hypocritical sign "12½."

While twelve is the number of sacred completeness, thirteen is a traitor or ringleader. At the time of religious feasts in Babylon, thirteen people incarnated the gods; the thirteenth, seated on a throne a little to the side and above the others, was put to death after the ceremony. The Last Supper is the most perfect example: Thirteen persons were at the table and one of them had to die. In addition, there were twelve righteous and *one* traitor, Judas. And, let's not forget, Christ was crucified on a Friday.

In some countries, the number thirteen is completely unlucky. In France it is more ambivalent. The choice is individual: Some value it and look for it, and others fear it. In gambling it is generally considered beneficent.

There must never be thirteen people at a table: The thirteenth will die within the year. This superstition, which comes directly from the Last Supper, is widespread.

"The Last Supper" (detail), by Leonardo da Vinci (Milan, Sainte-Marie-des-Grâces).

SEVENTEEN AND EIGHTEEN

Both being odd and primaries, these numbers are very well liked by gamblers. In general, all numbers that end with seven are magical and well liked in matters of chance.

Reflections

Shadows and mirrors are linked by the notion of doubling. An apparent being cannot alone explain dreams or death: He must have a double who can escape the terrestial envelope. Whether it is called a soul, guardian angel, or superego, it is very much there: Spectres, phantoms, shadows, and reflections, at once visible and immaterial, are proof of a double.

SHADOWS

Shadows are always present, but only the sun or another source of light, like a fire, can reveal their presence; it is believed they survive a little longer than a man and wander in the Kingdom of Shadows in the form of larvae or goblins.

A person's shadow must never be walked on or it will be hurt. (This gesture is also generally considered an insult.) A stone that falls on a man's shadow is an omen of imminent death.

A shadow is precious and it must be protected in certain places haunted by forces of the night. Shadows feed off of each other; in cemeteries, at certain cursed crossroads, and in the proximity of places where witches' Sabbaths are held, it is advisable to cross yourself in order to protect your shadow. Whoever makes a pact with the Devil gives him his shadow as security: This is how sorcerers are recognized.

In Italy, even in the last century, the shadow of a man or child was "buried" in the foundations of a new house—a substitute for the walling up of human sacrifices can be seen here. Out of respect and fear of this walled-up shadow, it is always best to cross yourself when passing near a building site.

In Africa the shadow of a hyena is said to make dogs mute.

MIRRORS

Mirrors, open doors to the invisible and the kingdom of the dead, have always had great powers of fascination. Although they are dangerous for those, like Narcissus, who let themselves be taken in by their charm, they enable us to know the future.

A newborn must never be placed in front of a mirror or he will become an epileptic. To avoid this evil, you must trace a cross on the mirror or hang a piece of broken mirror on the child's back. Whoever looks at himself in a mirror risks becoming entranced; before looking into it, you should utter certain magic words that will ward off this effect. A young bride must, at all costs, avoid looking at herself in a mirror before leaving for the church, unless her gown is being fitted. In Scandinavian countries, a woman is said to permanently lose her beauty if she looks at herself in a mirror by candlelight. Whoever makes faces at himself in a mirror is defying the Devil and will see the Devil at his death bed: In addition, his face risks getting stuck in one of these grimaces if the wind begins to change.

Breaking a mirror is a very bad omen: It is a sign of death or at least seven years of bad luck. If, in doing this, your double is killed, you will die; if it is only wounded, it will be seven years before your body is completely renewed. In England it is sometimes said that whoever breaks a mirror loses his best friend. In the theater, a real mirror is never put on stage: Since theater is already a reflection of life, in effect, you would be asking what the reflection of this reflection would be.

"The Nightmare," lithography by Colin, 1826 (Bibl. des Arts Déco)

A mirror, especially if it is convex like a crystal ball, condenses the image of the beyond and allows the future to be read. In the Middle Ages, people wrote on a convex mirror with blood. Then, by holding this mirror up to a full moon, they could see what was written on the mirror (their destiny) written on the moon.

A mirror allows a young girl to see the face of her future husband. In Scotland a girl eats an apple in front of a mirror with her eyes closed; when she has eaten the apple, she opens her eyes and over her shoulder she will see her future husband. In Hungary at midnight on New Year's Eve, if a girl dips a mirror in a spring, she will see the image of her husband. She can also, under certain conditions, place the mirror under her pillow. But if, on the night of the Epiphany, you write the initials of the three Wise Men on your forehead with your own blood, you will read in the mirror the hour and circumstances of your death.

In Persia the bride and groom entered the wedding hall by two different doors and first looked at each other in a mirror placed in the center of the room: They then saw each other such as they would be in Heaven. In many countries it is said that a couple who first see each other in a mirror will be happy.

Divinitory and linked to water, especially in Africa, a mirror is used in many magical practices that involve attracting rain. Mirrors were used in the French countryside to chase away hail and sudden showers.

Since it reverses space, left and right in particular, a mirror can transform certain hostile forces into friendly ones. In China when a person died on an unlucky day, a mirror was placed on the door to reverse the influences.

You must beware of mirrors in a dead person's room: To see your own reflection there is a death omen. In general, the mirrors are veiled, not so much to keep the dead person's soul from getting lost there as to keep the shadows of the dead, attracted by the death, from coming through the mirrors to trouble the living. In the Caribbean, however, a dying person's finger is rubbed against a mirror to aid his soul in delivering itself.

Vampires are not reflected in mirrors and a basilisk dies when it sees itself in one.

For some a *camera* lens is equal to a mirror that has the power to take hold of the reflected person's soul. Therefore, these people refuse to have their picture taken because the photo imprisons a part of themselves stolen by the lens. Young engaged couples are sometimes reluctant to have their picture taken because they think their marriage will never take place.

In addition, enemies can always bewitch you by sticking pins in a photo of your face or body.

Sacred Places

Certain places carry a magical power, the origin of which has been forgotten. The miraculous fountains of Ireland and Brittany are only continuations of ancient Celtic or Ligurian places of worship, even if in the meantime they have been placed under the patronage of a Christian saint. A hearth, a crossroads, a cemetery, or the banks of a pond are the favorite places of spell casters or those who seek to exorcize a spell. Sanctified, these places or monuments have kept a certain aura of past cults: They facilitate contact with supernatural forces. Many of them were even sanctified in blood: Menhirs, where women went in search of fertility, were sacrificial places; churches themselves were often built on sites where blood had flowed since ancient times. And let's not forget that it is under gallows that mandrake grows.

CEMETARIES

A cemetery is the only meeting place between the world of the living and that of the dead. It must be respected because the domain of shadows can attract to it the living who risk wandering there. The tombs must be carefully maintained so that the dead are content there and remain in their place.

A tomb whose surface remains rounded and is covered with nettles signals that the soul of the dead person is damned. In addition, you must walk around a grave three times so that the deceased does not come back to haunt. Graves are dug from east to west, so that the dead person's head faces the west and the feet are turned toward the east, ready to rise up when the news of the Last Judgment comes from the East. Several persons can be buried in the same tomb, but what is seen in an open tomb must never be spoken of. Some affirm that the first body buried in a new cemetery is immediately claimed by the Devil.

A cross on a grave is intended to keep demons away.

It is inadvisable to dig into the ground where a man has been buried or plant anything there. A grave must never be walked on, especially the grave of an unbaptized child. In addition, you risk setting a ghost free when you visit a grave. A coffin cannot be moved until the body has completely returned to dust.

It is inadvisable to risk going into a cemetery at night except perhaps on the odd hours. On the night of All Saint's Day, all the names of those who must die during the year can be heard. The first night after his burial, the deceased is called upon by the next most recent deceased to take his turn at guard duty at the cemetery gates. Most often it is a man and a woman who watch over the sleep of the living. They are replaced when a new person is buried.

In cemeteries at night, little flames called *will-o'-the-wisps* flicker there. For some these are damned souls that seek to attract the living; for others, they represent the souls of land surveyors that did not honor their contracts and are condemned to eternally measure the land. In any case, they are dangerous, especially during Advent. You must avoid whistling at them and to get rid of them, put a needle in the ground and run away. They will escape through the eye of the needle.

To cure a drunkard, you must give him the powder of a small bone of a corpse stolen from a cemetery during the full moon.

CHURCH

This building that each Christian frequents for his baptism, wedding, and burial is a place of privileged contact between unknown forces and man. The portal, the holy water basin, the baptismal fonts, the pews, and the weathervane atop the steeple—all can be a sign of approaching births, weddings, or deaths. Since churches are most often constructed in the shape of a cross, they remain the primary place for exorcisms and conjurations.

When the portal of a church squeaks or grinds for no reason, it foretells that a coffin will soon cross its threshold. The Anglo-Saxons believe that those soon to die can be seen entering the church at midnight on October 31st. You need only sit under the porch to see and count them. In Scotland it is believed that it is possible to save them: As the name of each of those condemned to death is called, a person hidden under the porch must take off an article of clothing.

A bird that flies into the nave during a service is a very good sign: It brings happiness and gifts. Perched on the steeple weathervane, a bird foretells a death for the coming week.

All the metal roosters perched on the steeples of churches will crow on Judgment Day.

Spells and Conjurations

Witches, sorcerers, and all those who, voluntarily or not, have the evil eye, can bewitch whomever they approach (that is, hand them over to demonic forces). Their action is most often revealed in the form of illness, decay, or even death. It is important to recognize these spell casters in order to protect yourself as much as possible from their sorcery. They are above all redheads, hunchbacks, monks, those who have a "bizarre" look, and all strangers. Those who covet your wealth or happiness, look at you insistantly, or point at you are to be feared. They rarely give their sign of recognition and allegiance to Satan (horns made with the index and little fingers pointed upward) where people can see them. They prefer to attack young women who have just given birth, newborns, children in general (especially boys, which is why in some regions they are dressed like girls), and young newlyweds—all must beware of "codpiece tiers" always lying in wait—cattle, trees, the earth, and more rarely, residences.

Sometimes a "normal" man, a superstitious man, himself puts sorcerers' practices that he fears so much, to the test: He concocts love potions or sticks pins in a lighted candle as a way of sending for the person he wants to be loved by. But he most willingly uses these means to take revenge on the sorcerers themselves: By beating a bewitched person's clothes with an elderberry stick, he also beats the sorcerer himself; by cutting an object or the earth with a sickle, he wounds whoever cast the spell; by poking pins in the heart of a dead animal, he makes the responsible person wither and die. If a normal man has involuntarily harmed another, he can spit in his own guilty hand to ease the pain of his victim.

In Corsica and certain Mediterranean countries, to find out whether an event is natural or due to sorcery, a person puts a drop of oil in water. If the drop remains stable, there was no intervention from malevolent powers; if it breaks up into little droplets, a spell was undoubtedly responsible for the event..

Symbolic hammering of a sick child's spleen by a blacksmith-bone setter, end of the 19th c. (Bibl. des Arts Déco)

When in the presence of hostile forces, or of persons having the evil eye or abnormal gestures, it is always best to conjure the spell. It is interesting to note that this word is still used for certain physical ailments: A wart or burn is "conjured" (proving that these ailments are of diabolic origin). The sign of the cross is always effective. The sign of the horns pointed downward in the face of danger or behind your back is also a great help. You can cross the index and middle fingers or else, with a closed fist, poke your thumb out from between these two fingers. Touching wood, whether it represents the god tree or the true Cross, is always positive, because it fills you with the strength to resist. But touching iron is preferable—metal has the power to chase demons away. It is best to throw something over your left shoulder after knocking over a salt shaker, whether it is a glass of vodka or a little salt; you can also spit, preferably three times. This must also always be done when nail or hair clippings are thrown out or at the site of an accident. Spitting protects against the evil eye in general; it is good to do it before undertaking any new activity or to protect against contagion. In the entire Mediterranean basin, it is traditional to spit when you pay someone, especially a newborn, a compliment: Devils might become jealous and take revenge. When a sorcerer is prowling around a house, it is a good idea to turn all the brooms upside down.

A barn is particularly subject to evil spells. Animals, not being able to conjure sorcery themselves, must constantly be protected. To ward off evil forces, you should plant a fig or elderberry in the farmyard, or nail a horseshoe, wreaths of beads, an owl, or some other malevolent animal to the barn door. Garlic, metal objects, and excrement have the same power, as well as flowers hung around an animal's neck. Spider webs must never be cleared from a stable or barn: Spiders protect the cattle from evil spells and illness. A ring also protects against evil influences: The first time a cow is milked, the milk must be made to pass through a ring.

Without speaking of magical formulas and charms, certain words in themselves have a demonic force and attract evil spells. All compliments are unlucky if you aren't careful to spit after saying them. There are many words that must not be uttered at a circus, in a theater, or on board ship. In enclosed places, these words take on a frightful force and inevitably provoke an accident. The word "rope" must never be used on stage, on board a ship, and particularly in the house of a hanged man. Although wishes for happiness and success are allowable on certain dates like January 1st, on certain occasions they are dangerous: To wish someone "good hunting" or "good fishing" is to condemn that person to returning empty-handed. The French word for "shit" is very beneficent on all occasions.

When it is certain that an animal is the victim of sorcery, make several signs of the cross, sprinkle the animal with holy water, make it pass through a fire, and then place three or nine grains of salt near it; it is also possible to successively pass three stones across its forehead. For man, conjuration has been ritualized in the form of exorcism where holy water, fire, salt, sacred words, and the sign of the cross are found. Baptism remains the foremost form of exorcism.

Spirits, Devils and Demons

The Devil is an honest man, he doesn't ask for something for nothing.

Breton adage

We will only briefly treat the world of spirits, which concerns the history of magic and religions more than our domain. It requires a dictionary all its own. But spirits, devils, demons, sorcerers, and phantoms make up an occult world subjacent to many superstitions, especially those concerning spells and conjurations. Most conjurations are aimed at defending us from incessant attacks by forces of the night.

Protective spirits intervene little in superstitions. There is no question of guardian angels. What is sacred forms a whole that, through a few simple substitutes like holy water, a crucifix, salt, and so forth, combats evil that itself takes on an infinite number of forms.

An intermediate category of spirits exists, composed of spirits who are neither good nor wicked and who leave man alone as long as he doesn't disturb them. These spirits are fairies, elves, White Ladies, gnomes, spirits, goblins, dwarves, and so forth. They get along well with humans who simply respect them.

Then there is the nocturnal world of Evil, whose only aim is to corrupt man. Here we find humans like witches and sorcerers who have made a pact with the Devil; others here are a part of the infernal throng despite themselves: They have been bewitched. They are the possessed for whom the hope of being exorcized still remains. Dead souls, phantoms, ghosts, ghouls, and vampires all seek to live again and martyrize the living. Finally, in the center is the king of the night, Satan, Lucifer, or Beelzebub, infinitely variable, assisted by other devils sometimes called demons—wolves, cats, owls, bats, witches, and sorcerers. All of them meet at the Sabbath, where Satan, a hermaphrodite, mates with witches, sorcerers, and animals. Being at once animal (he-goat), human (too human), and devil, Satan is everywhere. Seeking to corrupt souls and destroy the work of God, he proposes pacts to believing men and women, then tries to dupe them.

But the Devil is sometimes well-behaved and in his regional forms of a Servant, Drac, "Galipotte" or "Matagot," he can be successfully tricked by certain clever men. Many legends attest to this. Finally, fortunately for humans, there are ordeals and other signs that allow sorcerers to be recognized and burned.

Square

A square composed of four equal sides, two horizontal and two vertical, is linked to both the cross and the circle. Tradition proposed a square earth in a round sky. The entire problem of squaring a circle is tied to these two elements. A square, horizontal, linked to material reality and the earth, is in opposition to a triangle, vertical, linked to spirituality and the sky.

The four cardinal points that form a cross can also form a square. The importance of this last point is known in astrology. A square is obviously linked to the number four (see Numbers and Figures in this chapter).

Among the many *magical squares*, the most well-known, composed of nine numbers (zero is only a recent invention) totals fifteen for each horizontal and vertical line:

$$
\begin{array}{ccc}
4 & 9 & 2 \\
3 & 5 & 7 \\
8 & 1 & 6
\end{array}
$$

Inscribed on jewelry or cloth, this makes a very effective amulet or talisman. When it is put on the feet of a woman giving birth, it facilitates delivery. Other magical squares are formed from letters and can be read horizontally as well as vertically.

A *cube*, a solid whose six faces form six equal squares, illustrates the same symbolism. It continues to fascinate gamblers in the form of dice.

Talismans

Amulets, fetishes, gris-gris, good-luck charms, mascots, pantacles, phylacteries, medals, relics, jewelry, perfumes, tatoos—all these objects or signs have the common purpose of acting on destiny and protecting their owner from evil influences. We will group them under the generic term "talismans."

Amulets, fetishes, and gris-gris are natural objects that neutralize evil forces. Sharks' teeth or certain shells, most often worn on bracelets and necklaces, are the most primitive forms of these talismans. Coral or coralline rings or jewelry assume the same function. A circle itself is a protector: Rings, necklaces, and bracelets are at the origin of conjuratory objects. A *gold ring* worn on the left ear was the emblem of certain guilds and, in addition, had a conjuratory function. Popular with sailors and pirates, it was even more highly prized by Breton farmers at the turn of the century—they saw it as effective protection against illness and drowning. It has come back into style in the past few years, but many handsome young men who wear it have forgotten its function. All jewelry made of metal wards off demons. Among the simple talismans, let us cite a knot tied in a handkerchief or the more elaborate trinkets, especially of coral, representing conjuratory horns that are often put around a baby's neck in the Mediterranean region. A hand of Fatima (the prophet's daughter) is highly prized in the Orient; in addition it has divinitory abilities. A Basque "higo," a closed hand, the thumb of which sticks out between the

Woman from the Limousin casting a spell by means of an animal's heart, end of the 19th c. (Bibl. des Arts Déco)

index and middle fingers, also wards off demons. Horns made of stag antlers are sought after by the Spanish. A simple piece of metal kept in your pocket can have the same effect.

32

True talismans are more complex and linked to magic. They draw their force from elaborate and complex rites that link them to the divine world. Holy medals, like those of Saint Christopher and the Virgin Mary, as well as relics, are a part of this idolatry often condemned by churches that also sometimes promote them. Many amulets or talismans have a specific function, often medical, and must only be worn on certain days and under certain conditions. The making of these talismans is itself linked to astrology. The material must possess a divine aura: pure gold is linked to the sun, silver to the moon and copper to Venus. A sacred formula can only be inscribed on a virgin parchment (one that has never carried old texts that have been erased). Written words carry a radiance in themselves, whether they are from a verse of the Bible, the Koran, or any other sacred words. Esoteric formulas like abracadabra, adonai, tetragrammaton, and so forth are most often made of initials and must be laid out in a square, triangle, or cross. The most common shapes of talismans and pantacles are a circle, pentagram, cross, and a snake biting its tail. Solomon's seal and a pentagram are the most practiced forms. Perfumes also require complex rites of fabrication. They are elaborated upon or worn only under certain celestial conditions.

Amulets, above all, have a specific conjuratory function—they are worn as a preventive measure. *Good-luck charms* have a positive function: They must, as their name indicates, bring luck and make destiny favorable. Gamblers' fetish objects and mascots, whether they are human or animal, are very personalized. They only have a positive value for their owner. Certain objects have acquired a more general power; their possessor is guaranteed good luck. The most well-known ones today are a four leaf clover (provided it was found by chance and not looked for, preferably during a full moon), a horseshoe, a lizard's tail, a wren's feather, an elephant's hair, or, for young women, a sailor's pompon.

Triangle

The physical incarnation of the sacred number three, a triangle symbolizes the major stages of human life—birth, maturity, and death—and harmony with the world of gods. In general, this perfect shape must not be broken: It would be sacrilegious. This fundamental belief explains the superstitions surrounding ladders: In effect, a ladder forms a triangle with the wall against which it leans. Walking under the ladder breaks the triangle.

A triangle can also be unlucky. In Brittany, a person is said to have more of a chance of encountering the Devil at a crossroads or in a field that has only three sides. Still today, one of the most inauspicious and mysterious places in the universe is called the "Bermuda Triangle," in the Atlantic.

A pyramid, precious to Egyptians, is formed from four triangles: They saw a pyramid as a point where the forces of the earth and sky converged.

Solomon's Seal or a six-pointed star is made of two opposing triangles. This essential, esoteric sign joins together a triangle whose point is directed upward, linked to the sky, fire, and the male element with a triangle directed downward, linked to the earth, water, and the feminine element. Solomon's seal, which synthesizes these opposites, expresses divinity.

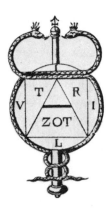

Minerals

The mineral world, whose formation and slow destruction man never sees, and whose general cycle of life, death, and regeneration he seems to be ignorant of, excites speculative thought and mythical imagination. The origin of this inert universe, indifferent to the passage of hours and centuries, asks perhaps the most disturbing questions. Some acknowledge an intimate relationship between mother earth and rocks or stones through an entirely plant-oriented conception of the inorganic world: Stones are connected to the earth by a vein that nourishes them from the depths of the earth's crust. Like trees and plants, stones grow over the years. But often their clothing is of a more or less magical, celestial origin, undoubtedly linked to the divine birth of man. All stones supposedly fell from heaven. Meteorites do actually fall from the sky, whence perhaps the confusion. Some stones are born of nothingness, but in general they come either from planets or lightning. For some people, they are tears from the stars (which is why each one corresponds to a planet). The "lightning stone" or prehistoric flint, whose origin has long been misunderstood, was supposedly a shred of cloud torn by lightning, then hardened. Pearls and emeralds fell from the sky into the sea. Crystals were fragments of the royal throne. Curiously, stone, inorganic by definition, on earth conserves the inner life that enlivened it in space. Some even attribute it with a human scent, an heir to the Kingdom of the Heavens.

The same thought, however, doesn't deny the static character of the mineral world: It puts the mineral world in opposition to that of plants, subjects it to the regeneration cycle, and makes it a symbol of permanence. Stones then are supposedly fragments of eternity: hard and inalterable, worn as talismans they confer magical powers that are also linked to their particular shape and color. In addition, stones worked at certain hours and on certain dates possess an additional power—a man's work shapes the various qualities. Aside from symbolic stones like menhirs, sacred rocks, and certain precious stones, metals—gold, silver, or lead— are a part of the same superstitious universe. Rarity only increases man's fascination. Sometimes the rarity alone justifies all the virtues attributed to gold or diamonds, for example, which have acquired prestigious social value.

Agate

There are many aspects of this veiny stone. It is always benevolent and has long been greatly valued as a talisman. A genuine agate was well known for cooling boiling water, a property by which it was recognized. When red veined, it is said to bear traces of the blood of the gods.

It is a stone that must be offered in June if it is to be beneficent— whoever will wear it acquires strength, health, and the grace and power to please. In Italy, as in the Middle East, it is especially known for its power to keep away the evil eye and to promote eloquence.

It has a reputation for protecting its owner from thirst and for sharpening vision. Its absorbing power makes it an excellent antidote for poisons and insect or snake bites. The design formed by these veins predisposes it to curing spider, viper, or scorpion poisons, according to the shape of the animal that can be seen in the veins.

Its astringent properties make it useful against dropsy and all hemorrhages. It cures stomach ailments when it has been cut in the shape of a triangle, and its dark varieties treat diarrhea. A woman will become fertile again if she drinks water into which a green agate has been dropped. In addition, if an agate whose feins form a tree is placed between the horns of an ox, it will bring fertility to the earth.

When it is burned it keeps away tempests as well as lightning. A man who carries an agate will be successful with all women, even if they didn't like him before.

A solid-colored agate makes an athlete invincible, especially if he took the precaution to hang it around his neck with a lion's hair. A black agate with white veins is the most sought after for combatting adversity and overcoming enemies.

A green agate or *chrysoprase* cures vision troubles and brings happiness in life. A *heliotrope* or bloodstone, green and red in color, is an excellent antidote for all poisons and protects against infidelity. *Sardonyx,* brown and red in color, is the stone of conjugal happiness when it is offered in August; it also protects against the evil eye and stomach ailments. Red agate or *coralline* should be offered in July—it calms anger and keeps away the evil eye and nightmares; it is the stone of love and friendship. A white *chalcedony* is born of dew, but it can also be found in the stomach of swallows—it guarantees vivacity of the soul and healthy eyes.

Jasper is an opaque variety of agate that, especially when green, stops bleeding and eases pain. A jasper stone is placed on the belly of a woman about to give birth. Jasper is also an excellent antidote for poisons and cures epilepsy and stomach ailments. In addition, it has the ability to attract rain: When a drought is prolonged, it is a good idea to put a vase of jasper on your windowsill.

Amber

Yellow amber is a fossilized, translucent, golden resin endowed with electric powers. In magical beliefs, it combines certain properties of gold with those of loadstone.

Amber concentrates energy and enables a person who carries some to be free of excessive moods and anger.

Amber rosaries, still used in Greece and certain Middle Eastern countries, enable their owners to find calmness and serenity.

Endowed with drying and absorbing properties, amber protects against the effects of fire and water, particularly conflagrations and floods. It also has the ability to keep away the evil eye.

Worn in a necklace, it protects against and cures sore throats, diphtheria, and goiter, and shields its owner from illness. Reduced to a powder, it is excellent against boils and keeps women from having miscarriages. When burned, amber eases difficult childbirths. Finally, all that is necessary to stop a nosebleed is to place a piece of amber on the nose.

Amethyst

Its name—"ametusios" in Greek means remedy against drunkenness—expresses its primary quality. Amethyst is the stone of sobriety, temperence, humility, and wisdom, far from earthly as well as spiritual passions and intoxications.

Amethyst makes a drunkard disgusted with his vice and protects those who must attend a banquet from the alcoholic fumes. Some believe that it draws this power from its violet color that is that of wine must.

It can constitute the best talisman against the evil eye if it is worn around the neck with a peacock's and a swallow's feathers; the names of the sun and moon must be engraved on the stone. "Amethyst with its pretty eyes" is also reputed to give you nice dreams and keep nightmares away. It reinforces memory and gives a taste for the sciences to its owner. Placed under a pillow, it cures gout.

So that this stone keeps all its magical power, it must be offered in February.

Coral

This animal that looks more like a stone or plant is at once linked to the earth, as a mineral, to water, its element, and to fire by its color. The "tree of waters" was supposedly born of a few drops of blood from the gorgon Medusa when her head was cut off. Let us not forget that this gorgon had the power to petrify with her glance and that her hair was filled with snakes: This explains the appearance of this "plant stone" and its power to cure bites from venomous animals. Another legend sees coral as the result of the putrefication of an algae that hardens when it comes in contact with air. White in the beginning, it turns red under the sun's action and from the kisses of loving nymphs.

Around the Mediterranean, coral is known for its power to keep away the evil eye and thwart all spell casters; children are made to wear necklaces of it and adults have coral amulets representing a hand making conjuratory horns or a closed fist.

It fortifies the heart of whoever wears it, brings him wisdom and reason, and rids him of fear. Hung with a sealskin on the mast of a vessel, coral calms tempests and keeps sailors from shipwreck. Reduced to a powder, coral wards off plague, hail, thunder, lightning, and whirlwinds. It also chases away rats, ants, caterpillars, and all vermin. It cures scorpion and asp bites for those who have taken the precaution of engraving it with the name of the lunar goddess Hecate or the shape of a snake. The same talisman protects you against undertakings by all your enemies.

Coral is gifted with a great power of coagulation. People who attach it to their navels are cured of all losses of blood. An excellent aphrodisiac, it cures dysentery, gout, epilepsy, and all skin and eye diseases.

Diamond

A diamond is the supreme achievement of matter—it is the image of perfection and incorruptability. Immutable and constant, it can scratch all other matter but cannot be scratched by anything but itself. When it is burned, it leaves no slag. This stone that symbolizes hardness combines purity with this due to its transparency. The "solitaire" condenses light and other forces and sparkles with all its "water."

At certain times, snakes gather to salivate and produce a diamond. It can also be found in precious metal mines where it glistens in the middle of gold, bronze, or crystal. Whoever engraves the name of Mars on a diamond can make himself invisible. Only blood from a he-goat allows the force of this reputedly invincible matter to be broken.

An image of purity, a diamond brings happiness with it. It wards off anger and lust, and allows reconciliation, especially between couples who should offer it to each other in April. Placed on the head or under the pillow of a sleeping woman, you can determine if she has remained chaste—an unfaithful woman reveals herself by groaning when the diamond comes in contact with her.

A diamond protects its owner from the evil eye, infectious illness, and the action of poisons. It also has the ability to calm tertian fever and cure colic. Whoever wears one will not have nightmares and will be protected from the action of his enemies and wild beasts, phantoms, succubuses, incubuses, and goblins will not be able to bother him. Set in a silver ring, a diamond has the same power and prevents insomnia. Finally, water in which a diamond has soaked cures apoplexy, gout, and jaundice.

Emerald

For Pliny the Elder, an emerald is the third most precious stone after diamonds and pearls. It is, however, dangerous. Being both holy and diabolic, it is Venus's stone, but also that of initiates for whom it symbolizes clairvoyance. An emerald is also the Pope's stone. The green color of "this dew of May" evokes both the regenerating power of spring and alchemists' lights.

A biblical tradition has it that an emerald fell from Lucifer's forehead during his downfall. Placed under the sign of the moon, it represents the justice of the king and must be offered on a Wednesday (if it is offered on a Monday it loses all its powers and can even become unlucky). Offered in May, it promotes happy relationships and is considered to govern the third hour of the day.

According to the Russians, it is an enemy of dirt and prevents its owner from being untidy. It becomes tainted upon contact with perspiration and breath and breaks into pieces upon contact with venereal coition. It is reputed to control sensuality, but some see it as an aphrodisiac. To help it keep its color, dip it in wine, then rub it with or soak it in green oil.

Linked to infernal regions, it promotes talents for divination and

"The Infernal Regions," by Desiderio Monsu, 1622 (Besançon, Musée des Beaux-Arts).

enables lost objects to be found. Whoever places an emerald under his tongue has the power to invoke demons and make them appear. A consecrated emerald is known for its power to set prisoners free.

Worn around the neck or on a finger in the form of a ring, it cures many illnesses—epilepsy, dysentery and tertian fever; it facilitates and hastens childbirth and stops hemorrhages. It wards off frights, demons, and sorcery, cures viper bites, and prevents physical failings. An emerald is a stone of knowledge that promotes labors of the mind and memory; it is considered to bring all spiritual as well as material riches. Whoever places it under his tongue is endowed with the gift of prophecy and if he wears it on his left arm, he will be immune to fascinations. Upon seeing an emerald, a cobra or viper's eyes spring out of its head, and a simple touch on the eyes with an emerald can cure a blind man and all vision troubles.

Blue, yellow, pink, or transparent emeralds are most often called *beryls*. Worn by children as amulets, it promotes their taste for the humanities. Litigants also like to wear them because they allow trials to result in their favor. In general beryls are good for the liver, hiccups, improving vision, and protecting yourself from control by your enemies. They promote peace in households. A sailor who has engraved the name of a sea god on a light blue emerald needs not fear tempests. Yellow beryls are considered to be the best and to bring strength, courage, and health; blue beryls are greatly effective against venoms.

Garnet

This red stone is sometimes discredited by certain people who see it as "the ruby of the poor." It is, however, very positive and draws its strength from its color that evokes blood. A garnet should be offered in January and brings constancy. It favors those born under the sign of Cancer and is considered to give those who wear it the illusion of being tall even if they are short. It has the ability to make its owner invulnerable and also to glow in the dark.

A *carbuncle* is a dark-colored garnet that children are made to wear to protect them from all dangers resulting from water—drownings, shipwrecks, or floods. Its color excites the mind and makes people joyful and likewise protects against neurasthenia and insomnia. It fortifies the heart and refreshes the brain, but it loses all its effectiveness if the person who wears it is fickle.

A *snow leopard stone* or "lyncurium" is a kind of garnet produced by lynx urine. Often confused with amber by the ancients, it was excellent against jaundice, colic, and fainting.

Glass

A lunar stone, "star droppings," a *crystal* shelters living souls at the heart of its mystery. A crystal ball is consulted in order to know the future or determine the nature of an illness—the spirits respond to the clairvoyant.

Extracted at night by the light of a full moon, *quartz* has the power to ward off sorcery. If it is in a silver setting, it protects against hostile persons and jugulates insomnia. It also guards against fear and ghosts. Worn as an amulet, this rock crystal smothers nightmares and cures cattle illnesses. You need only soak it in water, then make the animals drink the water.

For some, crystal glass is supposedly a stone from rain that fell from the sky during a storm; for others, it is supposedly a diamond that isn't completely "ripe." Its purity has make it a symbol of the Immaculate Conception. Reduced to a powder and mixed with food, it promotes the arrival of mother's milk. It gives fantasmagoric visions to whoever looks at the world through its transparency. But a person must never be looked at through a piece of broken glass—there would be a risk of a sudden separation. Breaking a glass or crystal vase brings seven years of happiness. It is also said that there will be as many happy years as there are scattered pieces.

Finally, crystal is reputed to cure kidney ailments.

Jade

In all the Orient, jade is considered to be lucky, as is an emerald, due to its green color. It symbolizes immortality, purity, and virtue and it is venerated in the same way as gold.

In Africa, it is thought to attract rain. It has the same power in Mexico, and when placed in a dead person's mouth, jade helps him cross the boundries of immortality.

In China, the nine openings of a corpse are plugged with jade and gold to prevent putrefication. It is the material of initiations and an emblem of power. It allows storms to be conjured and, like green jasper, attracts rain. It is an object of sacrifice and the favorite material for the making of talismans. Its green color makes it a symbol of plant growth. Certain ritual objects must be made of jade:

"Pi" disk, green jade, China, Han Dynasty.

- a "pi" is a flat disc with a hole whose diameter must equal half the width of the ring. A "pi" concentrates celestial influence.
- a "ts'ung," made of yellow jasper, represents the earth; it attracts rain and protects houses. It is made up of a hollow cylinder on the inside of a square.
- a "kuei" is a rectangle that ends in a triangle and symbolizes both a house and its roof and sexual union.

- a "chang" is a tablet of red jade that represents the sun's fire.
- a "hu" is a tiger of white jade.
- a "huang" is made of black jade; used in necromancy, it has the shape of a ring cut in two or three pieces.

In the West, alchemists often confused white jade with a philosopher's stone and saw the dew drunk from a jade chalice as an elixir of long life. The Celts made jade rings, similar to a "pi," that were supposed to symbolize both the sky and the forces of thunder and lightning.

When you wear jade, it is reputed to cure kidney and bladder ailments—formerly, greenstone jade was called "nephrite" which in French also means nephritis—and protects against the action of venoms.

Jade was used to make epileptic attacks cease, because the more rare white jade was in general considered a good luck charm.

Magnet

The rather late discovery of magnetite, an oxide of iron and its various properties, fascinated man. Loadstone, of course, symbolizes the attraction of love, the process of this attraction, and the seduction. It was widely used in magic and medicine where it was attributed with the property of attracting pain to itself.

The invention of the compass whose magnetized needle or calamite is able to direct itself toward the North Star only accentuated the magical character of this by-no-means precious stone.

Loadstone, black and shiny, should be worn around the neck or else set in a ring. It is a stone of love that needs only be called upon: "Magnet! Make me loved by whom I love!" to be immediately obeyed. Placed in a woman's bed, it calls her immediately to love.

Curiously, this same stone has the reverse properties—magnetite is the stone of chastity when it is worn set in a silver ring. If this stone is placed on a woman's head, you will know her feelings toward her husband: If she is chaste and honest she will embrace her husband, but if she is dishonest and unfaithful, she will violently push him away. But a man who coats himself with an oil that a magnetite has soaked in will see his virility reinforced.

Loadstone brings strength and courage. Magnetite plates confer their strength on the food and guarantee vigor and health. The stone attracts pain to itself and can be used to treat all ailments. It is sought after by those who have gout and, placed on a woman's thigh, it facilitates childbirth.

For some, if a weapon rubs against loadstone, it is immediately poisoned, but for others, on the contrary, wounds provoked by this weapon will be painless and without blood letting.

Whoever reduces magnetite to a powder, then places it on live coals at the four corners of a house will see all those who are sleeping flee. This process was sometimes used by thieves.

At the South Pole, a magnetized mountain exists that attracts all pieces of iron that pass near it—nails holding the hull of a vessel come out and the ship sinks. In order to approach the South Pole, you must take the precaution to make a craft whose elements are of wood.

Metals

All metals are the results of transformations by iron that draws them from an ore. Sometimes being of an infernal origin, minerals are purified and progressively attain absolute perfection (gold). One of the goals of alchemy was to obtain the transmutation of metals into gold, particularly when starting with lead. For the ancients, each of the seven main metals was linked to a planet and, like the planets, was unequal in power. The most perfect was gold, linked to the sun, then came silver, linked to the moon, mercury to Mercury, copper to Venus, iron to Mars, tin to Jupiter, and finally lead to Saturn. All metal talismans must be made by simple fusion at the apogee of its planet's influence and worn under the same conditions.

Metals are living beings in whose bodies flow blood and sexed beings—it is from their union that alloys such as brass and bronze are born.

Alchemist, engraved wood from the 16th c. (Musée d'Histoire de la Médecine)

BRASS

Brass is an alloy, therefore born of the union of other metals, but although it is of bastard origin, it was considered sacred by the Hebrews as well as the Greeks and Romans. Known for its resistance, it incarnated the ideas of incorruptability and immortality. Due to its resonant quality, it was the material chosen for the making of bells or it was often replaced by another alloy with the same property, bronze.

In certain regions of France, when a cow is milked for the first time, it is recommended that the milk be gathered in a brass container if the cow is to be a good milker in the future.

In general, alloys are associated with the astrological sign of Sagittarius.

COPPER

Copper, whose red color evokes solar fire, is connected with the planet Venus. It is a sacred metal in Africa where, when worn as a bracelet, it cures rhumatisms and other illnesses. Whoever wears this metal must, however, beware of water—its relationship with the goddess Venus brings on a fear of drowning and the dangers of flooding. Copper, favoring those born under the sign of Taurus, is often associated with the color green. Some claim that its ore can be uncovered with the help of a forked stick from an ash tree.

GOLD

Gold represents the perfection of matter—it is the mineral light equal to the sun and must be reserved for the representation of the heavens. White for the Chinese, this metal is the product of all metals; it was the constant preoccupation of alchemy to succeed in finding the path of this transformation. Gold is the symbol of spiritual wealth, love, light, and knowledge, but also of domination. It is particularly beneficent for those born under the sign of Leo. It is the metal reserved for ritual sacrifices, from the priest's knife that slits a lamb's throat to the Druids' sickle that gathers sacred mistletoe. The base of Oriental icons is always gold to signify the image of celestial perfection, and from this solar mythology, tradition took up the halo and the blond color of Christ's hair. Gold has been corrupted, however, by those who only see in it, like silver, earthly wealth.

Gold is a universal good-luck charm—its only fault is that it prolongs childbirth, so a woman must take off all her gold jewelry when giving

"Arbor Scientiae," engraved wood from the 16th c. taken from the work of alchemy by Raymond Lulle (Bibl. de l'Anc. Faculté de Médecine de Paris).

birth. Some say she can keep her wedding ring on for this operation, but others say that it also must be removed.

At midnight on Christmas night, a golden bough appears in all hazel trees, but whoever doesn't succeed in cutting it before the twelfth stroke of the clock disappears with the bough. Gold ore can be uncovered with the help of a hazel tree stick whose two ends have been supplied with iron.

IRON

Iron finds itself misplaced in the heirarchy of metals where it has an equivocal reputation—it is the image of robustness, but also of excessive hardness. It is both sacred in its function of conjuring evil forces and linked to death in the form of weapons of which it is an essential element. In opposition to the Golden Age, the Iron Age is that of violence and wickedness. Its compound, steel, has its same value—being shinier, it is used in the making of weapons and mirrors.

The use of iron is forbidden for certain sacred works—it cannot cut the mistletoe gathered by Druids, and the stones in the temple of Jerusalem were supposedly never to have been touched by it.

This metal has the well-known property of warding off demons and chasing away the evil eye. In Anglo-Saxon countries, when evil forces are encountered or when you want to attract luck, it is more common to touch iron than wood. In order to protect a house where a child has just been born or where someone is dying, it is a good idea to cross iron near doors, windows, and chimneys (that is, put two knives or sickles in a cross): They will wound the witches that attempt to approach the house. To avoid certain encounters, particularly those with a parson, it is advisable to touch a key. This object, like a nail or horseshoe, draws its value from the power of the metal. But in eastern France, jingling a ring of keys on Wednesday is said to make you go insane.

A wrought iron bracelet is reputed to facilitate the conception of a child and he who wants to avoid toothaches for a year must bite a piece of this iron on Easter Eve.

In order to make iron or steel like copper, place some crushed quicklime and alum together on a linen; place the iron or steel on this linen and put it all in a fire for about one hour. If you only want to soften iron, simply get it red hot in a fire, then rub it with a feather dipped in water that is floating on top of human blood. When it has been rubbed long enough, the iron will become soft and be able to be worked. A decoction of chamomile and herb Robert leads to the same result. (See also Weapons, Keys, Nails, and Horseshoe.)

Iron favors Scorpios whereas those born under the sign of Aries are in more direct contact with steel.

LEAD

Lead incarnates both weight and malleability. For alchemists it is the water of all the metals and permits all transformations—you need only go through white lead or mercury to arrive at gold.

Lead is linked to the sign of Capricorn and can be uncovered with the help of a forked stick of pinewood.

A young girl can let some melted lead drop into some water while thinking about the man she would like to marry; when the lead dries it will take the shape of the tool that characterizes her future husband's trade: a hammer for a blacksmith, a needle for a tailor, a sickle for a laborer, and so forth.

MERCURY

Mercury is also known under the names of liquid silver and quicksilver; for alchemists it is the "tree of life" or the "wood of life." It represents an element of mixing and adaptation and corresponds to the sign of Gemini.

A ring that makes you invisible must be made from a solidified mercury base. All talismans made with mercury as a base cure fevers and protect against memory losses. Finally, whoever slips some mercury under the pillow will, when he wakes up, find the solutions to all the problems that were troubling him.

SILVER

Silver is linked to the moon, water, and the feminine element. Second metal in power, it signifies light, royalty, purity, and fame. Its color is white; it favors the sign of Cancer. In the form of coins, silver acquired a negative aspect and an excessive taste, for it leads to greed and cupidity.

The bones of Egyptian gods were made of silver and supported flesh of gold.

Silver cannot be bewitched—its presence in jewelry or a talisman can only accentuate the power of those objects. On the other hand, if the piece of jewelry being worn is of silver and it begins to tarnish, it is a death omen.

Most superstitions having to do with this metal and referring to its wealth are dealt with under "Coins" (chapter IX).

Saturn: Allegorical engraving taken from the "Indagine Chiromantia," 1531 (Bibl. Nat.).

Onyx

This black stone saddens man's heart because, by its color, it is a reminder of mourning and the night. Whoever wears it goes into a profound melancholy.

At night, it promotes frightening dreams and dreadful, supernatural visions. During the day, it creates disputes and provokes anxiety. It is also fatal for pregnant women.

Others affirm, however, that onyx upholds a couple's fidelity and sometimes helps dissipate sadness that has already taken hold of a soul.

Opal

"An opal: stone of misfortune, infamous gem."

Despite the conviction of the poet, an opal, translucid or neutral, has an ambivalent meaning. It is but a reflection, a receptacle of the soul or body that approaches it. Thus, this living stone shines with increased lustre on a person full of energy and in good health and brings him happiness. Someone who is weak and nervous by nature, on the contrary, will suffer from this jewel.

An opal must be offered in October; it then allows all hardships to be overcome. But others call it "tear stone" and only wear it in combination with diamonds to avoid misfortune.

An opal betrays your state of health—it becomes dull when a person who puts it in contact with his skin risks falling ill.

A black opal is said to be a good-luck charm.

Portrait of a Savoy princess (detail), by the Maitre de Flemalle. Flemish school, 15th c. (New York, private coll.)

Pearl

A feminine, pure jewel of perfect beauty, a pearl was born of the ideal union between the sea and the sky. Several myths embellish this basic sketch. A pearl is supposedly a drop of morning dew fertilized by the moon that fell into a shell. It is produced by contact between rain and the sea, lightning and the ocean. For others, a white bird, fertilized by the sun, dives into the sea and bears a pearl in the eighth month.

According to Orientals, a pearl worn as a talisman supposedly has fecundating and aphrodisiac properties. But everywhere it cures feminine melancholy. Mounted on a pin, it treats hemorrhages, insanity, and jaundice and immunizes against venoms. It is still believed that it eases cardiac pain. In general, powder from pearls assures health and prosperity.

Since pearls resemble tears, they must not be mounted on an engagement ring. But this stone is often offered to a newborn to guarantee him a long life.

Ruby

A ruby shines in a dragon's only eye, but it also joins lovers who choose it. It is believed to protect children from the dangers of water.

It is a powerful talisman due to its beneficent red color. Offered in July, the sun's month, it is helpful in forgetting sorrows of the heart, brings courage and joy, and revives the memory.

A ruby protects against epidemics and activates blood circulation. In addition, it keeps lightning away. Placed under the tongue, it quenches thirst. Worn on the skin, it indicates health and prosperity. Worn on the little finger of the right hand, a ruby gives the illusion that you are bigger than life. But a ruby must never be worn on a Thursday—it will change color and bring misfortune.

If this stone suddenly loses its initial hue, it is a sign that a woman is going to die.

When the veins of a ruby outline a snake or a spider, the stone has the power to ward off hostile animals.

Sapphire

Its blue color confers a particular magical character on it. A sapphire is supposedly a celestial jewel, a reflection of divine beauty. It incarnates human hope, so it is believed to cure blind men and help prisoners escape!

A sapphire shields against the greatest hardships: poverty, betrayal, hatred, and error. It multiplies the courage and joy of whoever wears it on his finger. It also radiates love and peace and moderates passions.

In the Orient, thanks to its color, it is a talisman against the evil eye.

Whoever offers a sapphire affirms his innocence or attests to his repentance.

Stone

Innumerable sacred stones exist: enormous rocks; strange edifices with human or animal shapes; flat, holed and black stones, some marked with divine imprints, and so forth

Each type has a particular function and the superstitious love to specify the unique value of such and such a stone. A few beliefs, however, concern the general quality of a mineral, whatever it may be.

In order to avoid the spreading of an epidemic in a flock or herd, the head of the contagious animal must be rubbed with three pebbles. You can also throw the stones in a bucket of well water, then make the cattle drink from the bucket.

Whoever seeks help must throw a stone into a church or cemetery.

Upright stones, like dolmens and menhirs, French or Irish, come from a simple symbolism—these masculine sexes aid in marriage, fertility, and childbirths. They are prayed to and rubbed and offerings are made to them.

The reverse, stones with holes, images of feminity, facilitate pregnancy and, worn around the neck, ward off illnesses. Hung around the neck and shoulders of a horse or donkey, they make the animals mute. Sailors think that these stones assure good fishing.

Certain rocks lie on the ground in a precarious balance—a child can tip them over, but they cannot be budged under the pressure of a dishonest, immoral man!

"*Lightning stones*" or "fire stones," which in reality were flint or prehistoric axes, fell from the sky during certain storms. A man who used them to kill or wound, in sacrifices for example, was thus acting in the image of God striking the earth with his murderous lightning. These stones protect against lightning and facilitate childbirth. Worn in a necklace, they cure vision troubles.

Bezoars, produced by animals, are supposedly stones that can be found in the animal's head, bladder, stomach, or chest. The properties of these stones for the most part refer to the imaginary bestiaries.

Red *eagle stone* hides itself in eagles' nests. Placed on the left arm, it excites love in men and women. Placed on the chest it slows childbirth, but on the knee, it precipitates it. A pregnant woman who wears it as a pendant cannot abort. Eagle stone also treats fevers and epilepsy. Finally, it allows a thief to be revealed—simply reduce the stone to a powder and mix it with some food; the guilty person will not be able to swallow a single mouthful of this preperation.

Black or yellow, *celandine* is hidden in the belly of swallows. This stone must be looked for in August, because it then confers a rare ability—double vision! When it is black, this stone protects against wild beasts and quarrelsome enemies. If it is wrapped in the leaves of the plant by the same name, it prevents visual troubles. Yellow celandine maintains wisdom and good moods. Crushed and enclosed in a calfskin and kept under your left arm, it protects against hereditary illnesses and epidemics.

A dragon's head conceals a *draconite*, assuring invincibility to whoever places it under his left armpit. It also cures all poisonous bites.

Topaz

This magical stone neutralizes poisonous liquids if it is offered in November.

A topaz activates body heat and thereby cures colds and flus that require increased perspiration. It also acts on blood disorders and hemorrhoids.

Worn as a talisman, topaz guards against greed. It promotes commercial operations and attracts money and friendship.

Turquoise

Offered in December, in general, turquoise is a pledge of health and prosperity. Whoever wears it on a finger will know no domestic quarrels and be assured of a painless death.

This beneficent stone changes color according to the health of the person wearing it—it tarnishes when illness is near. It also increases its owner's sexual drive.

The favorite talisman of sailors, turquoise protects against drownings. It is also said to guard against falling off a horse. In the Orient, it wards off the evil eye.

In order to reconcile with enemies or to coax them, it is best to give them a gift of turquoise—they will not be able to resist its appeasing charm.

"The Woodcutters," by Bruegel the Elder (private coll.).

Plants

For a poet, the plant kingdom is a mobile, animated universe that maintains direct or symbolic relations with man. It corresponds to the lower level of Creation and reaches toward the animal world as man reaches toward the Divine. But it also identifies with the life cycle: The growth, regeneration, and death of trees, for example, sums up human destiny in a few years. Man feels close to this mortal kingdom that he integrates into his daily life: Nature is both the scene and source of beauty that gladdens the soul or inspires intelligence and God's gift; at every moment it is ready to nourish its guests. Plant festivals, such as the summer solstice, celebrate the earth's revival as much as the impatient hope of the worker who awaits the profits of his labors.

Plants are used in numerous superstitious practices and give birth to almost as many beliefs. All their resources—leaf, stem, juices, scents, saps, barks, and flowers—were exploited or vaunted. A direct relationship between the planets and the plants that obey their laws was established: Venus and flowers; Mercury and bark and grains; the moon and leaves; Saturn and roots; Jupiter and fruits; and Mars and stems.

Trees are fascinating to mankind because they seem to belong to three antagonistic worlds: Their roots plunge into the earth's bowels; their main branches cover up the ground; and their foliage soars up into the heavens. Thus they connect the domains of the inert, living, and the benevolent. The Tree of Life illustrates this belief—its sap is born of dew from the sky and its fruit assures immortality. No doubt, this perfection characterized the tree of Paradise by which Eve sinned. The tree's vegetable cycle again evokes all of woman's power for bearing fruit and the flux

55

from birth to death. Today it is popular to plant a small tree at a child's birth, and a "maypole" is decorated to celebrate spring. Finally, one of the most common protective gestures is to "knock on wood." Even dead trees conserve very powerful magical properties. Flowers are especially inspiring because of their beauty and medicinal virtues, virtues that only partially concern the superstitious domain. They are receptacles both of the earth that nourishes them and of the sky that quenches their thirst. Everywhere flowers have been put in relation to stars, passions, colors, ideas, and so forth.

Floral symbolism will therefore be extremely rich. However, we must evoke the traditional art of the Oriental bouquet that is inscribed in a religious vision of a plant. Fundamentally, a bouquet recreates the symbolism of a tree—a first, lower bough corresponds to the earth, an upper bough to the sky, and the median bough to man, the intermediary between nature and the divine. Claude Seignolle established a Manichaean list of the most well-known trees and plants that facilitates a general vision of this magical universe:

God made:	The Devil made:
Rye	Buckwheat
Cabbage	Thistle
Carrot	Hemlock
Oats	Darnel
Wheat	Sedge
Clover	Dodder

God's works:	The Devil's forgeries:
Pear tree, apple tree	Thorn
Chestnut tree	Horse chestnut
Vine	Bramble
Genista	Furze
Rosebush	Sweetbrier or "Devil's rosebush"
Walnut	Acorn

Basil

Associated with the legendary basilisk of the Bible, the basil plant did not, however, inherit all its malevolent characters. In fact, it profits from a double meaning: sexual and funereal.

Warn on the chest, basil attests to a young girl's virginity; it withers if she attempts to deceive her friends. But a married woman can put a leaf in her hair as a sign of love without any risk. A young man who is going to visit his fiancée takes a few sprigs of basil in his pocket because this plant is well-known for attracting sympathy. But he doesn't offer the sprigs to his beloved—that would be a scornful gesture.

A basil leaf is given to she-asses and mares that don't procreate. A pregnant woman holds a few of its roots and a swallow's feather in her hand to facilitate delivery.

In Africa, basil leaves ward off bad spells and cure traumatic shocks. Also, they are supposedly valuable as an antidote for scorpion venom.

In addition, this plant is said to make eye ailments disappear and purify the air in houses.

A symbol of mourning in Greece, basil also suffers a sad reputation. If it is heartily insulted, it will grow higher every day!

Crushed and hidden under a stone, it begets a scorpion. Chewed and placed in the sun, it gives birth to little worms.

Bramble

Some recount that brambles kept an inn that went bankrupt due to an excess of credit. Since then, they hang on to people in order to get reimbursed! If they grab a girl's dress, it's a sign that she will marry a widower.

Passing under a bramble bush cures flus, rhumatisms, and burns.

Mulberries became red by the blood of two lovers who killed themselves under its branches. But planted at the side of a house, it brings luck.

Carnation

Its cultivation was introduced to the West by king René of Anjou. It comes from the Orient where it is often considered a funeral flower. Due to its strong scent, a carnation symbolizes ardent love, but it is bad to wear it in a buttonhole on Tuesday. It protects those born under the sign of Aries.

This flower is absolutely taboo on theater stages and he who offers one to an actor will bring him bad luck. We don't know if the reason for this superstition is to be found in its strong odor that bothers the actors, its Oriental origin as a flower of the deceased, or else the idea of the evil "eye"* that its name might let us suspect.

*The French for carnation is "oeillet," the word for eye is "oeil."

Clover

Clover or sainfoin attributes its strength to its use as a pillow for the baby Jesus; it is said that it begins to flower on Christmas night. Its leaves stand erect when a storm is approaching.

But a *four-leaf clover* is especially interesting to superstitious people—it is perhaps the best-shared talisman in the West. It brings luck especially if, after discovering it, you offer it to someone. Whoever finds this miracle plant will meet with love the same day and escape military service. On the evening of Saint John, it confers supernatural powers.

Some affirm that Eve stole a four-leaf clover from the Garden of Eden before taking the path of exile. For others, it only grows beneath the gallows and feeds from the blood of the hanged. It must be gathered before midnight, because it then assures the best luck in gambling.

Clover is still believed to become green again every Christmas.

Each leaf supposedly has a significance: The first brings fame; the second, fortune; the third, true love; the last, health.

A *five-leaf clover*, even more rare, guarantees all the possible good fortunes of the world.

Daisy

This solar plant has the power to predict the degree of love someone feels for you—you must turn toward the sun, then when the toll of noon sounds, pick the daisy's petals saying, "He/she loves me a little, a lot, to distraction, not at all"; the answer only has value for the first of these flowers picked in the year.

Known for its abortive properties, a daisy can prevent some fevers when you take the precaution to eat the first one that you see in the year.

Fern

This sun plant is called "Saint John's hand" in France and "Devil's brush" in England. In both these countries, however, fern is considered a sacred plant resistant to magical charms.

It must be gathered on the night of Saint John, on the summer solstice, and you must have an empty stomach, bare feet, and be wearing a shirt. At midnight, a red flower that illuminates the darkness is said to blossom. Supposedly, this flower is highly sought after by the Devil. A few minutes before the decisive moment, whoever wishes to pick it must trace a circle around the fern, then detach it from the plant without turning his head around or answering maleficent calls. Whoever turns his head will never again be able to put it back in its normal position! A fern flower protects against all spells and especially allows the discovery of hidden treasures. If, when thrown into the air, it spins, then falls perpendicular to the ground, it is a sign that some wonder is concealed there.

A fern seed, easier to obtain, also conceals impressive powers. The night of Saint John, it detaches from the leaf—whoever finds it can make himself invisible at will. But, whoever passes without seeing it loses his way, even if he has known it for years. Or yet on this night, you can climb a mountain, then put this precious talisman in your coin purse—the coins will recreate on their own as they are spent. This seed, like the flower, has the virtue of invisibility. It enables you to win at all games of chance and strength. When crushed, fern seed takes care of stomachaches. Slipped in your pocket, it guarantees the perenniality of the love someone bears for you.

Whoever steps on a fern plant the night of Saint John will hear a concert of birds. But a pregnant woman risks aborting if she walks on its leaves. Mattresses and pillows are made of ferns to treat rhumatisms, rickets, and enureses. Hung over house doors, fern leaves keep lightning away. Cut or burned, they attract rain. Whoever spoils a fern will have a confused mind. In order to protect yourself from snake bites, cut a branch of this plant with your teeth.

Finally, a "Saint John's belt" is made with woven ferns—it cures all illnesses.

Garlic

For many inhabitants of Mediterranean regions, there should never be a day without garlic. This universal panacea for illnesses, placed under the sign of Mars, was called a "foul smelling rose." Its great prophylactic and conjuratory qualities were compensated for by the ill effect it had on the breath of whoever consumed it. Access to temples was prohibited to those impregnated with its odor. But garlic was, however, used in certain religious ceremonies due to its power to attract troubled souls.

Eaten in April, garlic guarantees strength, courage, and success for the day. When cooked the night of Saint John and consumed the next day, it protects against malevolent influences for the year, and for the Italians, keeps poverty away. In the Middle Ages, eating raw garlic was considered one of the best protections against plague and epidemics. Still today, it is reputed to combat drunkenness.

Garlic cloves are placed near a newborn's cradle to keep away witches and demons, as well as snakes that are repelled by its odor. Hung on doors and windows, in East Europe it is known for its ability to drive vampires away. For many Mediterraneans, carrying a few cloves protects against unexpected attacks of insanity. Scandinavian shepherds rub their hands with blessed garlic before milking their animals and hang a few cloves around the animals' necks to shield them from trolls.

To keep children from having troubles due to worms, tie a garlic necklace on them. In the Antilles, whoever wants to be cured of jaundice must wear a necklace of thirteen garlic cloves for thirteen days. On the thirteenth night, he must throw it over his head at a crossroads—if he can go home without turning back, he is sure to recover his health.

Garlic. Miniature from the 15th c. taken from "Tacuinum sanitatis" by Ibn Botlan (Bibl. Municipale de Rouen).

The consumption of garlic helps women to remain chaste, but it is also useful around the bed of a woman giving birth. It protects her from wicked forces and facilitates childbirth.

In Egypt, it was placed in the pessary in a woman's womb; if her breath smelled of garlic the next day, it was an assurance that she was expecting a child.

He who does not want to "reek of garlic" must eat a raw bean, a mint leaf, an anis seed, a coffee bean, or some parsley.

Hellebore

Since the Middle Ages this flower has enjoyed a solid medicinal reputation—it alone cures incurable illnesses, insanity in particular. It is also used to treat rabies and epilepsy.

Eaten in the morning before breakfast, it develops a child's intelligence.

It also allows harvests to be foretold: If the plant has four tufts, it's a sign of a good crop; three, the year will be mediocre; two, catastrophe is near.

A hellebore seed is said to resuscitate scorpions.

But the black flower, called "Christmas rose," that grows in spite of frost, must be distinguished from the white flower. The former is supposedly venemous and maleficent; whoever picks it falls into a sinister sadness. The latter, on the contrary, protects against miscarriages and leprosy. But, if it is cut to decorate a vase, it attracts lightning.

Herbs

Certain so-called simple herbs have been celebrated since antiquity for their recognized and many-times-defined medicinal value. Some affirm that they were first discovered by the gods themselves; others uphold that they were all found on the Mount. Among the most famous, *Saint John's wort* and mugwort occupy a prime place. Very aromatic and blue-violet in color, they serve in the making of crosses or crowns placed over doors to drive off sorcerers, evil spells, or devils. They are considered to be the Christian transposition of the ancient herbs of the summer solstice. In effect, on that date, they attain their full bloom and therefore the summit of their magical power.

The gathering of Saint John's wort and mugwort demands a very precise ceremony so that the plants accept putting themselves into the service of man. They must be gathered at dawn at the moment when they are still under the influence of the moon. The person must not yet have eaten, said his prayers, spoken, or washed his hands. He recites some magic words and most often walks backwards. If the gathering takes place after sunrise, the herbs will be poisoned. But it is also said that they are then purified by the dew that is equivalent to baptismal water.

Herbs belong to a living tradition. From this fact, their definition varies according to regions or herbalists. In general their list comprises ten flowers: artemisia, burdock, chamomile, couch-grass, ground ivy, lycopodium, St. John's wort, orchid, water pimpernel, and vervain. Others add houseleek, yarrow, and sage.

Named after Artemis, lunar goddess, *artemisia* neutralizes the evil eye and protects houses from lightning and robbers. It annihilates the evil effects of water, fire, or poison. In China, it is offered to newlyweds as a good luck charm. In Italy, women place a cross of artemisia on their roofs on the eve of the Ascension. They believe that Jesus blesses it that night, then goes back up to Heaven. Sometimes it is kept in the barn to calm the creatures that are too aggressive.

This herb enters into numerous magical recipes, such as walking sticks, and potions for untying codpieces (see Impotence, chapter VII). A crown or necklace of artemisia is worn to dance around a Saint John fire, then it is thrown into the coals in order to protect oneself from illnesses for a year. Artemisia also indicates the outcome of illnesses when a few of its leaves are placed under a suffering person's pillow. If the person falls asleep immediately it is a sign of recovery.

By its lunar force, this plant can accelerate menstruation and childbirths and prevent miscarriages. It makes vision clearer and cures kidney ailments and epilepsy. When a gun is bewitched, its barrel must be washed with an artemisia decoction on the fifth day of the month of the year to exorcize the spell. Arrows adorned with artemisia are also shot in the direction of the four cardinal points on January 1—they protect a family for twelve months.

Burdock or "giant's ear" cures skin diseases and syphilis and keeps hair from falling out.

Dedicated to the sun, whose color it reflects, *chamomile* must be drunk in an infusion on the night of Saint John—you are then assured of not committing any grave sin for one year. It also treats fevers and snake bites.

The *couch-grass* weed has proliferated on earth since God, in order to punish Adam's disobedience, cast this fatal spell on man. Therefore, it can never totally be gotten rid of. Despite this, ashes from a Saint John fire spread on the ground are said to be able to annihilate it. If couch-grass grows on a section of the earth despite your efforts, it is a fatal sign for your future.

Ivy, associated with Bacchus, the god of wine, prevents intoxication no matter what quantity of alcohol is consumed. Its intertwined branches make it an image of love and tenderness and, as such, a beneficent plant. But it presages misfortune if it dries out suddenly. Formerly, a little chewed ivy was spit in the eye of a rooster wounded in a fight, because its leaves were reputed to cure eye ailments. Those leaves also allow the future to be predicted. Gather ten on All Saints' Day, throw one away, and put the others under your pillow, and all your dreams will come true.

The double, globular tubercle of an *orchid*, called "crazy male," represents virile force. Therefore a decoction of this plant revives amorous zeal.

St. John's wort is nicknamed "St. John's beard" or "fairies' herb" in reference to its magical virtues. In effect, it secretes an odor of incense that calls to mind its origin. Hung on the doors of houses, it keeps away the enemies of God. People who are possessed are made to breathe it. It is affirmed that it calms the sadness of disappointed hearts. Finally, it is reputed to heal all deep wounds and its wine fortefies the female organs.

Vervain, sacred talisman of Rome, was sprinkled on altar stones and the steps of temples. It chases away evil spirits for it is an herb of divine love. Enemies who drink an infusion of vervain together will reconciliate.

Camomile. Miniature taken from the manuscript of Abulcassis, Italy, 15th c. (Bibl. Nat.)

Whoever rubs himself with its leaves will see all his wishes come true. But reduced to a powder and exposed to the sun, it provokes quarrels when it is spread around at a meeting. It is still said that when planted for seven weeks, it begats worms that are fatal to man. Placed in a pigeon house, it attracts all the pigeons in the vicinity. Whoever wants to cure an epileptic must give him a few vervain leaves and a peony grain. Whoever wishes to increase his sexual power wears a plant on the chest. Vervain root favors the growth of vines and trees.

When the herb is placed in a child's pocket, the child will grow up to be polite, intelligent, and agreable. In a house, it guarantees a family's prosperity. Finally, worn around the neck it cures scrofula, ulcers and urinary ailments. Sap from vervain, thick and similar to sperm, inflames love; mixed with honey and warm water, it gives you good breath and unblocks respiratory passages. Seven vervain leaves are put in the hollow of a walking stick.

Sempervivum or houseleek is said to protect the house upon whose roof it grows. That is why it is called "Jupiter's beard." Like vervain, it keeps away fevers and evil spells. On the eve of Saint John, young girls gather as many buds of this herb as they wish to have lovers. They give each bud a name, then go to bed. In the morning the bud that has adorned itself with a flower designates the future husband.

Whoever rubs his hands with houseleek juice will be insensitive to pain, even that from a branding iron. In Wales, it is believed to make you invincible and keep you from being wounded. The first Friday after a child's birth, he is given a little crushed houseleek in water to drink to protect him from convulsions the rest of his life. Also, whoever eats some houseleek cannot be subjected to the tying of a codpiece.

This plant must not be pulled up from the roof of a house because it protects the family from infections. The wife of a sailor hangs it on a beam when her husband goes to sea; if, seven days later, the plant has dried out, it is a sign of a shipwreck. Finally, houseleek is thought to make cows mate.

Yarrow, "soldier's herb" or "Venus's eyebrow," heals deep wounds and can make a woman start menstruating again.

Sage reigns over the medicinal plants like a rose dominates all flowers with all its beauty. Sacred herb of the Romans, it is not content with healing—it revives the body and increases physical vitality.

Sage. Miniature from the 15th c. (Bibl. Nat.)

Gathered with the right hand after a sacrifice of bread and wine, it dispels sorcery and treats eye ailments. It is also affirmed to calm miseries of the heart. It assures pregnant women of an easy pregnancy. Sterile women go to bed for four days and drink its juice, then they have intercourse with their husbands—a child will be born of this union.

This flower is used in numerous magical preparations such as arquebusade water or celestial water. Its vital force is supposedly so powerful that it is said to resuscitate dead infants.

If sage is put in a glass flask under some manure, it will beget a worm or a magical bird. This bird has the tail of a blackbird; its blood, rubbed on someone's stomach, makes him or her lose consciousness for more than fifteen days. The bird must be burned; its ashes thrown into a fire provoke a clap of thunder, and thrown into a lamp they cover the walls with imaginary snakes. Devil's herbs, plants having one leaf marked with a black spot, are found in Brittany. They grow in little paths that are rarely frequented. The sinister mark is supposedly that of the Devil's thumb. The Devil, in attempting to pull up this plant in order to put it more in plain sight, ran into Divine resistance. Whoever uproots this herb will find a treasure. It leaves a mark on the skin, but it erases itself if the person is of good moral character.

Still in Brittany, a golden herb is gathered like mistletoe in the rest of France with a gold pruning knife. Whoever touches it with his foot understands animal talk.

A mysterious plant, called an "oblivion herb," irresistibly attracts all those you wish to capture in your net if you carry the herb in your pocket.

Tormentil or "devil grass" leads whoever treads on it astray. Even the most informed traveller will lose his way. He will only be saved if he finds some herb Paris whose seeds, in falling, show the direction to follow. This beneficent herb also cures colic.

Laurel

The legendary laurel was born of a metamorphosis of the nymph Daphne whom the gods changed into a plant in order to take her away from Apollo. It is also placed under the sign of Esculape, Apollo's son and the god of medicine. Like mistletoe, laurel stays green in winter, incarnating immortality. Laurel crowns consecrate military or intellectual victories and have become the symbol of glory. In China it is believed that a moon hare makes an elixir of immortality under this plant. However, it seems that originallly a laurel crown was especially appreciated as a lightning conductor! It is said that in fact lightning never strikes laurel.

Hung in doorways, this plant wards off illnesses; placed under a pillow, it stirs up wonderful dreams. Laurel blessed on a Sunday cures a feverish person. If its leaves are chewed, it confers the gift of double vision.

On a wedding day, the house where the reception is going to be held is decorated with laurel—it brings the young couple's future under the best auspices. Laurel is also put in the church on the Saturday of Holy Week.

This plant is also supposedly endowed with prophetic powers. If its leaves wither on the bough, it is a sign of death. A handful of its leaves are thrown into a fire—if they crackle as they burn they announce either good luck or an abundant harvest, but if they don't make any noise, it's a fatal omen.

Lily

Both marine and lunar, a fleur de lis inspires mythical imagination sensitive to symbols of purity and virginity. It is said to be born of a drop of milk that fell to the ground from the breast of Zeus's wife, Hera. Aphrodite, jealous, dressed the lily up with a pistil like a donkey's penis. Because of this double origin, lilies have an ambivalent significance. Although it was the symbol of the kings of France and the "flower of flowers" for the Greeks, it concealed a sort of evil, magical poison.

Placed in a vase containing cows milk, it dries up all the cows in the area. Mixed with sap from a laurel and put under manure, it produces worms. If these creatures are put in someone's pocket, that person will not be able to sleep. If someone is rubbed with them, he will catch a fever.

Damaging a fleur de lis brings misfortune, especially to a man, because by doing this he threatens the purity of all the women in his family. It is offered to newlyweds as an assurance of a happy life.

It also reveals whether or not a girl is still a virgin; a yellow lily must be reduced to a powder, then mixed with food. If immediately after this meal the girl feels the need to urinate, it is a sign that she is still such as God made her.

Mandrake

For botanists, *Mandragora Officinarum L.* is a solanaceous plant, like potatoes, characterized by the toxicity of its tubercle and fruits that can, however, be used in very small doses. Its berries have always had a reputation for being aphrodisiacs, but its tubercle, that can take on a vaguely human form, has greatly inspired magicians, alchemists, and sorcerers. The French name "mandragore" gave rise to the deformation "main de glore" (hand of glory) with multiple powers and the radical "man" is found in the German and English names for this plant. Circe and the other magicians know all the powers of this plant that are magical as well as erotic.

Mandrakes are sexed—a male can be recognized by its white color and a female by its blackness. Both have the same powers and assure wealth, power, fertility, and knowledge of the future to their owners.

Mandrake is the little man of the earth who is born under gallows from a criminal's last ejaculation, preferably a virgin. Only magicians know how to uncover it and know that its gathering is a dangerous operation—a mandrake cried, retracts, and demolishes itself when someone tries to pull it up; whoever is imprudent enough to attempt this operation will be made blind and insane by a bolt of lightning.

Male and female mandrake. Miniature taken from a 17th c. manuscript (Bibl. de l'Arsenal).

In order to pull the little man out of the ground, you must go to a gallows at midnight on a Friday accompanied by a black dog; tie the mandrake root to the dog's paw, then call the animal. The dog will be struck dead when pulling out the plant. Some specify that three circles must be made around the plant with a sword beforehand and that when it is being pulled up you must put your back to the wind and face toward the West. Another method consists of wetting it with urine or menstrual blood before gathering it. Other magicians specify that this operation must be carried out in bare feet and that the magical place must be protected with squares, circles, and seals and by perfumes determined by the dominating stars. It is also good to cut an owl's throat and pull up the mandrake by seizing it with the end of a shroud. During this extraction, ghosts are lying in wait ready to devour whoever makes a mistake during the ritual or came for dishonest reasons, such as for the taste of wealth.

Once it is pulled up, the root must be placed on a bed of red soil, any green leaves that are attached must be cut off, and a red berry placed on it for a month and two juniper fruits placed on it for eyes. It is kept like this in a glass jar that is exposed to the sun and that you must not take your eyes off of; each day it must be watered with human blood. At the end of three days it begins to palpitate, its eyes and mouth open, and, in four days, it attains the adult stage and can be utilized—it can speak and foretell the future, double its owner's wealth, open all doors for him, even those that were bolted, and make his wife fertile even if she was sterile beforehand. Upon the death of its owner, a mandrake goes to its master's youngest son and obeys him on the condition that he respected the last wishes of the deceased.

Some believed that after having pulled up a mandrake root, it was necessary to let it rest at the bottom of a grave in a cemetery for thirty days and that it was there that it came to life.

A dried mandrake root is worn as a talisman in a little sachet worn around the neck; placed under the sign of Saturn, it favors its possessor and brings him fertility and wealth. Mandrake extract mixed with that of wine dregs, henbane, poppy, and a little musk, then poured over an apple, plunges whoever eats it into a deep sleep.

A bestiary of the Middle Ages tells us that elephants mate after eating mandrake.

Mistletoe

Gallic Druids gathered mistletoe from sacred oak every year on the sixth day of the moon which then corresponded to the beginning of the year. A French expression "New Year at the mistletoe" is witness to this even though this plant is especially celebrated on Christmas day. Mistletoe undoubtedly acquired part of its magical value from its apparent immortality since it grows, green and flowering, in the heart of winter on a dead tree. This magical value is also due to its growing in bouquets of three branches, the number three being a revered number. The Druids believed that it was sent directly from heaven and gathered it with great ceremony, never cutting it with a vile metal, but with the aid of a gold hedgebill or with their bare hands. They attributed it with curative virtues and offered it in a talisman to believers. In Germanic tradition, mistletoe, placed under the sign of a goddess of love, maintained the fraternity of man, but also assured invincibility and guaranteed against wounds on the battlefield.

Decoctions of this plant are given to animals to promote their fertility. People drink it as an antidote. Its virtues come to light only if its branches were gathered with the right hand. Mistletoe also cure epilepsy—an afflicted person drinks it in an infusion or carries a few blessed leaves on him. It is still believed to cure jaundice.

Some attach a few branches to the door of newlyweds to bring them happiness. Others place some in front of their bedroom to ward off nightmares. But even more numerous are those who kiss under the mistletoe at Christmas as a sign of love. A woman who has never been kissed under

Druid gathering mistletoe, engraving from 1840 (Bibl. des Arts Déco).

these conditions before her marriage risks having a hard time throughout her married life. But it is also affirmed that mistletoe branches that have witnessed too much gushing forth cast an evil spell on those who kiss beneath them. To exorcize this spell, the branches must be burned on the twelfth night after Christmas.

You must never take all the boughs off of a mistletoe plant—it will bring misfortune. Oaks are believed to flower on the night of Saint John, at which time girls place a white sheet at the base of one and gather the pollen from its flowers. Then they place some of the pollen under their pillows at night and dream of their future husbands. A single mistletoe branch can play the same role.

If some mistletoe is hung in a tree with a swallow's wing, all the cuckoos in the area will rush to that place. A bouquet of mistletoe is given to a cow that calved after Christmas in order to protect the cattle from epidemics.

The golden bough, endowed with immense medicinal virtues, is supposedly a branch of mistletoe whose green leaves turn yellow at the new season.

Mushroom

It was long believed that these mysterious, sometimes malevolent plants reproduced by spontaneous generation. In some countries they are called "sons of God." Most beliefs about mushrooms have to do with determining which are edible and which are poisonous or "bleaching" the poisonous plants.

Good mushrooms are believed not to change color when they are broken or crumbled. They should always have an agreeable odor and be endowed with an annulus or ring.

Deathly mushrooms, on the other hand, smell bad, are never attacked by slugs, and turn an onion brown when it is rubbed on their caps. Some maintain that the shinier and more colored a mushroom is, the more poisonous it is; others affirm exactly the contrary.

It is believed that metal has the power to attract the poison. If a piece of silver tarnishes when it is boiled with a mushroom in water, it is a sign that it is bad. But it can be left to marinate: The poison will stick to the silver and the mushroom will become edible.

In order to make a mushroom inoffensive, it must soak in water with a few pinches of kitchen salt. Some are content to wash it with boiling water that "purifies" the plant.

A mushroom is sometimes used as a love potion since it contains an aphrodisiac powder.

Nettle

Not well liked by a person out walking or child whom it sticks, nettle is, however, essentially favorable. It is the primary herb of bravery and whoever holds it in his hand along with a yarrow will never know fear or ever again be afraid of ghosts.

In eastern Europe, children jump over nettle on Saint John's eve in order to be stout. Gathered before sunrise, it chases away evil spells. It is worn dried as a talisman to keep away the evil eye and protect oneself from lightning. Thrown in a hearth fire, it protects a house from the effects of a storm.

He who urinates on nettle nine mornings in a row will never suffer from excesses of bile or liver ailments. If a nettle leaf is dipped into a sick person's urine, it can determine whether or not he will survive: If the leaf remains green, he will get well shortly, but if it dries out, he is condemned. Eating nettle is reputed to ward off fevers.

Nettle, Botanical plate from the 18th c. (Bibl. des Arts Déco.)

Nettle seeds are famed aphrodisiacs and they also facilitate childbirth. In certain regions, nettle leaves are fed to hens so that they will lay more eggs.

Whoever rubs his hands with a mixture of nettle juice and serpentine will be able to catch fish bare-handed without any difficulty.

However, nettle can be negative: In fact, when it grows on a grave, it is said to indicate that the soul of the person who lies there is damned.

Parsley

This plant was judged propitious by the Greeks who consumed it at funeral banquets or took it as an offering to the gods. The Romans, on the contrary, who planted it around graves, considered it evil and capable of provoking epilepsy or striking those who approached it with sterility. A mother who ate some while she was still breastfeeding saw her milk dry up immediately.

Today, however, parsley is reputed to enlarge the breasts of wet-nurses and make their milk more abundant. In Sicily, when a child starts to choke while drinking his milk, custom has it that you stick a sprig of parsley and tobacco in his anus while spitting three times.

In France, you often hear of a pregnant woman preventing parsley from growing or even killing it; this belief is perhaps partly due to the abortive properties attributed to it, but carried on you, a little dried parsley protects against nausea.

Parsley takes a long time to grow because it must go see the Devil seven times before deciding to come up. Also it must be assured that the person that planted it is pure and not wicked! It is advisable to have it sown by a child or an idiot; elsewhere it is said that it is sufficient if you are not a liar or else keep a silver piece in your pocket during the operation. Some people who do not refuse to eat parsley do refuse to plant it under the pretext that it is unlucky and attracts misfortune, but this reason hides their fear of not seeing it come up. You must not give away parsley from your garden—this would be to give away your luck; transplanting it is reputed to attract misfortune.

In the Middle Ages, a sorcerer who wanted to kill an enemy could be satisfied by pulling up a parsley plant while uttering his enemy's name.

Poppy

In this section we will deal with corn poppies, celandine, and poppies, which are all three plants of diabolic latex placed under the sign of the moon.

A white poppy is a hallucinogenic plant; its extracts serve in making opium, morphine, and heroin (whose effects are not under the jurisdiction of superstitions). Note, however, that since antiquity, poppies have been reputed as prophetic and were often used by diviners.

As a general rule, a corn poppy is evil and it is best to beware of it. Whoever stares at its center goes blind. This flower was punished by God for its pride and vanity: He authorized Satan to touch it with his fingers, leaving their black marks on the base of its corolla.

A corn poppy does, however, enable you to determine the degree of love another person feels for you—simply snap a petal between your fingers; the louder and dryer the noise, the more you are loved.

A yellow celandine, that must not be confused with the stone by the same name, is often called a wart herb since its juice permits the removal of warts as well as corns and calluses. Swallows have the habit of giving eyesight to their blind young by placing a celandine leaf over their eyes. Also this flower, a violent poison, passes as a cure for blindness, plague, and dropsy. Worn in your shoe, it cures jaundice, if you took the precaution of not putting on socks or stockings.

Corn poppy. Engraving from the 18th c. (Bibl. Nat.)

Celandine has the ability to make you invincible and make you win trials if you carry some on you with a mole's heart. Being diabolic, when celandine is placed in a sick person's room, it cries or makes the sick person cry when he is going to get well, but it laughs or makes him burst out laughing when he is condemned.

Pumpkin

Like a cucumber or gourd, a pumpkin, by its shape, size, and many seeds, represents fertility. In China it reigns over the plant world.

You must never point at it with your finger, because the pumpkin will rot on the spot.

Planted on Good Friday, it grows thick like an oak.

Its seeds help repress excessive amorous fervor. Crushed and mixed with oil, they are said to remove freckles. Finally, they are talismans of health and prosperity.

On the eve of All Saints Day, Americans carve a pumpkin, giving it a human face. Then they light two candles to light up the eyes and place the pumpkin on their doorsteps. It greets wandering souls and wards off evil spirits—this is the feast of Halloween.

Rice

In the West, custom has it that rice is thrown on newlyweds as they are coming out of the church as a sign of prosperity—this rite comes from Oriental beliefs that see this grain as the primary substance of purity. Rice corresponds to what wheat and bread represent to European populations. Arabs see a grain of rice as a drop of Mohammed's perspiration, and the Chinese burn a handful of it to assure themselves of an abundant crop. Rice is also thrown on newlyweds in Indochina where it is presumed to ward off evil forces. It is an object of worship in India and serves as an offering to trees and gods in all the Orient.

Rose

The most symbolic of them all, a rose incarnates the chalice that received Christ's blood or the precious liquid itself. Life is prolonged by this flower that grows near heros who died on the battlefield. The Romans decorated graves with roses in order to defy Death. Moslems believe that it was born from Mohammed's nail clippings. A rose is attributed with seven petals—each one corresponds to a day of the Creation and a metal. In addition, its beauty and fragility have made it a scepter of love like the lotus in the Orient. Poetically, it is likened to the face and body of a woman.

Whoever eats rose petals has some hope of acquiring a little of the rose's beauty. If you snap a petal between your fingers, the louder the noise, the more you are loved. If all the petals fall from a rose you are holding, it is an omen of death. They bring misfortune when they are scattered on the ground.

"Rosa Centifolia Bullata," by Redouté, 19th c. (Bibl. des Arts Déco.)

A red rose is believed to aid in conception if a woman wears it around her neck in a little sachet. On Saint John's feast day, a girl picks a rose and wraps it in white paper. She opens the packet on Christmas Day. If the flower is well preserved, she wears it in a buttonhole and marries the man she desires. A rose of Jericho is said to blossom on Christmas night and sometimes at a child's birth.

When a rose seed, a mustard seed, and a weasel's foot are placed together in a net, they attract fish, but hung in a tree, they make it sterile forever. Deposited in a lit lamp, these items give the people present the illusion of being covered with soot. When this mixture is thrown on a dying cabbage, it makes the cabbage green again. If it is mixed with olive oil and sulphur, then rubbed on the walls of a house, the house will appear to be aflame.

Rue

Being a poisonous plant, rue plays a protective role against witches and vipers and lifts the sorcery that strikes someone with mutism.

It symbolizes sadness and repentence—it is thrown in the face of a betrayer as an insult. In addition, it grows much better when it is harmed or if it is hidden in a secluded corner. Supposedly the ideal place to plant it is under a fig tree.

Placing sprigs of rue in your socks or house attracts happiness, but you must not offer them or you would be giving your luck away. The most beneficent leaves are those on which butterflies have laid eggs.

A weasel that wraps itself in rue need no longer fear a basilisk.

Whoever eats four sprigs of rue accompanied by a fig, a nut, a little salt, and nine juniper berries for breakfast immunizes himself against pain for that day. Rue also cures eye ailments and vertigo.

"Moonlight on the River in Seba," by Hiroshige, Japan, beginning of the 19th c. (Paris, Musée Guimet)

Trees and Bushes

From the sacred oaks of the Donone forest in Greece to those of Saint Louis in the Bois de Vincennes, from Apollo's laurel to the olive tree of the Acropolis, a tree is a monument linked to history and religious rites. It is—no pun intended—genealogical: If a tree is planted at a child's birth, the growth of these two will be parallel; each town, each house, and each noble family has its guardian tree whose death is feared. The fall of a family tree announces the end of the lineage. There are many rites surrounding trees, but a cult in connection with them cannot be spoken of. They are the figuration of a transcending power: God is worshipped by means of a tree. The symbolism of the cross is linked to this worship and, in the superstitious mentality, it remains a crime to chop down a tree. Whoever cuts a branch risks seeing one of his limbs amputated in a short time. A tree, linking air, earth, and water together, adds fire to these elements when it is struck by lightning. Its wood protects against all sorcery and fascinations and must be saved. Illnesses result from a fascination or a possession. Therefore, nails are pounded into trees, new ribbons hung from the nails, and flat stones tied to the ribbons to exorcize the evil.

The *apple* tree was venerated by the Gauls and remains a magical tree for the Normans who affirm that its roots must be watered with cider if the tree is to grow stout. If an apple remains attached to its branches all winter until the following spring when the tree blossoms, it is a sign of approaching mourning for one of the inhabitants of the house.

An apple, which is likened to the fruit of the tree of science, has a much worse reputation although it is considered a universal panacea in the eyes of popular medicine. This forbidden fruit symbolizes both desire and the taste for knowledge—when it is cut open, its seeds outline a five-pointed star. A young man is advised not to offer an apple to a young woman because she will immediately go share it with another.

In order to protect a cellar fron snakes, deposit six apples around in it before the harvest. After the harvest, these apples must not be thrown out, but burned in the hearth. A curious superstition says that whoever devours a green apple will get lice.

In many mythologies, the *ash* tree has an importance equal if not superior to that of the oak. An image of immortality and fertility for Scandinavians and Germans, for the Kabyles it was the first tree to appear at the time of Creation. For them it is also, above all, linked to a woman and no man shall plant it. If he carries out this deed, he will soon see a male in his family die.

An ash is known for its ability to ward off snakes; an infusion of its leaves is reputed to combat venoms.

A young English girl who puts an ash leaf in her left shoe will marry the first man she encounters. When this tree doesn't produce any fruit, it announces the approaching death of a king or important figure in this world.

A forked ash stick allows underground copper mines to be discovered.

An *aspen* was used to make Christ's cross and its leaves still tremble with horror today. To cure a fever, simply drive a nail into its trunk.

For some, a *beech* tree supposedly furnished the wood for the Holy Cross, but it is more probable that it was an aspen. It is a magical tree that cannot be struck by lightning and that gives pleasant dreams to whoever sleeps in its shade. A beech is the only tree a bear cannot climb; fairies are fond of it and dance around its trunk. Those who are good observers notice a perfect circle where the grass doesn't grow at the foot of some beeches—the circle is an infallible sign of the presence of fairies, and the tree must then be approached with much respect.

Birch is used in making torches that are lit to accompany newlyweds to their home on their wedding night—it will bring them joy and happiness in their union. A cross of birch placed on the front door of a home protects it from the Devil's doings; you must carry a piece of its bark to protect yourself from spells. Northern populations are familiar with the many curative virtues of its sap, used under the name of "birch water."

A *cherry* tree will bear much fruit if you take the precaution to have the first ripe fruit of the season eaten by a woman who has recently given birth to her first child. Its fruits, healthy and pleasant tasting, are endowed with divinatory abilities—whoever shoots a cherry pit from between his thumb and index finger and hits the ceiling of the room where he ate the cherry on the first try is sure to get married shortly. In the United States at the end of a meal a girl counts the number of pits in her plate while saying, "Married this year, next year, someday, never." The last pit will give the answer of her destiny.

"To be sure that a vineyard produces a good wine, a cherry tree must be planted in the middle of it."

Cherry tree in blossom, painting on wood. Japan (Paris, Musée Guimet).

A *chestnut* tree bears a mealy fruit that serves as food for the poor. A chestnut is a funeral food that should be left as an offering near the deceased. In certain regions of Italy, the ritual meal of the eve of All Souls' Day must include this fruit.

Kept in your pocket, a chestnut or horse chestnut guards against rhumatisms and circulatory problems.

A *cypress* is a beneficent tree that symbolizes immortality— it was from its wood that Egyptians made their sarcophagi. Its presence in cemeteries protects visitors from will-o'-the-wisps and wandering souls. It is very beneficent to stand under a cypress because the air surrounding it is free of all noxious vapors.

An *elder* is a magical tree that is intentionally left to grow on farm surroundings where it protects man and animals. It is known for its capacity of warding off moles as well as snakes. Anyone who is a victim of a spell must beat his clothes with an elder stick—each whack that he gives strikes the sorcerer. Elder wood must never be burned in the hearth because this act will prevent the hens from laying. Whoever hits a domestic animal with an elder stick will see the animal soon perish.

Elderberries are sovereign against warts and allow many illnesses to be cured.

The *elm* does not bear any fruit. Known for its longevity, it often replaces the oak in villages as the tree of justice. It is linked to funeral cults like the cypress and the yew that also live a very long time and are presumed to be immortal.

It is linked more to man, as opposed to the vine that entwines it that is consecrated to woman.

A *fig* is ambivalent, being both sought after for the protection it can bring and the savor of its fruit, and feared as if it were cursed. Venerated in Palestine and Greece, it was a life-giving tree whose fruit, in the words of Plato, was "the philosopher's friend." For the Romans, on the contrary, a fig was essentially impure to such a point that a temple had to be totally destroyed if a fig accidentally grew on its roof. Some offered its fruits to the gods and the dead; others saw it as the tree of Judas.

Like hawthorn and laurel, a fig has the privilege of never being struck by lightning. It is still planted in farmyards of southwestern France where, like the elder more to the north, it protects the inhabitants and cattle from evil influences.

A fig's surroundings are reputed to be deadly and sleeping under its shade is supposedly fatal, but to conjure this effect, simply eat three of its leaves and slit its trunk. Burning its branches in the hearth dries up a nursing mother's milk. It is inadvisable to pass between two fig trees, especially for a girl who wishes to get married within the year.

The best way to calm a raging bull is to tie it to the trunk of a fig tree. If the tree is sick, to give it back its strength simply burn some of its own leaves at its base on Saint John's Day.

A *fir*, the king of the forests for the Germans, is, like all conifers, the image of eternity. At Christmastime still today, it is offered glittering ornaments, ribbons, or egg shells. A Christmas tree must be burned before the twelfth day that follows this celebration, or else there will be a death in the family. Some people say, however, that it must not be burned at all. When a fir is struck by lightning, it announces the approaching death of a powerful person.

The precocious flowering of a *hawthorn* evokes the joy of spring-like revival. It is a protective plant that is offered to couples, placed near the cradle of newborns, and hung on the door of houses to protect them from sorcery. Witches get caught on and are torn by its points, that served in the making of the crown of thorns. If it is respected by lightning, especially when it is in bloom, it is undoubtedly in memory of the burning bush.

A hawthorn cures fevers, and whoever places a branch in front of a calvary is assured of meeting with luck in gambling.

A *hazel* tree is used in the making of forked rods used by witches or magicians. A straight, unwrought branch without buds must be used, and whoever knows how to use it has the power to find hidden sprigs and buried treasures.

A hazel is a magical tree that hatches a golden bough each Christmas night. Hazelnuts, which some see as the image of a child in its mother's womb, are a sign of fertility and should be offered to couples at the time of their wedding. Hazelnut years are reputed to be favorable for fertile marriages. In certain provinces of eastern Europe, however, these years are also said to be abundant in prostitutes. Finding a doubled hazelnut announces wealth or twins.

According to certain traditions, *holly* is supposedly a creation of the Devil, who wanted to mimic the laurel that God had just invented. But more often, on the contrary, holly is a favorable and beneficent plant that is associated with sacred mistletoe at the time of New Year's celebrations. Always green and covered with fruits during the cold season, it is an image of eternity. Some see its prickles and red berries as a symbol of the crucifixion.

Holly without prickles, or knee holly, is very favorable for women, whereas regular holly is more beneficent for men, but both keep away evil spirits equally. It is good to mix holly into bouquets.

A girl who picks a holly leaf counts its prickles, saying, "Girl, wife, widow, nun"—the word that corresponds to the last prickle announces her destiny.

Hornbeam wards off evil powers—a forked rod made of its wood is sovereign against the evil eye.

A *juniper* tree aided the Holy Family at the time of the flight into Egypt. It is very beneficent and its presence wards off demons. Its wood was used by alchemists to heat up their retorts. Juniper fires were known for their property of shunning epidemics. Popular medicine knew the many therapeutic powers of its berries and its ability to ward off snakes.

A *lilac* is linked to May and must only be offered with precautions. A white lilac offered to a woman by a young man announces the purity of his intentions, but it must never be given to a sick person because he risks having a relapse. A mauve or blue lilac announces a request in marriage.

The *linden*, consecrated to Venus, is a tree of fidelity and friendship—its scent evokes the sweetness of living. It was, however, used in witchcraft, but especially for the Germans it remains a protective and guardian tree of villages and families. It is celebrated on May 1st with dances organized around its trunk.

A *maple* tree is very lucky in North America—newborns are carried under its foliage to assure them strength and vitality.

The *myrtle*, from which crowns for newlyweds and heros are made, is a tree of glory and fame, but also of happy loves. When it blooms in a garden, it brings luck and happiness to the entire house.

The *oak* is the king of trees and was of great importance in mythologies of western Europe. It is consecrated to Zeus, and in its boughs the Druids gather mistletoe for New Year's Day. Saint Louis held his court of justice under an oak, and all oaths taken under this tree, especially if it is formed from two twin trunks, cannot be broken without danger. A trial placed the two litigants under an oak; whoever was touched by the first leaf to fall was presumed innocent and won the trial. Traditional medicine made use of the oak's bark, as well as its leaves and acorns.

Cutting down this tree or simply cutting off one of its branches can bring only misfortune.

To relieve or cure hernias, you must embrace an oak. This act also assures women that they will have a virile husband and many children.

Whoever passes over the cavity of a hollow oak is assured of having vigor and health.

A small parasitic insect, a gallfly, creates galls on oak leaves that are often found on the ground. Whoever finds one of these little balls must open it—if there is a larva inside, he is assured of becoming acquainted with wealth; if it is a little fly, he can expect some bad news; finding a spider inside announces famine in the region.

The *olive* tree produces a lucky and magical oil that protects against drunkenness and reinforces the virility of whoever drinks it nine days in a row. The foremost tree of Islam, sacred for Jews and Greeks, an olive tree has a purifying power and combats sterility. Its bough crowns the heads of heros and symbolizes peace.

A *pine* tree is of great importance in the Far East where its wood serves in the making of ritual objects.

"The Great Pine," by Paul Cézanne (Musée de Sao-Paulo).

In certain countries it was planted at the birth of a girl, as opposed to a cedar for boys. A pine rod allows iron ore buried in the soil to be revealed.

The *walnut* is a complex tree that is planted at the birth of a child in Germany. But around the Mediterranean, it is also reputed to give refuge to witches who dance around its trunk at their Sabbath. Whoever sleeps beneath a walnut tree will see the events of the coming year in a dream, but he or she also risks not waking up.

Gathering its leaves on Saint John's day keeps lightning away and protects whoever carries a few of them from attacks by vermin, lice in particular.

Like the hazelnut, a walnut is a triumphant sign of life and fertility. If a walnut is placed under a witch's chair, she cannot get up, but few dare to do this for fear of vengence. Walnuts with three fruits in them are highly sought after because they protect against witchcraft and are excellent good-luck charms that are good to keep in your pocket. Finally, oil drawn from these nuts is a sacred liquid and it is important that it be respected.

The *willow*, especially if it is weeping, is the symbol of affliction, unfaithful love, and betrayed trust. Whoever carries a piece of its bark on him will be protected from such suffering. This tree is also known for its gossiping—whoever betrays a secret in front of it will hear it repeated in the wind shortly afterward.

In the Far East it is said that a girl who sleeps in its shade risks finding herself pregnant. In Russia, whoever plants a willow digs his own grave.

Worn as a talisman, bark from a willow wards off nightmares and all terrors that are born of the night.

Like the cypress, a *yew* tree produces a rot-proof wood that is used in the construction of churches, where it signifies immortality. Yews, which live to be very old, are also linked to funeral rites and are often found in cemeteries. It is a bad omen to chop one down or cut off one of its branches.

A person out walking who falls asleep under a yew risks forgetting the reasons for his outing and finding himself without a memory when he wakes up.

Water Lily

This friend of the nymphs, which evokes the birth of the world springing from primordial waters, is most often considered a poison against love and should be eaten by those who have condemned themselves to chastity.

However, placed under the sign of the moon and acquatic powers, it is also valued as an aphrodisiac. Worn as a talisman in a sachet around the neck, it promotes virility.

In Africa, a water lily decoction is said to bring the milk back to mothers or wet-nurses whose milk had dried up.

In Asia, a *lotus* is a symbol of beauty that rises up pure from stagnant and unhealthy waters. It represents wisdom and a consciousness of time, because at once it presents the past, present, and future (the bud, blossom, and fruit). Buddha is represented in the center of an eight-petaled lotus and Brahma is represented in the very form of a lotus.

Wheat

Despite its widespread, intensive use, wheat remains a misunderstood plant of mysterious origins. Therefore, it is considered a gift of God, the primary nourishment assured to man since the beginning of time. Ancient peoples devoted a cult to it strictly associated with that of the Mother Earth. Sowing, harvesting, and garnering festivals appeared in the fore-

"Summer" or "Ruth and Boaz" (detail), by Nicholas Poussin, 1664 (Musée du Louvre)

ground of most Western agricultural calendars. The vegetative cycle of wheat symbolizes both fertility, assured by the union of the earth and sky, and the eternal new beginning of seasons and years—in brief, human life.

It is believed that on the third night of May, a small red insect falls from the sky and nestles down in the wheat for two or three days—it is the assurance that God will provide for a good crop. In China, wheat seems to be protected by a particular constellation of eight black stars that correspond to the eight kinds of grain. On Easter Day bread is baked, then hidden until sowing time. On that day the bread is fed to the horses—it guarantees a good crop and keeps these animals healthy. Also, to obtain a good crop, you must get up at midnight of Saint John's Day and gather seven wheat ears that are still green. Some plant a few grains of wheat in a pot on Saint Barbara's Day.

On the evening of a wedding, the groom's mother, aided by other women of the family, puts handfuls of wheat grain on the bride's head. Then the groom takes a few grains and disperses them over his body. In Corsica, before a wedding feast the bride sits on a cup of wheat and each of her attendants pours a few grains on her head. These practices are aimed at assuring a couple's fertility.

In Italy, on Saint John's eve, a girl sows a little wheat in a pot that is then hidden from the sun's rays—nine days later, it is put back in the light. If the shoots are green and stout, it is a sign that the girl will find a handsome, rich husband; from then on a red ribbon is tied around the pot. If, on the other hand, the wheat grows yellow or white, it is thrown out because it indicates a disastrous conjugal future.

*The Annunciation (detail), by Leonardo da Vinci
(Musée des Offices)*

In Germany, grains of wheat are placed on a horse's back to invigorate the horse.

Wheat grains blessed by the parish priest have the power to ward off storms, tempests, and fevers. Thrown over the shoulder, some average grains get rid of warts—as many grains must be thrown as there are warts.

On the night of the Adoration, wheat helps predict the future—twelve grains must be taken, representing the twelve months to come, and thrown, one by one, into the fireplace. Those that fly the farthest when they pop foretell the happiest months.

"The Courtesans," by Carpaccio, Venice, 1455–1525 (Venice, Musée Correr).

Animals

A large part of the animal world is made up of very ancient cultural practices linked to animism. Animism is above all a "psychological conception" of the universe (Freud in *Totem and Taboo*)—it was one of the first organized manifestations of the religious spirit. There an animal is not neutral—it is good or evil, pure or impure, or lucky or unlucky, often both at once. In addition, beliefs in metamorphoses and metempsychoses have licensed this domain: Many animals are reincarnations of human beings or the vehicle of transmigrating souls. They are also the mask or appearance chosen by gods, spirits, and especially demons.

Animals are also the expiatory victims that are sacrificed (oxen, bulls, roosters, and so forth) or chased away after being charged with sins of the community (scapegoat). Animals are signs of destiny, privileged instruments of divination. The best divinatory animals are the spider, raven, cuckoo (all birds are, more or less), dog, horse, rat, lizard, snake, and fish. Either the study of their behavior or observation of their intestines (haruspices) is used for omens.

All this animal symbolism was established in the West in the Middle Ages by the *bestiaries*. There animals took on an allegorical value that has varied little since. The three basic animals of the bestiaries are the lion, ox, and eagle, symbolic representations of the evangelists (the fourth being a winged man). "I saw four living beings and beheld that their contenance bore the resemblance of a man. Each of them had four faces and each of them four wings . . . the likeness of their faces was that of a man in front, then of a lion on the right of the four, of an ox on the left of the four, then of an eagle in back . . ." Ezekiel, Book of Revelations, IV.

These bestiaries came from the *Bible* and the *Physiologus*, a Greek work from the second century. That most of the animals are from the Middle East or the Indies explains the importance in Europe of animals of great symbolic weight, such as the lion, ibis, elephant, or monkey. Little by little the bestiaries were Europeanized with the apparition of the fox, dog, and so forth. A bestiary dating from 1350 describes five gentle animals (stag, doe, fallow deer, roe deer, and hare), symbols of virtue and the Church, in opposition to five foul animals (wild boar, sow, wolf, fox, and falcon), symbols of vice and the Antichrist.

Works of God:	Works of the Devil:
Eagle	Wood Owl
Turtledove	Jay
Finch and Nightingale	Sparrow
Swallow	Bat
Blackbird	Thrush
Lark	Sparrow hawk
Codfish	Lesser spotted dogfish or dogfish
Mackerel	Ling
Conger eel	Toadfish
Sea Robin	Ray
Sole and Plaice	Spider Crab
Spiny Lobster	

The preceding lists, established by Claude Seignolle (*Les Évangiles du Diable*), clearly show the division of animals into pure and impure. The favorite animals of those who practice witchcraft are the messengers of the night and of death: the cat, screech owl, bat, toad, and raven.

Ant

Although ants are gregarious and industrious, just like bees, they are less appreciated by man because he doesn't profit from their activity.

It brings bad luck, however, to destroy an ant colony; if ants build their dwelling near yours, they promise you security and wealth.

When a bird's nest is found, it is best not to speak of it out loud, especially near a stream, because ants will run to it.

Their eggs eaten with honey guarantee love.

Ants supposedly never sleep.

An ant transporting its eggs to a new place is a sign of bad weather.

Breaking a newly-laid egg over an anthill cures jaundice and fevers.

Basilisk

Born of an egg from a seven year old rooster and hatched by a toad, this biblical animal presents itself in the form of a snake, with or without wings, having the head, neck, and feet of a rooster. Another tradition says that every year roosters lay an egg from which a crocodile that kills man with a glance is born. A near relation of the snake and dragon, the basilisk incarnates absolute evil and allies itself with the forces of death. It kills with its hissing; its corpse poisons whoever eats it; and it is struck dead when presented with a mirror. Alas, this malevolent animal fears only "the weasel wound in rue"!

Bat

Being nocturnal animals, bats are connected with unknown spirits; both bird and mammal, they appear to be the image of lust and bisexuality and are reputed to be impure.

Bats lose their sight in front of bright light. If you rub your face with bat's blood, you will be able to see as clearly at night as during the day. Having a bat's right eye in your pocket makes you invisible.

If a bat flies near you, beware—someone is trying to betray or bewitch you. If one flies around a house three times, it foretells death or at least a calamity. If it hits the window pane of a sick person's room, the person is going to die.

If a bat flies into long hair, it takes hold and cannot be gotten out.

A bat is nailed to barn and shed doors to keep witches away.

This malevolent animal is also respected; for some, its life represents that of a man's. To kill a bat is to shorten your life or the life of another human being.

Bats can even be a sign of luck—carrying a bat's bone is an excellent talisman.

Bear

Jung, the psychoanalyst, was once on a visit to the Indians of New Mexico. They asked him what was the animal of his clan. He answered that Switzerland had neither clans nor totems. When the discussion was over, the Indians left the room by a ladder that they descended as we descend a staircase: with their backs to it. Jung went down, as we do, facing it. At the bottom, the Indian chief

89

silently pointed to the bear of Berne embroidered on his visitor's jacket: the bear is the only animal that climbs down with its face to a tree trunk or ladder.

Andre Malraux, Anti-memoirs*

A bear cub is born shapeless, so its mother remodels it by licking it. Unless they have been "ill-licked," bears are known for their gluttony and courage.

The bear. Anonymous watercolor, 16th c. (Bibl. Nat.)

Whoever gets on the back of a bear is cured of fear forever; if he is an infant, he is only cured of hay fever.

Bear fur constitutes an excellent talisman against blindness.

In Finland, before killing a bear, you ask its forgiveness for your act. In the United States, bears are said to have litters only every seven years and when they do, all the newborn animals around perish.

Bee

Close to man in their social organization and productive activities, bees, like man, are supposedly natives of the Garden of Eden. They are often the little servants of God Almighty. They are wise creatures having a special knowledge of the future. Christianity made bees symbols of virtue and chastity. Their heirarchical community structures explain their use as an emblem of royal or imperial power. Their direct usefulness, the making of honey, completes this benevolent view.

Bees are not known to exist in Ireland.

A virgin girl can, without danger, go through a swarm of bees, but if a dishonorable woman approaches a swarm, she will be stung.

*Translated by Terence Kilmartin.

Bees like to participate in their owner's life—the hives must be adorned with a piece of a bride's veil or a black crepe, in the case of death, in order to keep them up to date with daily life. In Alsace, the former French province, a family member announced a death to the bees in these terms: "Your master is dead!"

Bees are particularly sensitive insects—they leave home if the hives are counted or sold without their being warned. Moving hives on Good Friday kills the bees.

Flying in a house, they announce a visitor; flying around the face of a sleeping child, they foretell a happy life. To give a hive to someone is also to bring him luck.

When bees swarm on a dead tree, it is an omen of a death in the family. Finally, if they leave all the hives, you had best get out an umbrella.

Beetle

The beetle is a sacred animal of ancient Egypt, being a symbol of both the sun and of eternal return. Its representation in the form of a ring or earring provides many amulets or talismans.

A beetle is a sign of death when it walks on your shoe or when it comes out of a shoe placed near a door. In Scotland, it foretells a misfortune when it enters a room where the family is gathered. But it must not be killed—that will only make the misfortune greater.

Beetles attract storms.

Birds

Being aerial, birds are in direct contact with the sky and with spirits. Birds gave rise to a most important form of divination: ornithomancia. There remain numerous followers of ornithomancia yet today.

In Brittany, birds are said to answer questions by their song. But man no longer understands their language.

A child who dies before being baptized is transformed into a bird until the day when John the Baptist baptizes him or her.

In Ireland, Australia, and Brazil, a black or gray bird that flies around a tree at night without stopping is carrying the souls of sinners who have not yet made their peace.

Birds that fly from right to left in even numbers are good omens; if they fly from left to right or in odd numbers, they bring bad luck.

A bird that enters and exits a room by an open window, that hovers

Drawing taken from the "Vallardi Album," by Pisanello, 1395–1450 (Musée du Louvre).

over a house, or hits against a window is a sign of death for one of the inhabitants.

If a caged bird dies the morning of a wedding, the marriage will be an unhappy one (Scotland). A bird that flies over a woman who is washing swaddling clothes announces that the woman's baby will soon fall ill.

In Great Britain it's a bad omen to receive bird droppings.

Upon hearing the cry of night birds, you should throw salt into the fire to ward off an evil spell.

BLACKBIRD

Despite its black feathering, a blackbird is more or less beneficent. Two blackbirds perched side by side are a good omen (except in Wales, where they announce a death near at hand).

If a blackbird's heart is placed under the head of a sleeping person, that person will unveil all his secrets.

Hanging the feathers of a blackbird's right wing by a red thread in an uninhabited house will prevent intruders from sleeping there.

Bull

A biblical animal that symbolizes expiation, the bull represents life and fertility in Crete and Egypt. Ambivalent, it is also evil in the form of the two gods Bal and Moloch. Both feared and admired, the bull has not laid itself open to supersititions.

Detail of the "Pasiphaë" by Pierre Lemaire, 17th c. (coll. des Musées Nationaux.)

Butterfly

Like a bird, a butterfly is a messenger. Its lightness is sometimes compared to that of a soul freed from its carnal envelope. In Ireland, seeing a butterfly fluttering near a corpse foretells eternal blessedness for the deceased. In Scotland, it is a good omen if a golden butterfly dies near a dying person.

A pink butterfly promises you lifelong happiness. If, on any day, the first butterfly you see is yellow, it foretells an illness; if it is white, luck. To see three butterflies together on a flower brings misfortune.

In Great Britain, if you want to have a favorable year, you must kill the first butterfly you see in the year.

Cat

This latter was a remarkably large and beautiful animal, entirely black, and sagacious to an astonishing degree. In speaking of his intelligence, my wife, who at heart was not a little tinctured with

*superstition, made frequent allusion to the ancient popular notion
that regarded all black cats as witches in disguise.*

Edgar Allan Poe, The Black Cat

Cats are recognized as having gifts of clairvoyance, cleverness, and
ingenuity. In most countries the black cat is considered malevolent.
Egyptian religion, which equates the male cat with the sun and the female
with the moon, grants cats seven to nine lives. To reward a cat for its
respect, Mohammed stroked it three times on the back, thereby assuring
it of always landing on its feet.

*"The Witches' Sabbath," by Steinlen, 19th c. (Bibl. des
Arts Déco.)*

A cat, no matter what color, participates in daily life. If it licks itself,
it announces a visitor. If it sneezes once, there is happiness in the house;
if it sneezes three times, the family will have colds. A girl who has stepped
on a cat's tail can abandon all hope of marrying within the year. No cat
that has been bought will be good for hunting mice. A cat that catches
birds does not catch mice.

One should not go to sea if a cat is cleaning its face—it's a sign of a
tempest. If a cat turns its back on a fire in the hearth, it foretells a
shipwreck. If a cat can be heard meowing on a ship, it's a bad omen.

Black cats are accomplices of the demon and they attach themselves
to people who have made a pact with him. In France, a "matagot" is the
cat that goes to the Witches' Sabbath. To chase away evil spirits, you
should burn a black cat on the first week of Lent or in Saint John fire. On

the other hand, throwing a black cat into a conflagration puts out the fire. In lower Brittany, when the Devil is mentioned at the intersection of five roads, a black cat will run up from the opposite road.

Every black cat hides a Devil's hair in its tail. They also have a single white hair that confers great power on whoever finds it.

In the Vosges Mountains of France, the left paw of a black cat put in a hunter's left pocket is believed to prevent him from aiming well.

Caterpillar

There are many ways of getting rid of them, but none for attracting them! At sunrise, you must walk around the garden three times and say to them: "Caterpillars and baby caterpillars, I am going; follow me." Caterpillars die if it rains during the octave of the Corpus Christi Day Mass. A woman who is menstruating kills the caterpillars around her.

In Yorkshire, throwing a fuzzy caterpillar over your left shoulder brings good luck.

Cattle

Sensitive to spell casters and evil spirits, cattle must be protected in the barn as well as at the fair or market.

When selling your cattle, take a sample clump of fur from the tail or hide of the animal in order to assure yourself of the best transaction.

When buying an animal, it is recommended that all the cattle be blessed. In Ireland, if, in going to the market to buy animals, a woman is encountered before a man, it foretells a bad transaction.

The Scottish believe that cows must be shaved behind the ears and at the base of the tail so that witches won't steal their milk. (See also Ox, Horse, Sheep, and Cow.)

Cock

By its morning song, the cock (or rooster) interrupts all nocturnal activity and thus exorcizes all malevolent forces. Its song puts an end to the Witches' Sabbath, frightens lions, and chases away vampires.

Since it announces the day, a cock is naturally a symbol of the sun. It is believed that on Judgment Day, all the cocks, even those on belfries, will sing and wake up the living and the dead. Its comb is an image of courage and power rivaling a lion's mane. A prophetic animal, a rooster has long been used by diviners who study its behavior and intestines. The weathercock at the top of belfries is supposedly a survival of a ritual sacrifice practiced at the ground-breaking of a house.

If a cock crows at twilight, it announces death. If it crows facing the door of a house, it announces the arrival of a stranger. In the Guienne region it is said that "If the cock crows in the evening, rain runs behind it."

Cock fight. Indo-Iranian miniature, 18th c. (Bibl. Nat.)

In Charente it is affirmed that a rooster, hatched by magpies, crows at all hours. For those in Lorrain, a rooster born on Good Friday will crow before others.

So that a medicine is effective, it is advisable to administer it at the rooster's crowing. In Norway, a rooster aids in finding drowned persons, because put in a boat, it crows as it approaches a body.

A black rooster chases away the rats in a poultry yard.

It is not proper to eat rooster on Thursday.

Cow

This animal, sacred in the Orient, is especially appreciated by Western farmers for its utilitarian virtues. Formerly a sign of prosperity in the countryside, it assured a household an essential complement to the diet in the form of milk and meat. The celebrated "golden calf" still symbolizes that abundance today.

For the Scottish, milk from a white cow is of inferior quality. Americans maintain that red cows have the best meat. A cow's milk sours if the farmer forgets to wash his hands between each milking. But, if a swallow passes under a cow's udder, the cow's milk will turn to blood.

Cows eat golden buds in order to make the best butter. The Bretons affirm that to protect a cow from a wolf, you must offer butter to Saint Hervé.

A cow will calve if you cut the end of its tail in fourths or hit it three times with a hazel tree stick.

Bretons say a cow must not be hit with genista—it will no longer give milk.

When a farmer buys a cow, he must take it away with a rope around its neck. If you are selling a calf, you must make it walk out of the barn backwards so that the cow doesn't become sterile.

A cow announces a death near at hand if it moos three times in your presence.

When a cow raises its tail, it's a sign of rain. But if it slaps its tail against a tree or fence, it's a sign of good weather.

Crane

A relative of the stork, it is likewise the image of fidelity and longevity.

If the feathers of its right wing are hung by a red thread in the middle of a new house, no one will be able to get sleep there.

A crane's heart placed under the pillow of someone sleeping will make that person tell all about what he or she did the night before.

If a horse is rubbed with water in which a dead crane has soaked, the horse will become white (dappled, if it is a mare).

Crayfish

Armor-plated and aquatic, crayfish can have certain powers over crops.

In order to save crops from late frosts, bury a jar filled with river water containing twelve crayfish in the middle of the field.

In order to preserve a harvest, fill a container with ten crayfish and water and expose to the sun, then plunge it in a field.

Cricket

It seeks the warmth of homes and thus becomes a protector of houses. If it leaves a house, it's a sign of illness or death to come.

If it gets quiet when you leave for a fair, in Provence, you will make bad transactions.

Cuckoo

Its song, heard only for a short period at the beginning of spring, has made the cuckoo a prophetic bird. The wish that is made when a cuckoo is heard for the first time in the year is always granted.

If, when you first hear a cuckoo in the year, you have money in your pockets, you'll have money all year long. In Wales, to hear its cry before April 6 is bad luck, but it assures a year of prosperity if it is heard on April 28. To hear it after August, particularly in September or October, is a diabolical omen; he or she who hears it will die during the year.

In Finland and Brittany, a cuckoo announces, to girls, marriage before the coming winter. In Alsace, girls ask it when they will be married—the number of cries corresponds to the years of waiting. In Scotland, it indicates the number of years left to live.

The cuckoo is so busy answering questions that it hasn't got time to build a nest and deposits its eggs in other birds' nests.

Dog

Linked to the beyond and in particular to hell, it exercises the same function there as on Earth—Cerberus guards the Devil's house. A dog smells death approaching and warns man with its howling. This corpse eater that has the power to see phantoms played the role of a scapegoat in the Indies and America.

The Chinese attribute a dog with seven consecutive lives. The Moslems say that it must not be killed because its life equals that of seven men.

To encounter a black dog brings misfortune, and, say the Normans, all dogs belong to the Devil except sheep dogs.

In order to determine if a sick person will get well, rub his teeth with a piece of food, then throw it to a dog. If the dog eats it, it's a good sign; if it refuses it, the person will die. A rabid dog that has just bitten someone must not be killed; if it is, the wounded person will not get well.

A dog that passes between two friends shakes up their friendship. A dog that runs between the legs of an English-woman lets her know that her father or husband is going to punish her for some reason. Also in England, to make an unknown dog follow you is a good omen.

If a dog eats some grass, rolls on the ground, or scratches for a long time, it is going to rain.

Dolphin

According to Aristotle, "Many stories circulate about dolphins that give proof of their amiable and gentle nature as well as manifest the deep attachments that they supposedly show for young boys . . ." The dolphin, as well as the porpoise with which it is often confused, is a friend of man. It loves music and saves shipwrecked people. Everywhere it is a good omen to encounter one.

Its presence announces good fishing, but when it approaches too near the coast, a tempest is not far away. If it goes back out toward the north, it's a sign of good weather; if it goes toward the south, it will be rainy and cold.

Dolphins transport on their backs the souls of sailors who died at sea.

Donkey

Although it is the image of ignorance and poverty, in all the Orient it is considered a sacred animal. In the West, the story of the donkey's skin and the dunce cap are the most well-known expressions of these characteristics. It is equally reputed for its virile power and stubbornness. Present at Christ's birth, it plays an important role in Christian bestiaries.

The Devil never takes the form of a donkey, because since Christmas

Donkey shaved by a barber. Glazed Faience plate. Italy, Pesaro's workshop, 16th c.

night the donkey has worn a cross drawn on its back. If a sick child is set on this cross and the donkey makes nine circles, the child's recovery is assured. Covering a child with a donkey skin keeps him or her from being afraid. Like its godfather the ox, the donkey speaks on Christmas night.

A donkey hides when it is about to die. Therefore, to see its corpse is a good omen.

If a man's head is rubbed with a donkey's hoof clippings, he will appear to have the head of a donkey.

A donkey's lung cures snake and scorpion venoms. "If the hairs around a donkey's penis are cut into some wine and you make someone drink them, that person will fart immediately" (Grand Albert).

When a donkey brays and wiggles its ears, it will rain.

In opposition to the virile donkey, the he-mule, a sterile animal, transmits its defect to all men who mount it bareback.

Dragon

This mythological animal joins the four elements. It breathes fire and makes use of it to destroy its enemies. It lives in underground caves where it guards treasures. It can also live in water, the sea serpent being but one of the avatars of the dragon. Finally, it has control of the atmosphere—a dragon is most often represented with wings. For Jung, the triumph of the angel over the dragon symbolizes the triumph of the self over repressive tendencies.

Flying dragon. French imagery, beginning of the 19th c. (Bibl. Nat.)

When dragon's teeth are sown, completely armed warriors are born of them.

"The dragon threw itself under the elephant, coiled its tail around its legs, and with its wings and claws hung onto its flanks while tearing its throat with its teeth.

The elephant then let himself fall on the dragon, crushing it to death. Thus did the elephant take revenge in killing his enemy." (Leonardo da Vinci, *Notes*)

Dragonfly

Light and elegant, the dragonfly is nicknamed "young lady." Whoever catches one is sure to marry within the year. It comes to the aid of fishermen worthy of its virtue by hovering over fish.

Duck

Its habit of only traveling in twos explains why it has become one of the symbols of conjugal fidelity. A bolster of duck down is the best guarantee.

If a female duck lays a dark brown egg, it is an omen of great misfortune—in order to escape it, kill the duck immediately and hang it upside down.

Like all animals that live near water, ducks are well-known meteorologists. In Savoy it is said, "When the ducks flap their wings in the stream, plowmen will soon have water."

Dung

Just like human excrement, animal droppings most often bring good luck if you walk on them with the proper foot! They frequently have curative virtues.

Stepping in dog droppings with the left foot brings good luck. In England, placed around a house, dog droppings guarantee happy days.

Dried dog dung cures dysentery. Dung of an ox or cow is a proven remedy against tumors of the testicle and sciatica. Finally, goat droppings dissolved in vinegar cure warts and boils. Mice dung mixed with honey make hair grow back.

Dung, particularly that of sacred cows, is reputed to keep phantoms away in India.

Eagle

The king of birds, it alone is capable of staring at the sun. An example of courage and absolute power, it was venerated by despots such as Napoleon and Hitler. An enemy of the snake that incarnates evil, an eagle is a symbol of the Resurrection for Christians. Tales and fables, on the contrary, portrayed a less sympathetic image of the eagle, robber of children.

Its blood gives vigor and courage to whoever drinks it.

Study of a heraldic eagle, by Pisanello, 1395–1450 (Musée du Louvre).

An old eagle flies so high that it burns its feathers; in dropping in the water, it again finds its youth, just like the Phoenix that was consumed in flames in order to be reborn.

Whoever steals eagle eggs will never have a peaceful soul.

Its flight was interpreted by the ancients. Today it is said that those whom it flies over will soon be given up in death. Likewise, an eagle's cry announces an imminent death.

Nailed to a barn door, an eagle keeps away evil spirits.

Its brain, glowing and warm, gives fantastic illusions to whoever eats it.

An eagle's power is so great that its feathers burn and spoil those of other birds when they are mixed together.

Earthworm

Used in ancient medicine, it fascinates man with its power of regeneration. From each piece of a cut up earthworm, a new worm will emerge.

Ground earthworms applied to cut nerves solder them together again.

Earthworm powder cures jaundice.

Egg

Being a dominant symbol of life, an egg allies the notion of cycles (eternal new beginning) and of germination. To assure the prosperity of a new house, eggs are buried in its foundation. Divination by eggs, or oomancia, was practiced for a very long time. An egg can also be negative, for it is linked to the rooster, toad, and especially the snake.

In order to protect a house from natural catastrophes and to hasten the recovery of an ill person, saves the first egg laid on Ascension Day. An egg laid on that day will never rot. Breaking a fresh egg over an anthill protects against fever; breaking a hard boiled egg over an anthill cures jaundice.

To see white eggs in a dream foretells happiness; broken eggs, misfortune. If the yolk of a hard boiled egg is taken out and replaced by salt, you will dream of the man or woman of your life after you eat it. If a girl wants to know what her future husband will look like, she breaks an egg on someone's head, then throws the egg in water—the face of the loved one will be outlined there.

An egg without a yolk brings unhappiness—it was laid by a rooster! An egg with two yolks foretells the death of a family member. Finding a very small egg is also an omen of death. It is bad luck to collect eggs or bring them into the house after night has fallen. In Japan, if a woman steps on an egg shell, she goes insane.

This is a general superstition: The shell must always be broken up after eating an egg and never thrown into the fire. Some break the shell of soft boiled eggs after having eaten them so that enemies are broken in the same way. Egg shells are not burned for fear of martyrizing Saint Laurent a second time—he was burned on egg shells. In Great Britain, it is said that if egg shells are thrown into a fire, the hen will lay no longer.

Sailors must never say the word "egg" at sea. The Scottish say that if egg shells are not broken, witches steal them and make vessels with which to run off fishermen's boats.

In Egypt and Rome, eggs were offerings because they were a symbol of the continuity of life. Christians made them the image of Christ's resurrection. It is from these that Easter eggs were born. The Druids considered sea urchin eggs as snake's eggs. The cosmic egg contained the world in its embryo—it was adorned with all magical virtues.

Elephant

Its size and extraordinary trunk have made the elephant a quasi-legendary animal in the West. The ivory of its tusks has always been highly prized.

Elephants only mate at night and in hiding. They rejoin the herd only after purifying themselves in river water. When they have a rendezvous with death, they leave from the herd and go die in a mysterious place, the elephant cemetery.

They kill flies that bother them by folding their skin, thereby crushing the flies.

A ring or bracelet made from an elephant hair keeps away evil spells. Decorated with gold thread, it is a particularly prized gris-gris in Africa.

Firefly

To catch sight of a firefly on the night of Saint John brings good luck, but to eat one makes you impotent. A firefly keeps milk from souring when kept in a house.

Fish

Linked to water, a fish represents life and fertility. Living in the depths, it is the image of intelligence and the unconscious. For Catholics, it is the symbol of Christ.

Eating fish makes children grow and makes them wise and strong. Its "phosphorus" brings wisdom and knowledge.

When eating a fish, you should cut from the tail toward the head.

A fisherman must never count the fish he has caught—he won't

A Chinese festival, illustration for M. de Guignes' "Voyage to Peking," 1808 (Bibl. Nat.).

catch any more for the rest of the day. If a fish you just caught falls back into the water, cross yourself with the right thumb on the left temple—you will catch two even larger fish in the next minute.

EEL

To eat an eel's heart gives powers of divination; to eat an eel makes you dumb. An eel in white wine is an excellent remedy for intoxication. (The eel is placed both under the sign of the fish and the snake.)

CARP

In China, a live carp is offered to students who are going to take an exam. The student must immediately throw it back into the water under the penalty of forgetting all he or she has learned.

JOHN DORY

The black marks that it bears on its two flanks are traces of the fingers of Saint Peter, who seized it to throw it back into the water.

Flea, Louse, Bug

Forgotten in the bestiaries and by diviners, these little creatures did nevertheless pester our ancestors.

Fleas are born in churches. If one of them bites you on the hand, you will receive a kiss or some good news (Germany).

Fleas abandon the body of someone who is going to die; if fleas are seen on a corpse, there will soon be another death in the region (Alsace).

In the Vosges, if you want someone to be devoured by fleas, you must put violets on his chest.

A flea will never penetrate a bed that was properly aired out on Good Friday. To chase them from a bed in the Dauphiné region, it is advisable to put a walnut branch there. Pliny preferred mare urine or rue for this purpose.

In Brittany, a person will have lice if he wears a shirt that was cut out on Good Friday. In the north, having lice is a sign of health.

Bedbugs never crawl into a monk's bed. "To make all the bugs in a bed die, take a cucumber in the shape of a snake, soak and steep it in water, then rub your bed—the secret is infallible." (Grand Albert)

Fly

Excommunicated by Saint Bernard, the fly pesters us to get revenge.

A fly that falls into a glass you are getting ready to drink from is a sign of prosperity.

In Rouergue, catching a fly in a dream foretells that someone will soon come to insult you.

String three eggs together and hang them over the front door on Ash Wednesday—this was Morvan's recipe for chasing flies away for an entire year. In Normandy the same result will be obtained by hanging a herring from the ceiling on Good Friday.

If all the flies are not chased from a room where a woman is about to give birth, she will have a girl.

Fox

The incarnation of cunning, the fox is both sympathetic and dangerous.

For the Welsh, seeing a single fox is a good omen; seeing them in a pack is bad. A fox that runs around a house foretells a disaster.

In order to keep foxes away from a chicken coop, drag a scraped pigskin attached to a hazelwood stick around the coop three times.

If a woman wants to protect herself from illnesses peculiar to her sex, she must carry on her a testicle taken from a live fox.

Frog

It is in opposition to its cousin, the toad, as much by its virtues as by its gossiping.

To make a sleeping woman talk, you need only put a frog's tongue on her heart.

To make yourself liked, carry a frog's decayed bones.

If, on its own, a frog comes in your house, it brings you luck.

In order to protect a field against birds, enclose a green frog in a pot of fresh earth and bury it in the middle of the field.

In order to stop coughing, spit into the mouth of a thicket frog and let it hop away (Champagne).

Frog skin can be grafted onto human skin.

Some peasants compare a frog's cry of pain to that of an infant. It is ill-advised to kill frogs because they are the souls of dead infants.

Being a cold blooded animal, it has the power to sterilize those who approach it. The ashes of a pregnant frog attached to a woman's belt stop her menstrual flow. If the ashes are hung on the neck of a hen, it will not be able to bleed. Hair will not grow on places rubbed with these ashes dissolved in water.

Goose

Sacrificed in Northern Africa on New Year's Day to assure a good year, in France it has a reputation for silliness. (See also Turkey, Hen.)

Whoever sees geese in a dream can expect to be honored by princes.

Green Woodpecker

Like the hoopoe and cuckoo, it is a prophetic bird. The number of times that it pecks against wood has a significance that man has forgotten. Now it is only known as a meteorologist: "When the green woodpecker cries, it announces rain!" and "When the green woodpecker complains, it will not be long before it rains . . . It sings to call the rain, which is why it is called the 'miller's counsel.' "

Gull

Its immaculate and luminous plumage puts it in opposition to the raven.

Whoever kills a gull goes blind.

Being a bird of the sea, it bears the souls of dead sailors, and the living respect it. Three gulls flying together foretell death for sea-faring people.

A gull that taps against the windows of a house warns the family that the man at sea is in danger.

Hare

The opposite of its cousin, the rabbit, the hare does business with the Devil, who often takes on its appearance. It is reputed to be so fearful that it is even afraid of the sound of falling leaves in autumn.

Eating hare too often makes you fearful.

Devils disguise themselves as hares in order to drink the milk from cows.

For a man going fishing and for a wedding party coming back from the Mass, seeing a hare is a bad omen. In order to exorcize the omen, Alsacians say that you must turn around three times when you encounter a hare.

A hare can only be hit with the left hand.

In Orléans, placing a hare's foot under the left armpit protects against toothaches.

If you carry a rabbit's foot under your right armpit, you will never encounter the white hare.

Hedgehog

Greedy and gluttonous, according to medieval legend it rolls itself in apples to carry them away. In Provence, it likewise seizes figs and grapes.

In Europe, hedgehogs are said to drink the milk of cows in the pasture.

Its presence in a barn keeps cows from calving. If a woman puts her foot on a hedgehog, she will give birth to one. (Therefore, it brings misfortune, and it is recommended that you kill them.)

It comes out of its hibernation on February 2 to test the weather. If spring is coming, the hedgehog stays outside. In the United States, it is believed that the wind blows in the opposite direction of its nest.

He-Goat

The favorite disguise of the Devil and associated with Dionysis and the god Pan, a he-goat is known for its ardent nature and lubricity. Thus, at Sabbaths, its greatest pleasure is to have its hindquarters embraced. A scapegoat takes the sins of the community upon itself before being rejected or sacrificed.

The English believe that a he-goat cannot be seen for twenty-four consecutive hours, because at one moment or another he must visit the Devil and pay him homage. Its hoof and hair from its goatee are talismans for keeping away the Devil.

A black he-goat in a stable protects the horses from illness. In Egypt, the place where a house is going to be built is wet down with goat's blood.

Some sailors believe that a goatskin hung on the mainmast promotes a safe passage.

Rubbing one's penis with goat's tallow assures a man of his wife's love.

Hen

Sometimes linked to the dog, a hen frequently appears in initiation or divinitory ceremonies. A sacrificial animal, especially when it is black, it is also a layer that must be protected against evil spells.

Black hens have the ability to find lost money. In Alsace a black hen is sacrificed at the time of exorcisms or when you want a wish granted.

A hen that crows like a rooster announces death. If it cackles near a house or doesn't lay at its usual time, it announces death. It is possessed by the Devil and must then be killed, otherwise, it will destroy its eggs or teach others how to.

A hen that lays an odd number of eggs brings misfortune—one of the eggs must be taken away. If all the eggs bear little roosters, it brings luck. All eggs laid on Good Friday guarantee strength and fertility to all the other hens on the farm if one egg is kept intact. A henhouse must be cleaned on Good Friday in order to chase away vermin for an entire year. A hen that hatches eggs on Midsummer's Day brings misfortune. To protect a brood, you should place a piece of iron in the shape of a cross or a ring in the nest.

Hens never lay again if their eggs' shells are burned.

If the hens squabble, so will the women at the wash-house.

An English custom says that a hen should be brought to the house of newlyweds as a guarantee against unhappiness.

For alchemists, a chicken symbolizes the three phases of work: red, white, and black (crest, plumage, and feet). The custom of the wishbone is long-lived. The wishbone consists of the two clavicles soldered together in a "V." Two people take hold of it, each pulling on a side; the one who gets the biggest piece when it breaks will see a wish come true.

In England, when a farmer is going to die, all the chickens roost at noon and not at their usual time.

Herring

Herring kept in brine, like codfish, has taken a big place in daily life with the Christian obligation of Lent.

Hanging a herring from the ceiling on Good Friday keeps flies away for the entire summer.

If a girl eats herring preserved in salt for three months, then goes to bed without saying or drinking anything, she will dream of her future husband.

For fishermen, if the first catch of the season is a female herring, it foretells a good season; if it is a male, a bad one.

Hoopoe

It is a mystical bird, celebrated everywhere for the virtues of its glance. According to the Koran, it was the messenger between Solomon and the Queen of Sheba and thus acquired its reputation of guide-bird.

Whoever wears its right eye suspended between his or her eyes will see hidden treasures. Wearing hoopoe eyes on your chest makes you gain weight without eating; worn over the stomach, they will reconcile you with all your enemies.

Its dried intestines are worn as talismans—in Tangier, they are hung up in boutiques to protect against robbers. Its head carried in your purse keeps you from being duped. Worn around the neck, its tongue regenerates memory and judgment.

When the stone found in a hoopoe's nest, a "traitor's stone," is placed on a sleeping man's head, it will make him avow all his secrets.

In Scotland, to catch sight of a hoopoe is a bad omen, for the souls of men condemned never to find peace take refuge in the body of these birds. Their cry incessantly repeats the word "bewitched."

Horns

Horns are one of the primordial elements of the infernal uniform. They were supposedly given to Eve by Satan. She then made a gift of them to her husband (hence the expression "to wear horns.") Therefore, it is not advisable to have a horn in the house. But the horn of an ox in the United States or of a stag in Great Britain and Spain will protect you from the Devil's eye. In addition, stag and she-goat horns have the virtue of whitening and cleaning teeth.

Cloisonné enamel. China, 16th c. (Musée des Arts Déco.)

In all Mediterranean countries, making horns with the index and little finger is the best way to keep away evil spells. Making horns with the index and middle finger is, on the other hand, a sign of mockery. (See Spells and Conjuration.)

Study of a horse, drawing taken from the "Vallardi Album," by Pisanello, 1395–1450 (Musée du Louvre).

Horse

Being sensitive to occult forces, the horse's behavior was studied in divinitory arts. In numerous civilizations, a black horse is death's companion and draws the chariot of the deceased.

To dream about a black horse foretells an approaching bereavement. If a horse that draws a hearse turns and stares at someone in a congregation, that person will die; if it stops in front of a strange house, prances, and kicks, a brutal death will strike one of the inhabitants.

If a horse comes out of the stable with its right foot first, all is well; if it comes out on its left foot, beware. If a horse stops without apparent reason, it is because it felt an infernal presence.

As a general rule, encountering a white horse brings good luck, but in the United States, a red-headed girl on a white horse is bad luck.

A jockey that mounts a horse with a white star on its forehead and a white hind leg has very good chances of winning.

Finally, a horse's tail is braided with ribbons to keep away evil spells.

111

Hummingbird

Sacred animal of Latin America, it serves as a refuge for dead souls and thus deserves particular respect. In the Antilles, when it picks at a girl's breakfast, she will marry during the year; if she is married, she will have a child within the year.

Hyena

A foul, wicked devourer of corpses, the hyena is a stranger to man. It changes sex every year and knows how to imitate a man's voice to attract its prey. In Egypt, its shadow brushing past a dog makes the dog mute.

Ivory

Of animal origin like coral, scales, or horns, this matter is favorable, along with wood and iron, and keeps away evil forces. Incorruptible and white, ivory incarnates purity, but Homer saw the image of a lie in its opacity.

All ivory bracelets, amulets, or jewelry are beneficent and bring luck. In addition, they have the ability to keep away all corruptions, cancer in particular.

He who wants to soften ivory in order to be able to work with it without difficulty must scrape it until it becomes white and without impurities. Then he boils it in sea water with six ounces of mandrake root. He then throws it into a mold and lets it cool by the morning dew three days in a row.

Kingfisher

Tradition has it that it served both as a bow and arrow to God. To see it is always a good omen.

It brings happiness to the house near which it builds its nest.

Kingfishers dry out the branches on which they perch.

Ladybug

Pet of God Almighty, Mary, and Saint John, it brings good luck if it lights on you. It is inadvisable to kill this insect blessed by God. Some say that it even understands human language.

If it lights on you, then flies away, there will be nice weather on Sunday. On Sunday, it brings good luck to whomever it rests on long enough to count to twenty-two.

It flies away in the direction from which a sweetheart will come.

In Burgundy, the little black dots on a ladybug's back indicate the number of babies to come; in England, they are a sign of happy months.

Lark

According to Gaston Bachelard, a lark's rapid flight joining the earth and sky makes it a foremost sign of sublimation. This kind animal brings support and assistance to lovers in particular.

Worn secretly in the right pocket, a lark's eye wrapped in wolfskin makes you charming and irresistable. Putting this eye in a glass of wine, she who drinks it will fall in love.

Brought to the bolster of a sick person's bed, a lark turns its head if the person will die and stares straight ahead if he is to get well.

Carrying a lark's foot assures victory over man and the elements. Because its song is very well known, tradition recommends swallowing three lark's eggs on Sunday mornings before the bells ring in order to clear your throat.

Lion

The king of animals owes its title to its reputation for courage and invincibility. The lion fears only the rooster who defies it with its red crest.

Only a cock's crow and the grinding of empty chariots can frighten it. A lion erases its tracks by sweeping them with its tail. It sleeps with its eyes open, and it gives life back to stillborn cubs by blowing on them.

Its eyes, worn under the armpit, keep away all savage beasts. Its skin makes you invincible.

A lion, which never harms a king, is a robber's best friend.

Lizard

A lizard is an ambivalent symbol: a near relation of the snake, it incarnates Evil; lover of heat, it allies itself with the sun. Man saw the image of immortality in its regenerative tail and in its periodic shedding. A lizard's tail is a highly prized talisman. The tail of a green lizard in a right shoe assures happiness and money. Girls who want to become good seamstresses must let lizards run across their hands—they impart vivacity in this way.

In the Vendée it is said that wherever you see green lizards there are no vipers. In Alsace, killing a lizard provokes rain the next day.

Eating green lizards cures skin diseases.

In Great Britain it is said that if a bride crosses a lizard on her way to the church, her marriage will be unhappy. In Languedoc, if a lizard bites a woman's breast, she will quickly lose weight. In Provence, they say that when a lizard nips a cow on the nose, the cow dies.

Magpie

It is the only animal to have refused entering Noah's Ark. It preferred to remain perched on the roof of the boat. Talkative, curious, thieving, and lying, it has a very bad reputation. More familiar than the raven, it has many of its characteristics. Everywhere, except in China, it is a bird of misfortune.

If it sings near a house or enters a room, it comes to announce death. If it is encountered when you are leaving on a trip, it would be best to return home. When it is seen, you must cross yourself, take off your hat, and bow (Great Britain).

In Germany, one magpie signifies misfortune; two, marriage or happiness; three, a good trip; four, good news; and five announce the near arrival of friends.

It is so cautious that the roof of a house upon which a magpie has perched is certain never to collapse.

Magpies quarrel before it rains. It is also said: "Magpie on a farm, snow in short term."

Eating the brain of a magpie makes you go crazy.

People of the Vendée believe that a male magpie is black and white and a female is white and black . . . but that's another story.

Maybug

These insects appear in great number only in certain years, thus people speak of "maybug years."

A maybug year announces a plum year. On the other hand, in Picardie it is said: "Great maybug year, poor wine year, great apple year."

In Normandy, a dog that eats a maybug becomes rabid.

Mole

"The mole is known by most everyone and it has admirable virtues and properties; if one of its feet is wrapped in a laurel leaf and put in a horse's mouth, the horse will immediately take flight and have fear, or if it is put

"The Mole Hunter" (detail), by Bracquemond, 19th c. (Bibl. des Arts Déco.)

in the nest of some bird, the bird's eggs will become useless and nothing will form inside. If you want to chase the moles from a place, you must take one and put it in this place with active sulphur which you burn; immediately all the other moles will gather around. In addition, if a black horse is rubbed with water that a mole has been boiled in, it will become white." (Grand Albert, *Of the Mole*)

The mole, an animal of the earth and the night, blind and clairvoyant, has always been intriguing. The mysterious signs that it writes on the earth remain difficult to interpret. All moles come out into the open air to hear the Angelus.

An elder tree keeps moles away; in the Vendée a variety of euphorbia, the spurge (called "mole grass"), is said to be more effective in this role. A molehill built in the proximity of a house warns that one of the inhabitants will soon be ill. In England, if a mole digs near a kitchen or bathroom, it is said that a woman will die in the house.

A mole's foot worn in a sack around the neck is an excellent talisman against illnesses, particularly cramps and toothaches.

A hand that has suffocated a mole, a "moled hand," has great curative virtues.

Mosquito

Its smarting bites have given it a reputation for aggressiveness. It is, however, sometimes an omen of good luck.

If, at sunset, a mosquito is allowed to get into a sick person's room, it will take the illness with it when it leaves.

When it flies close to the ground, get out your umbrella. If it flies high in the air, it announces good weather.

In order to cure mosquito bites, rub them with vinegar, oil, butter, onion, garlic, or lemon peel and . . . blow on them.

Moth

A messenger like its daytime companion, the moth is directly linked to death. When it is white, it is the soul of a dead person; it brings misfortune to kill it. If a black moth penetrates a house, someone will die within the year.

If a moth enters a house, in general it announces important mail for the next morning.

Mouse

Less diabolical than its superior, the rat, a mouse is however an animal that must not be trusted. It is a bad omen to encounter one on a trip. The arrival of mice in a house announces an approaching death, and when they are very prolific, they announce a war or invasion near at hand (Alsace). When a mouse squeaks near a sick person's bed, there is no longer any hope for that person.

They are often the souls of assassinated people, or, when they nibble clothes, the incarnation of some evil Devil. In Scotland all other mice are said to leave the house if you take one by the tail and hang it over the fire until it is roasted. A toad enclosed in a vase will also make them flee.

Fried or roasted, a mouse cures colds and measles. If a mother wants her child to have black eyes, she must eat a mouse during pregnancy. Finally, if a tooth is tossed into a mousehole, a new tooth will grow back in its place.

In Germany, encountering a white mouse brings luck.

Nests

Man easily identifies a nest, refuge built little by little by birds, with his own home. Whoever destroys a nest brings on himself a sudden death.

You must never declare that you have discovered a nest—ants or cuckoos will take advantage of it.

If you have a headache, perhaps a bird has taken a hair from your head to build its nest. In Austria, this same petty theft gives you pimples.

For the Indians of the Andes, a "MACUA" nest is woven with fine hairs from women. If this nest is diluted in perfume, the mixture makes you irresistible to the opposite sex.

Nightingale, Redstart, Robin Redbreast, Wren

The perfection of its song has made the *nightingale* a symbol of poetry and love. Eating its heart makes you sing as well as it does, but also it makes you sleep less than four hours per night. It is also said that he who eats a nightingale's heart when the wind begins to change goes insane.

In Alsace, killing a *redstart* also turns cow's milk red. If a redstart enters a sick person's room, there is no longer any hope for that person (Lorrain).

A *robin redbreast* tried in vain to unhook Christ from his cross. A drop of holy blood fell on its breast. Whoever kills or puts a robin in a cage is doomed to misfortune. In Alsace, cow's milk is said to become red when a robin is killed.

A *wren* is a Druid to the Irish and a little king to the Welsh and Bretons. To kill it brings misfortune. In England, whoever kills one will break a bone; in France, he will go directly to hell unless it is a child, who will be immediately covered with pimples if he touches a wren's nest.

A wren's feather is a good luck charm prized by gamblers; in addition, it has the ability to protect against drowning. Wrens' feathers were greatly sought after by sailors and fishermen; consequently, this bird, that elsewhere it was necessary to respect, was massacred en masse.

Oriole

This fire-yellow bird brings only happiness. To hear it sing in a blossoming peach tree is a very good sign, but it is inadvisable to take it out of its nest.

Owl

A nocturnal bird of prey like a screech owl, it is an omen of sterility and death.

In Alsace, an owl is a messenger of death; if it makes its cry heard near the room of a sick person, there is no longer any hope of recovery.

Nailed to a barn door, an owl keeps rats away.

In Normandy, an omelet of owls' eggs is fed to a drunk to make him reasonable again.

Ox

Calm and laborious, it is in opposition to the bull and has long been an animal of sacrifice. Like the donkey, it was present at Christ's birth and warmed him with its breath.

It speaks on Christmas night, but only children born during the year can hear it. In Normandy, those who are carrying a newborn in their arms also can hear it.

In order to keep an ox from eating in the barn, hang a wolfskin over its tail. (See Cattle)

Oyster

Despite its famous pearl, an oyster inspires few superstitions.

It opens during the full moon. A crab then tosses it a pearl or twig to keep it from closing and eats it.

American sailors wear a piece of its shell as a talisman.

In England, if you eat oysters on August 5, you are sure to never die of hunger.

Pig

The hog, an animal without fur and omnivorous like man, was rejected by Judaism and Islam as impure. The *pig* of the European countryside is too useful to come to this negative point.

In Ireland, pigs are known to have the ability to see the wind. A pig that runs with a straw in its mouth announces a storm.

If a pig is struck with an elder branch, it will die immediately.

In Alsace, encountering a herd of pigs in the morning is bad luck, but to find yourself in front of a sow and her litter is a sign of coming success. Seeing a wild boar is a bad omen.

The word "pig" is not said on a boat.

Pigeon, Dove

Its peacefulness and whiteness have made the dove the favorite representation of the Holy Ghost. It symbolizes the peace and happiness of couples. Only a young pigeon is the figure of ingratitude—it seeks to kill its father in order to marry its mother.

Encountering a pigeon or a dove is always a good omen—a couple will announce an upcoming wedding. The flight of twelve doves over the head of someone out walking promises him or her wealth very soon.

A man's skull placed in a pigeon house attracts all the neighboring pigeons.

Quail

A quail symbolizes the peacefulness of households—if a husband wears the heart of a male and his wife that of a female quail, their agreement is assured! In addition, a quail's heart in a wolfskin moderates the amorous temperament of whoever wears it.

Rabbit

Young rabbits, who are born with their eyes open, have the ability to keep the Devil away. Their nocturnal games ally them with the lunar gods. Particularly prolific, they are the promise of prosperity and success. Thus a rabbit's foot became a universal talisman. When it is suspended over a cradle or placed on a newborn's skin, it will protect the child from all sorcery. Gamblers and thieves also make great use of it. But be careful; bad luck awaits you if you lose your foot!

In Great Britain, repeating the words "white rabbit" three times quickly on the first day of the month guarantees a happy month. Seeing a white rabbit near a house is, on the contrary, an omen of death. Miners who encounter a white rabbit on their way to the mine count on a catastrophe.

Sailors avoid saying the word "rabbit" before going to sea; on board, if this animal must be referred to, it is necessary to use another word.

The rabbit also plays a role in Christianity since it is charged with bringing eggs to children on Easter Sunday.

Rat

This animal is attributed with great intelligence and divination abilities. This companion of Satan, prisoners in their cells, and sailors is linked with night and also with the plague. It has given rise to numerous legends.

Rats are divided into clans and governed by a multiple master, the "king rat," composed of rats tied together at the tail and fed by their congeners. This multi-headed king was linked to the Holy Trinity.

Engraving on wood from the 16th c. (Bibl. Nat.)

When a child loses a tooth, he or she must toss it at a rat and ask it to bring one that is prettier and more solid.

If rats attack furniture, particularly that in a bedroom, it's a sign of death.

In order to chase them out of a barn or loft, sprinkle three corners of the room with holy water—they will leave by the fourth corner. But, don't forget, if all the rats leave a house, it will collapse.

Rats always leave a vessel before a shipwreck or fire. To see the rats leave a vessel before it sets sail is a sure sign that it is going to sink.

When rats penetrate a new boat, on the contrary, it's a very good sign.

Raven

Prophet!" said I, "thing of evil—prophet still, if bird or devil!
By that heaven that bends above us-by that God we both adore—
Tell this soul with sorrow laden, if, within the distant Aidenn,
It shall clasp a sainted maiden, whom the angels name Lenore—
Clasp a rare and radiant maiden, whom the angels name Lenore?"
Quoth the raven, "Nevermore."

Edgar Poe, "The Raven"

This sorcerers' bird, gifted with prophecy, undoubtedly owes its ability to inspire terror to its black plumage and its particular cry. Very rare in Europe today, it is replaced by the much more amicable crow. But the superstitions persist.

Whoever sees them pass must count them to know his or her future: one raven, sadness; two ravens, happiness; three ravens, marriage; and four ravens, birth.

A raven flying three times around a field foretells the owner's death. In Brittany, two ravens are linked to each house—one predicts births, the other deaths.

Salamander

Toward my fifth year, my father found himself in a cellar where laundry had been scalded . . . In looking at the coals, by chance he saw a little animal, similar to a lizard, that was indulging in a joyous frolic in the middle of the most ardent flames. My father, having recognized immediately what it was, called my sister and me, showed us the animal and gave me a rude slap which brought on a deluge of tears. He wiped them softly and said to me: 'My dear child, I did not strike you to punish you, but only so that you would remember that this lizard that you caught sight of in the fire was a salamander, an animal that no known person has ever seen.'—With that, he kissed me and gave me a few quattrini.

(*Benvenuto Cellini,* Memoirs)

This batrachian symbolizes the spirit of the Fire. When hung on a pothook, a salamander makes everything put in the fireplace boil. Like the phoenix, it was reborn from its ashes. By its coldness, it has the inverse power to put out fires.

A salamander bloats cattle by blowing on them. Encountering one is a very bad omen.

Scorpion

Maleficent and fleeing light, hardened and armed, a scorpion is one of the Devil's creatures. It kills its mother and kills itself when it is surrounded. In Africa, it is considered more dangerous to women than to men. It must never be mentioned—its name alone unleashes evil forces.

To dream of a scorpion, lizard, caterpillar, or centipede announces a misfortune that will come from a betrayal.

Screech Owl

Athena's bird, it incarnates wisdom and intelligence, but its nocturnal life allies it with birds of prey, witches' companions. Its cry is most often interpreted as an omen of misfortune.

If it perches on the roof of a house, you should tie its wings and feet and then hang it upside down in order to keep danger away. Whoever looks in a screech owl's nest becomes morose and unhappy in life.

When the screech owl's cry is heard, salt must be thrown into a fire. In Wales, its hooting announces that a girl has just lost her virginity. In France, it announces the birth of a girl to a pregnant woman. Its hooting at the full moon foretells death.

If a screech owl's heart and right foot are placed on someone who is asleep, that person says everything that you want him or her to say.

Nailed to a barn door, it keeps away misfortune.

When screech owls sing, it's a sign of good weather, at least that is what's said in Brittany.

Seal

Oily and unseizable, it is sometimes taken for an image of virginity or else the subconscious. In the Faroe Islands, female seals shed their skins and appear in the form of alluring women. (See Siren.)

Sheep

The lamb, identified with Christ, is sacrificed at paschal feasts. Like God on earth, a shepherd watches over his flock. Some shepherds take a piece of wool in their coffin to excuse themselves before God on Judgement Day, for no shepherd should leave his flock.

A shepherd must not count his animals—that is a wolf's part.

People of the Cevenne region never shear their sheep on Corpus Christi Day because the animals would die. As for the people of Provence, they are suspicious of this absurdity.

In the Lower Alps, it is affirmed that crossing a flock brings luck, but to pass it is a very bad omen.

A small bone from a sheep's head has the value of a talisman for shepherds.

On Christmas morning, sheep turn toward the east and bleat three times.

In order to remedy insomnia, you can always count sheep, but is that really a superstition?

She-Goat

In opposition to a he-goat, according to the superstitious, it has a rather good aura. A white she-goat, especially if it appears on the right, is an excellent omen. Three black she-goats in a flock attract wolves.

Children brought up on goats' milk will be fretful and jump around continually.

Consuming five she-goat dungs in white wine, eight mornings in a row before eating, cures jaundice.

Siren

This mythical animal—or woman—is known to all sea-faring people. Half woman, half fish, or else half woman, half bird, it attracts travellers with the sweetness of its song before drowning them. Beware of the siren's song.

Snail

Everyone knows that when going looking for snails, it is best to put your jacket on inside out.

Snake

A snake is one of the fundamental archetypes found throughout all civilizations. Ambivalent, it symbolizes both knowledge and absolute Evil. It is the object of cults and the emblem of medicine. A snake biting its tail is the image of eternity. Since Adam and Eve, it is the favorite messenger of the Devil. It is always a bad omen to encounter one. In Germany, it is a particularly bad sign to see one fall down a chimney. Never compare a snake to the size of your arm—your arm will immediately be covered with scales.

A snake never bites pregnant women. On the contrary, a snakeskin placed on a woman facilitates childbirth. Having a snake on you relieves toothaches. When hung around a sick person's neck, snake teeth cure fevers. Its head and teeth are excellent talismans in gambling.

In Alsace, snakes are chased away on February 22, Saint Peter's Day. In order to drive them off, it is sufficient to plant elder trees. Cornelian and jade protect against bites; aconite and mistletoe cure them.

A grass snake sucks cows' udders. It finds its way into a sleeper's mouth and very easily sees into his stomach. It is a very good omen to encounter one. If you want to be assured of triumphing over your enemies, kill the first grass snake you see in spring—to let it live would lead to disaster. Its skin must be hung in the chimney—it will make an excellent talisman.

If you spit on a viper before eating, it will die instantly. Emeralds protect against viper bites.

The Sea Serpent reappears regularly in the world. In Norway, it is said that a boat musn't pass between two of its coils—the boat would be crushed between them.

Sparrow

Present at the Crucifixion, it encouraged the Romans to make Christ suffer by repeating: "He lives, he lives." To punish it, God tied its feet together with invisible string; ever since, it can no longer walk, it only knows how to hop.

When it gets into a house, it announces death, but it is bad luck to catch it, put it in a cage, or kill it. A sparrow never eats from the hands of wicked people.

In Brittany, it spreads news from one tree to another; when a sparrow is killed, someone will go without news from a loved one. Others claim that a tree dies with the bird.

In England, it is the symbol of gods of the home.

Spider

In the center of its web, the spider, like God in the center of the world, weaves destiny. On the whole, "If you wish to live and prosper, let the spider live." But mind the time of day, for as the saying goes:

> Morning spider, sorrow
> Noon day spider, profit (worry in Alsace)
> Every spider, hope . . .
> or yet: immediate spider, gift.

In Alsace, the worry that it announces is a function of its size. Except in the morning, it is a good omen to crush it with the right foot.

Killing a spider brings unhappiness and rain. Moslems never kill a spider because a spider saved Mohammed by spinning its web around a cave where he had taken refuge.

Finding a spider in your clothes foretells a return of money. In Scotland, it brings a fortune in descending the length of its thread.

In England and Brittany, it brings cancer if it brushes the face of someone sleeping. A daddy longlegs gives a death notice to whomever's shoulder it touches. A Tarantula bite fixes a person in the disposition of the moment.

Spider webs must not be cleared away from stables or barns because they protect the animals. In addition, their webs are said to stop hemorrhages when applied to wounds.

Stag

It is especially valued for its horns that have the virtue of regenerating each year. Deer horn powder, an aphrodisiac, promotes fertility and rebirth.

Encountering a stag, however, is most often considered a bad omen.

Finally, stags eat crabs to get rid of spider venom.

Stag Beetle

The head of this insect, worn as a talisman, guarantees happiness, thanks to its horns that protect against evil spells. If it isn't killed on sight, it comes and sleeps in your bed.

Stork

This bird of good omen supposedly flew around Christ's cross, showing him its sympathy. A messenger of spring, it symbolizes birth and brings newborns. It is also curiously well-known for establishing itself only in free states.

When it is old, its young look after it and nourish it until its death. If it flies over a house, it's a sign of an upcoming birth. In Alsace, it is explained to children that a stork bit a pregnant woman's leg and she had to take to her bed.

In Egypt, storks prevent wives from deceiving their husbands by giving them a great many pecks.

In Munster, the cat sometimes replaces the stork in the function of mid-wife.

Swallow

A swallow doesn't make spring, but it is its messenger. Thus, it brings love. It is a beneficent bird, sometimes nicknamed "God's hen," that must be respected.

In Flanders, it is said that when swallows fly close to the ground, it's good-bye to dust. If they fly high in the sky, there will be good weather. In Brittany, killing a swallow starts a rain that lasts four weeks.

In Alsace, a swallow's nest in a stable, barn, or house brings happiness. A swallow's nest on a house protects the house from fires and storms. If you destroy a swallow's nest, one day you will fall from a tree.

Eating swallows when they are in heat inclines you toward love. In the Berry, in order to be loved, you must offer a ring that has stayed in a swallow's nest for nine days.

If a swallow passes under a cow's belly, the milk will turn to blood. Killing a swallow ruins cows' milk. In Germany, a woman who steps on a swallow's egg will become sterile.

The stones found in its nest, worn in a amulet, assure very good sight. But swallow droppings on the eyes make you go blind. A swallow's nest reduced to powder and mixed with honey is an excellent remedy for inflammations. Cooked in white wine, it cures sore throats.

In France, if one of these birds perches on your shoulder, death is near at hand.

Seeing swallows fight among themselves is a sign of mishap.

Swan

Being of both the sun and moon, this immaculate bird symbolizes strength and light. Its famous song announces death because it is reputed to sing only one time, before dying.

In Scotland, three swans flying together presage a disaster.

A swan can only hatch its eggs during a storm.

Toad

Having the infernal face of a frog, it is one of the Devil's incarnations. It is also said that it feeds off the earth and avoids sunlight. Its look has powers of fascination. It has a stone in its head that in traditional magic has the value of a good-luck charm.

If a toad crosses the path of a bride on her way to the church, the couple's happiness is assured. In the Girond, a toad was nailed to a boat's framework when it was being built to protect it from evil spells. Finally thieves believe that a toad's heart keeps them from being surprised at the moment of a break-in.

If misfortune persists in a household, take up a stone from the threshold—perhaps there is a toad under it.

A toad's heart placed on the left sleeve of a sleeping woman makes her confess all her secrets. The edge of a sickle becomes unusable if it is used to cut a toad.

In Lorrain, it is said that if you eat an egg on Good Friday or Easter Eve, you're sure to find a toad in it.

Supposedly, he who has gone to a Sabbath three times has a little toad on the white of his eye.

Tortoise

This animal is found in numerous cosmogonies. The tortoise, carrying its house with it, symbolizes stability. It is known for its longevity. Its brain is reputed to make whoever eats it immortal. A tortoise shell bracelet protects against evil spells.

In order to relieve gout, hang a tortoise's right foot on the sick person's right foot—likewise for the left foot.

Turkey Cock

Its head, bare of feathers, and red wattles that hang from its crop have made it a phallic and prolific symbol. Like the peacock, the turkey cock struts and puffs itself up. Often ridiculous, it is the "turkey of farce."

A man who wishes to regain his sexual vigor must watch three turkey cocks puff out their necks three times in a row.

To see or possess turkey cocks in a dream signifies approaching insanity for a friend or relative.

In Europe, the turkey hen represents silliness. A stupid girl is called a "little turkey hen" or a "white goose." A Christmas turkey is a substitute for goose. Like the lamb at Easter, a Christmas turkey (or goose) must be white and immaculate.

Turtledove

Like the pigeon and dove, the turtledove, always encountered in couples, is a symbol of fidelity. To dream of turtledoves indicates perfect accord in marriage or an upcoming union. However, this "wild pigeon" marks all that it touches with sterility.

If its heart is worn in a wolfskin, it extinguishes lustful fires and amorous desires. If a turtledove's feet are hung on a tree, the tree will never bear any fruit.

When a hen hatches a turtledove's egg in addition to her own, only roosters will be born.

Engraving on wood from the 17th c (Bibl. Nat.)

Unicorn

Half antelope, half rhinoceros, it has a white body, blue eyes, and a red head surmounted with a twisted horn. Although it is a bastard, it incarnates purity.

Only a virgin can approach it. If a girl who isn't really a virgin is sent to it, it will kill her.

Its horn, confused with a narwhal's tooth, protects man, particularly against all forms of poison.

Vampire

According to Central European traditions, vampires are supposedly incarnations of the dead who, by night, leave their tombs to suck the blood of the living. These superstitions, already frequent in popular and scholarly literature, were revived by the cinema, the success of which witnesses the continuity of human phantasms.

Vampires leave their coffins from midnight to sunrise; they present themselves in the form of a man or a bat. In its coffin, a vampire is recognized by its florid complexion, gorged with blood.

Vampire from New Caledonia, drawing according to nature by Mesnel, 19th c. (Bibl. des Arts Déco.)

Only a crucifix or cock's crow has the power to make vampires disappear. However, a garlic clove can keep them away; the fearful keep cloves at the heads of their beds. In order to annihilate a vampire, you should drive a stake into its heart and then burn its ashes. But all "vampirized" people eventually become vampires.

A vampire cannot be reflected in any mirror.

Vulture

A divinatory bird, it never kills; it devours abandoned corpses and, because of this, everywhere announces death.

According to Pliny the Elder, it smells death three days in advance.

When it hovers over a house, it announces an approaching death.

Burned vulture feathers keep snakes away. Its heart repulses the Devil.

Wasp

Unlike the bee, this aggressive insect has a bad reputation. Thus, killing the first wasp you see in the year brings luck for the months to come.

Certain formulas are witness to the fear it inspires: "Bee, hornet, or wasp, stop your sting like the Blessed Virgin stopped her child," and "May this creature become sweet like the milk of the Blessed Virgin Mary in the mouth of Our Lord Jesus Christ."

Weasel (Belette in French)

It is called "belette," petite belle (little pretty one), in order to flatter it because it is feared so much. When you encounter it, you say, "Belette, belette, what a pretty lady you are!"

If you encounter it, you must stand still, slowly pick up three small stones, throw them in front of you, and cross yourself seven times.

It is impossible to capture a sleeping weasel.

A weasel's two testicles wrapped and tied to the thigh of a woman carrying a weasel bone make her sterile. According to the ancients, a weasel conceives by the mouth and begets by the ear.

If a dog that barks continually is given a weasel tongue to eat, it will ultimately be quiet until its master's death. Eating a weasel heart while it is still beating gives you the power to foretell the future for one year.

It kills the basilisk with the odor of its urine, which sometimes kills the weasel itself.

This animal is considered frightening because it is in opposition to all forces of life, such as speech and reproduction; its very cry announces imminent death. Its antithesis, the white ermine, would rather be killed than dirty its fur.

Werewolf

At night, certain men are transformed into wolves; in the Poitier countryside, they were called "cursed beasts that go on a spree," commonly known as werewolves or lycanthropes. They are metamorphized after bathing in a fountain. When a werewolf is killed, it takes on human form again.

Bastards are, more than others, subject to this illness. A werewolf-man is recognized by his flat fingers and the hair covering his hands.

If young ladies are accompanied home from a ball, it is because of werewolves . . .

The werewolf. Illustration by Maurice Sand for George Sand's "Rustic Legends," 1857 (Bibl. des Arts Déco).

Wolf

Savage and satanic, it is the animal ridden by sorcerers on their way to a Sabbath. It is linked to both death and fertility.

A wife who is not satisfied with her husband must carry the marrow from a wolf's left foot.

A pierced wolf's tooth strung on a strand of rope protects a child from fear, rage, and anger. Attached to a horse's neck, the tooth makes the horse indefatigable.

A wolf's eye also protects children.

The tail of a dead wolf hung over a barn keeps its congeners away.

In order to keep evil spells away from a new house, its door hinges must be lubricated with wolf fat.

Wolfskin shoes protect against chilblains.

Dreaming of a wolf indicates an approaching betrayal.

When a woman catches sight of a wolf behind her, she unties her belt and lets it drag while saying, "Watch yourself, wolf, that the Mother of God doesn't make you a friar."

In England, if a wolf sees a man before being noticed, the man becomes a mute. Encountering a wolf before the day begins provokes a suppression of the voice.

In Auvergne, a shepherd who sees a wolf eating a ewe must immediately put a fistful of hair in his mouth in order not to lose his speech.

The word "wolf" must especially not be said in December, because you risk seeing one turn up.

And especially don't forget: "When a wolf is spoken of, its tail is seen!"

Woodworm

These insect larvae that gnaw on furniture and beams are also called "death clocks." In Alsace, they are said to bring misfortune to those who hear them.

The winds, detail from "The Birth of Venus," by Sandro Botticelli, 1485 (Musée des Offices)

The Weather

The stars and atmospheric phenomena have for all time been translated by man like a language of supernatural forces. Tainted by symbolic value, they were at the base of numerous religions, such as sun worship and Greek or Roman rites. Of unknown immensity, the celestial canopy shelters most of the gods of this world. Natural manifestations as simple as rain or hail have long remained unexplained—they were signs from Heaven, gifts, or wrath of the gods. Violent or infrequent, like lightning or an eclipse, these manifestations have roles as omens or warnings. Founded on observation, beliefs concerning the weather govern daily life—they are extremely frequent, but as varied as climates.

Aurora Borealis

This rather rare phenomenon symbolizes the return of the powers of the day in the middle of the night.

This sudden illumination of the sky presages the misfortunes of war, blood, pillages, and fire. But the Eskimos consider it a game of ball among the dead.

Comet

Considered a cosmic irregularity, a comet announces a disaster or series of cataclysms. Some affirm that it is lit by God to warn man. For others, it is ignited by the sun's rays or is only a wandering star that falls to the earth. It takes on various appearances, such as a plentiful beard, a hairy head, or a long, slender tail.

Comets have a reputation for heating the atmosphere; they kill the weak and lustful, particularly princes. But they also raise the temperature of human blood several degrees, rushing man into wars and revolutions. Comets bring drought that is favorable to plague and famine.

It is said that the world was once drowned by a comet and that another will one day burn the earth, marking the end of time.

Comet years are reputed to be good years for wine.

Dew

More subtle than rain, dew is the quintessence of water and a symbol of regeneration. It is compared to a pearl, a tear, perspiration from the sky, and saliva of the stars. Pure and beautiful, it has the power to lend its gifts to men and women.

In general, dew is sovereign against eye sorenesses. Gathered at dawn on the first of May, it preserves a woman's complexion.

Dew gathered in the morning can exorcise a spell cast on a farm animal.

In China, it is affirmed that dew gives life to the dying.

Whoever rolls in it catches a fever.

The sound of bells makes the dew disappear.

Eclipse

The sun took on the color of a sapphire and it wore the moon in its first quarter on its upper portion . . . Everything seemed bathed in a vapor the color of saffron. This spectacle, man understood very well, presaged that some lamentable evil was going to befall mankind. And in fact, the same day as The Apostles' birth, in Saint-Peter's church, a few of the Roman nobility called upon, raised up against the Pope of Rome, wanted to kill him, did not succeed at all, but did nevertheless chase him from his see . . .

This was the solar eclipse of June 29, 1033, described by a contemporary. But the eclipse of the moon is even more frightening. Seven arrows must be shot in its direction in order to ward off its evil spell. It is said that sorcerers by their incantations, make the moon fall on the earth.

Therefore, one must yell louder than they so the moon doesn't hear the magic words.

The Chinese believe that a toad devours the moon—arrows must be shot toward the sky to chase it away.

Hail

Dangerous for cultivated land, hail is evil and everyone seeks to drive it away.

A virgin girl can stop a cataclysm by putting three hailstones on her breast.

If a cutting instrument is placed in the garden in the direction of the sky, it will divide one of the hailstones and turn the storm to rain.

Hail does not fall on a house in front of which three grains of salt have been deposited.

In order to spare the crops, the keys from the seven neighboring houses must be assembled on a thin cord and placed in a circle, then each person goes around the circle of keys three times. Also a mirror can be held out toward the sky.

In the South of France, people protect themselves from hail by putting a turtle on their backs. In the Juras, it is sufficient for the village priest to throw his shoe into the air.

In Egypt, a more sophisticated method prescribes making four nude women lie on the ground with their legs raised.

Lightning Bolt

First an expression of the gods' anger in ancient religions, the lightning bolt, brutal and murderous, appeared to be an instrument of Satan to the Christians. Man has also sought to protect himself from it. To the extent that the lightning bolt is a divine punishment, it never strikes a sleeping person or the same place twice.

In Germany, it is believed that wood struck by lightning protects barns on the night of May 1. In the United States, this wood is never used to make a fire in the fireplace because lightning will strike it again.

A harvest will be plentiful if lightning strikes on the twenty-seventh day of the month and poor if it's on the twenty-ninth day.

At a place where lightning has struck, "Devil's pebbles" or "lightning stones" that have the shape of hatchets or arrowheads are found. In the South of France, these prehistoric vestiges are buried in an underground passage, a cave, or at the foot of a tree because it is believed that they drive away evil spells. In the Alps, on the other hand, people are eager to break them, otherwise the hatchet or arrow returns immediately to form a second bolt of lightning. Alsacians affirm that if a fragment of one of these hatchets is put into a wound, it confers an invincible power on the wounded person. He can then kill with a single closed fist while exclaiming, "May lightning crush you!"

In order to protect a house from lightning, you must:

- gather a snake's skin around your head,
- sleep on a feather bed,
- feed a fire in the hearth,
- throw some salt and laurel leaves into that fire,
- clothe yourself in natural silk,
- put the pothook from the hearth on the window sill, and
- put a bouquet of artemisia under the attic joists.

"A Flock Struck by Lightning." Wash drawing from the beginning of the century (Bibl. Nat.).

Holy water from the Pentecost, Candlemas candles, and ashes taken from Palm branch, Saint John, or Yule log fires all drive lightning away.

When surprised by a storm, taking refuge under a tree should be avoided unless it is a beech, walnut, or hawthorn. Also, walnut leaves can be carried.

Lightning Flash

In opposition to the destructive lightning bolt, a flash of lightning is a fruitful symbol. When the Devil decided to destroy the earth with thunder, the Virgin Mary created a lightning flash to warn man so he would have time to cross himself and remove the malefice.

As a sign of respect, the tongue must be clicked three times at the sight of a lightning flash. But to look at one makes a person go insane, so it must not be mentioned just after having seen one.

When a lightning flash appears, all mirrors are veiled and the scissors are hidden.

An infant exposed to lightning flashes runs the risk of catching scabies.

Moon

This cyclical star influences the rhythms of the sea and of women. Venerated in numerous religions, the moon most often incarnates a feminine element, except for certain nomadic peoples who travel at night. It makes nature wax and wane in its image. The moon doesn't diffuse its own light, but it does diffuse that of the sun. It reigns over the kingdom of shadows that receives dead souls. All sorcery, magic, and conjurations are practiced during a full moon. Both open and closed, the crescent moon symbolizes Heaven and Resurrection for Moslems.

All that grows above ground must be sown when the moon is waxing and all that grows below the ground when it is waning. It is also said:

"The Goblins," engraving from the 19th c.

"When the moon is waning, sow nothing." One must never marry or give birth when the moon is waning.

The full moon, a privileged moment of exuberance for diabolical forces, drags in its tracks insanity and murder. It is well-known for curing illnesses, and it is good to begin treatments at this time. A young girl who would like to know when she will marry holds a silk handkerchief at the face of the full moon, and the number of moons that appear correspond to the number of years of waiting.

At the first appearance of the new moon, you must spit in your hands and rub your face so that the lunar cycle will be favorable. It can also be greeted with respect by stirring the coins in your right pocket—at the next full moon the amount of your wealth will have doubled. If it is looked at over the right shoulder, then three steps are taken backwards—it will bring a message of love. Elsewhere, if it is seen through the leaves of a tree, it is beneficent. But to see it for the first time through a window or any other glass object is a terrible omen. Two new moons in the same month foretell bad weather for a year. In Brittany it is said that if a wash is done at this time, the linen comes out shrunken or torn.

Babies conceived at the waxing moon will be boys. At its waning, neither nails nor hair should be cut.

The ten days that follow the new moon are the most tainted with superstitions:

- First Day: It is the best day for beginning a new adventure. A child born on this day will live a long time, happy and prosperous, but if it falls ill, the suffering will be long and very unpleasant.
- Second day: It is unfavorable for financial transactions and sea voyages.
- Third day: It is a very inauspicious day for newborns as well as criminals. The latter run the risk of being caught red-handed.
- Fourth day: All new building constructions must be undertaken on this day; the child born on this day will have a sharp political career.
- Fifth day: This is the best day for women to conceive.
- Sixth day: This is the best day of the month for fishing and hunting.
- Seventh day: A boy and girl who meet have every chance of falling in love.
- Eighth day: If you fall ill, the affliction will be mortal.
- Ninth day: Don't expose yourself to the moonlight, because it will make you ugly.
- Tenth day: A man born on this day will never have a tranquil soul.

The moon, the "eater of souls," attracts the souls of the dead, but also the spirits of the living, who, dispossessed of themselves, go insane.

Dreaming of moonlight can make you go blind.

By the light of the moon, my friend Pierrot,
Lend me your quill in order to write a word,
My candle has died, I have no more fire!
Open your door to me, for the love of God!

This popular song, well-known in France, would seem to be allied to ancient pagan ceremonies held at the full moon, during which the priests sought to obtain an oracle from the heavens. The last two verses recall lamentations of a world obscured by the silence of the gods.

The moon directs the ebb and flow of the sea. Seafaring people say that the souls of the dying go out with the tide.

The April moon is the moon that follows the paschal period. Gardeners accuse it of burning or "reddening" the young plants and buds: "Frosts of the April moon burn a plant's shoot." The disappearance of the April moon concludes winter: "When the April moon has passed, frosts are not feared at last."

Planets

The ancients knew of seven planets: the sun, the moon, Mercury, Venus, Mars, Jupiter, and Saturn. Still today, each one is characterized by a particular meaning that links it to man and the cycle of the days.

The system of these planets illustrates the constitution of the human body. The sun and moon, the eyes of the sky, are linked, one to the right eye, the other to the left. Saturn and Jupiter listen with their two ears. Mars and Venus, both sensual, preside over the two nostrils. Mercury, the chatterer, presides over the tongue.

Finally, each planet corresponds to a day of the week. Sunday is the sun; Monday, the moon; Tuesday, Mars; Wednesday, Mercury; Thursday, Jupiter; Friday, Venus; and Saturday, Saturn.

This system is also dynamic because it participates in the formation and renewal of terrestrial riches. The earth has the body of a woman and receives from its male, the sky, all its vital forces. The sun deposits a dew on the ground that Venus fertilizes. The moon, like a brain, directs the moods of the earth. Jupiter and Saturn nourish them, and Mercury, in the form of rain, washes them away.

Rain

Rain, the most banal sign of the sky, fertilizes the earth. But in the form of an absolute deluge, it seems to express the anger of the gods.

Its benevolent influence is often wished for. People seek to forecast or provoke its coming. Rheumatisms and corns on the feet are good alarm signals. Wheat and barley wilt. Salt clumps, bread gets soft, and fat runs. A cat that is cleaning itself rubs a paw behind its ear. A slice of buttered bread falls on the wrong side. If the rain is slow in coming, you must soak a broom in a bucket, drown a holy relic in a river or lake, or even burn some ferns. If all else fails, it is always possible to sing out of tune.

If it rains on a wedding party as it comes out of a church, it is a very good omen—the couple is assured of a long happiness or of many off-spring. If it rains during a burial, it means that the soul of the deceased has reached Heaven.

Rainwater cures eye illnesses. Money washed in this water will never be stolen. In Wales, it is believed that an infant laid in rain water will speak sooner than others. The Anglo-Saxons believe that the rain of July 15 necessarily lasts forty days. In fact, on this date they celebrate Saint Swithun, an obstinate personage who made it rain for forty consecutive days to keep the monks from moving his body that was buried at the door of a cathedral.

Throughout the centuries, rains of milk, toads, stones, or blood always preceded great catastrophies: fires, invasions, wars, earthquakes, or inundations.

Sudden showers are very sensitive. The first one of the year must be greeted with respect or it will take revenge and become a deluge. When they have lasted too long, they must be presented with a mirror to make them go far away.

Rainbow

This bridge between the sky and the earth, a seven-color stairway, is also called "tail in the sky" or "Devil's garter." Despite its beauty, it is rarely a good omen: In Greece, "Isis' scarf" foretold war.

One of the rainbow's ends pumps water from rivers and ponds to nourish the clouds. In Languedoc, it is believed that water, crossed by the colors of the rainbow, is poisoned. The sailors of the North believe that a rainbow inhales a vessel that crosses its rays. In order to protect his crops, the peasant who fears drought must exclaim, "Rainbow, rainbow, don't drink our water!"

The sight of a rainbow poisons its witnesses. In Czechoslovakia, it is said that if a rainbow is pointed out with a finger, it will begin to thunder, and the finger will be struck and fall from the hand. In Austria, a worm grows on the end of that same finger.

In Yugoslavia, whoever crosses the end of a rainbow changes sex. If you succeed in throwing an object across its rays, the object will turn to gold. Finally, there is supposedly a pot of gold at the end of each rainbow.

In general, to ward off the evil spells of this arch, it must be broken: Trace a cross in the air with a knife, spit in your hand, or make a circle with the saliva and cut it with your finger while saying, "I will cut you, sharp as a bell."

A rainbow is particularly feared in Scandinavian mythology, for it is the path toward God to which children's souls are drawn. Therefore, its presence predicts the death of a child.

Snow

Its color makes it a symbol of purity, but linked to winter and the great hostile cold, it also illustrates the death of nature and man.

A peasant, however, prefers it to frost, because he believes that snow protects the earth: "If December is under snow, the crop is protected." Or it is said: "December with its white feet comes, a snow year and a good year." If the snow is slow in melting, it is because a new storm will not be long in coming.

Snow must never be brought into the house of an ill person because he will die within the hour.

"The Census at Bethlehem" (detail), by Bruegel the Elder (Brussels, Musée des Beaux-Arts)

Star

The stars correspond to human souls; good or bad, each person has his own. In Scandinavian regions, stars are thought to be windows of the world destined to renew the air of the sky's spheres. They are also little doors open toward the beyond.

A star is insulted when it is pointed out by a finger—the finger will remain fixed in that position. Stars must not be counted or white spots will appear on your fingernails.

In Anglo-Saxon countries, to see the first star of the evening brings good luck. Young men of Charente who want to marry count ninety-nine stars, nine days in a row. They will marry the first girl that they meet on the morning of the tenth day.

Shooting stars are considered to represent human souls, but their movement has various interpretations. For some, these souls are coming back to earth to occupy the bodies of mortals or to give life to newborns; for others, they're dead souls en route to Heaven; still others think they are all proceeding toward hell, except those on August 15. Elsewhere it is affirmed that these souls are coming out of Purgatory to reclaim humans, an action of grace in their favor.

Illustration of Grandville for "The Stars," 1849, (Bibl. Nat.).

Shooting stars are also supposedly the matches of the Devil's pipe. In certain regions of the United States, they are believed to be missiles sent by God to stop man from invading the sky.

Their presence can announce a baby's birth as well as someone's death. In any case, it is customary to make a wish at the sight of a shooting star, but it must be thought of before the star disappears. Wishes made the night of Saint John, on the third star and with a piece of gold in the left hand, are by far the most effective. But the Sicilians prefer to cross themselves.

The pole star is the only fixed star in the northern hemisphere. Therefore a cult was devoted to it because it symbolized the Milky Way, abode of the gods. For the people of the great north, it represents the sky's naval or the pillar of the world.

Sun

An object of worship, the eye of God, or God himself, the respected sun, appealed to or feared, remains a too distant force to have inspired daily beliefs.

It is forbidden to make an insulting gesture in its direction, like pointing. It only shines for the Righteous: thus a bride bathed in light will have a happy life.

The Sun's chariot, allegorical engraving on wood taken from the "Indagine Chiromantia," 1531 (Bibl. Nat.).

A child born at sunrise will be lively and intelligent, whereas one born at sunset runs the risk of being slow and stupid.

If the sun hides its face it is an omen of disaster. (See Eclipse.)

Only an eagle can look directly at the sun.

Tempest

It especially threatens seafaring people who see in it the wrath of Neptune; his trident answers Zeus' lightning bolt. Therefore, people seek to coax these terrible and inconstant sea gods by a ritual sacrifice that, formerly bloody, today amounts to breaking a bottle of champagne against the hull of a new boat. Likewise, mast decorations, flags, and banners are reminiscent of the flower garlands the ancients conspicuously hung out to please the nautical gods. Bow figures, such as nude women or sirens, play the same role.

Precursory signs of a tempest are studied with attention. Gulls that fly far inland or porpoises that play close to a vessel warn sailors and fishermen. In Cornwall, to see a white hare or the bare feet of a woman with abnormally long toes on the wharf is a very bad omen.

Elsewhere it is known that a tempest will blow after the marriage of a sinner, a hanging, or the death of a great criminal.

In order to prevent the shipwrecks that tempests drag in their tracks, it is best not to set sail on a Friday unless there have been three

145

breaks in the foam before reaching the high sea. It is also inadvisible to throw a stone in the direction of a vessel leaving port or to lose the bucket or mop used to clean the deck. Women are warned of danger by knocks at the door by an invisible being or the sound of gulls hitting against window panes. A cat that turns its back to a fire foretells of the same catastrophe.

Thunder

Lightning engraves divine anger in the sky, but God can also express himself by word of mouth in the form of rolling thunder. Sacred drums, used by the military and at executions, have taken up this menacing rumble.

Heard in the distance, thunder is a good omen for the person going on a trip. Its significance changes according to the day of the week. On Monday, it announces the death of a woman; on Sunday, that of a notable, rich person, noble, or priest. The thunder of Tuesday is a sign of a good crop; that of Wednesday presages the death of a dishonorable person. On Thursday, it is a sign of abundance of all goods; on Friday, it announces war; and Saturday, drought and epidemic. In England, it is said that thunder that rumbles on the first Sunday of the year makes it known that a member of the Royal Family will die shortly.

When thunder is heard, the priest must be called. He can drive it away by blowing on it. The bells are rung and a blessed bullet is shot into the sky to kill the sorcerer who is the cause of this misfortune. It is also good to call upon Saint Barbara and Saint Donatus to drive away the storm.

As experienced in meteorology, thunder has a prophetic value according to which months of the year it manifests itself in. It is a bad sign in January, where it also announces the weather for the months to come: "Storm in January, grieves the farmer." Or even: "When it thunders in January, it thunders all the months of the year."

A storm is unlucky for wine growers in February: "If it thunders in February, put your wine barrels in the attic," but appreciated by farmers: "Thunder of February fills the granary."

"When it thunders in March, the farm is enraged," but opinions are divided according to regions: in the south of France, a storm is a good omen: "When it thunders in March, oxen and priests are fat." But in the north and east, "When it thunders in March, the cows' milk is drawn."

Thunder is very well received in April: "If the rain of April is worth its weight in gold, it's a real treasure when the thunder rolls," and "Thunder in April, open your barrel."

Likewise in May: "When it thunders in May, there's hope for the granary."

In June, it is hoped that the storms aren't too numerous: "If it thunders in June, year of straw, year of hay," but "If it thunders in the end of June, there will be no wine."

July announces the weather to come: "From a warm July comes an autumn during which it often thunders."

Associated with the warm weather of August, a storm is welcome if it brings neither great rains nor hail: "If it thunders in August, great prosperity everywhere but much illness."

Alsacians say that if it still thunders in September, at Christmas the snow will be high. In general: "In September if it thunders three days, it's a new lease for autumn." Stormy weather is celebrated in October in wine-growing regions: "In October thunder, vineyards prosper." In November it announces a mild winter: "If in November it thundered, the winter is aborted." Likewise: "Thunder at Christmas, no winter."

Wind

Turbulent and instable, it is just as much a little breeze as the master of a hurricane or tempest. It is often considered the breath of God and the incarnation of time. No one, however, has seen the wind. In Brittany, it is

"Fishing Boat on a Turbulent Sea," Japanese print by Hokusai, 1760–1849 (Paris, Musée Guimet).

known that certain sorcerers can make a wind from languor that paralizes the country. The wind fertilizes hens and mares, but of all the animals, only a chameleon feeds off the wind.

The wind can be very frightening, especially for sailors. Sorcerers know the wind's secret: They sell to sailors a strap with three magic knots tied in it. When the first knot is untied, a light breeze comes up; the second starts strong winds; and the third unleashes a tempest. Most often a sailor makes three knots in his handkerchief to attract the wind. When he unties the first, the wind grows strong; the second knot abates a tempest; and the third establishes an even calm. Whistling can also attract the wind, but when a tempest rages, the only thing to do is to whip the foam until its cries bring back the calm.

A boat that is transporting eggs or a dead body will meet only with adverse winds.

King Henry of Sweden made a pact with the Devil: The wind blew in the direction where he had turned his hat.

Everyone knows that to piss into the wind provokes the Devil.

Farmers fear the effects of the wind less directly, but they know that the wind brings frosts as well as good weather. January winds announce rain for July, those of March or May are not to be feared: "A windy May doesn't make for a scarce year." The wind establishes itself in fall: "At the feast of Saint Dennis (October 9), the wind makes its nest!" The direction in which it blows is important to know. Winds from the north and east bring the cold, those from the south heat, and from the west rain. The dominating wind of the year permits the coming crops to be forecast. As a general rule, that wind is the one that blows during the reading of the Gospel on Palm Sunday. The wind on New Year's Day will blow for half of the year and that of Easter Eve "forty full days." Moreover: "When a magpie builds low, over all the year the wind will blow."

The Calendar

From the natural cycle of the seasons, man, very early on, juxtaposed a rational and abstract division of time that assured him at least the illusion of mastering this still unexplained phenomonon.

All human experience has proven the necessity of days of rest for active men and women. Each civilization set these periods in time; thus were born taboo days in early societies—the Christian Sunday rest, the Jewish Sabbath, and the Moslem Friday. In general, man divided time in terms of agricultural activities, social practices, such as holidays and leisure, or ritual practices. The world cycle—century, year, month, week, day, and hour—are just arbitrary periods of which we have forgotten the "fabricated" character. Little by little, certain days, like Friday the 13th, or certain periods, like Holy Week, took on a new meaning that seems natural to us today. Superstitions regarding time started long ago but are still open to speculation, particularly superstitions about birth and death.

The present wide diffusion of horoscopes based on the very ancient science of astrologers is an example of the permanence of this fascination with Time.

Ascension

Like many pagan feasts based on the lunar calendar of our ancestors, Ascension, the day of Christ's rising to Heaven, became mobile on the Christian's Julian calendar. Ascension Day is the Thursday that follows the fifth Sunday after Easter; it falls between April 30 and June 3.

In Wales, it is inadvisable to work on Ascension Day—you expose yourself to great misfortune; in Alsace, whoever neglects this advice risks being stricken down.

Eggs laid on Ascension Day will never rot. Saving an egg laid on this day guarantees a farm's propserity for the year.

It is said that you can always make out the outline of a sheep in the clouds on Ascension Day. If it rains on this day, superstition says it is a sign of a bad crop and of an epidemic for the cattle. If there is good weather, the summer will be long and warm—"Rain on Ascension, everything withers right up to the harvest"; "If it rains on Ascension Day, all goes to hell"; and "Water on Ascension brings 'bangon' (tumors in sheep)." Ascension also marks the end of cold weather ("On Ascension, the last shiver") from which comes the following advice: "On Ascension, good woman, shear your sheep."

Assumption

Assumption, the day of the Virgin Mary's ascent into Heaven, is always on August 15. It announces the end of the crops and of the good season ("In mid-August, farewell beautiful days!"). In the South of France, it is said that autumn rains will soon begin: "On August 15th, rain comes out from behind the bushes." And everywhere it is believed that rains that start on this feast day will be of long duration: "When it rains on Our Lady's day, it rains until Christmas." In brief, according to the French saying, "The Virgin of August 15th does or undoes all."

The laying of eggs is said to diminish during this period: "Between the two Notre Dames, keep all your eggs, madame." In the countryside it is affirmed that "On August 15th the cuckoo loses its song; it is the quail that takes it up again." For Alsacians: "From the sun on Assumption, much wine, and good, too."

Candlemas

February 2nd is called "Feast of the Candles" because it corresponds to the Purification of the Virgin, for whom church candles are blessed. It is also a door between the old season and the new season. A medieval calendar, based on the seasons, had spring beginning on the Candlemas.

In Alsace, holy candles from this day are saved to be lit at the time of a grave illness or a storm. They ward off evil spirits. In general, a holy candle from the Candlemas protects a house and its inhabitants. In the

French-Comte region of eastern France, whoever can keep a candle lit from the church to his or her home is sure not to die during the year.

Originally, the Candlemas preceded Lent—the French custom of eating crepes corresponds to the last festivities preceding fasting. (It was also the tradition during that time to chase prostitutes out of their district and organize cock fights—both these practices have become obsolete.) If on the first try, you succeed in flipping a crepe onto the top of the buffet, the year will be a happy one. But, if you eat the crepes after 8 P.M., you will have bad luck. In order to be rich, you must hold the pan handle and a piece of silver or gold in the same hand; you can also toss up in the air seven crepes in a row.

If you rub a crepe on your face before eating it, you won't be stung by a wasp for an entire year. If you share crepes with the hens, they will be good layers.

In the Yonne region of France, planting crosses of twigs in the fields on this day is said to assure good crops. Bears come out of their dens on the Candlemas and test the weather. If it is freezing or snowing, they remain outside and wait for the arrival of good weather; if the weather is nice, they go back into their dens because they know the sun will not last. Wolves also come out of their lairs on the Candlemas; if they go back in, winter will last another forty days. "On the Candlemas, if the lark ascends singing, it takes six weeks for it to come down again." Finally, according to a "well-known" saying: "On the Candlemas, winter dies or comes alive again."

Carnival

The term "Carnival," borrowed from the Italian "carnevale" (a form of "carneleva" or "remove meat"), is linked to the idea of abstinence. Literally Carnival is the first day of Lent; the last three days before Carnival are

Mardi Gras amusements, French engraving from the 17th c.

Fat Sunday, Fat Monday, and Fat Tuesday (or Mardi Gras). The date of Carnival varies between February 3 and March 9.

In its nonliteral meaning, carnival is linked to ancient pagan winter feasts of magico-religious origin, associated with the rebirth of sunlight on the winter solstice. It is a time of secular rejoicing that existed during ancient times and continued after the coming of Christianity.

In ancient Rome during a carnival that lasted for nine days, people wore masks to frighten the dead shadows (lemures) that were being belched forth from hell. The mask had an exorcizing function. (Still today, masks play the role of exorcist—politicians have replaced the Lemures, spectres of the dead of yesteryear.) An animal or mannequin was burned to purify the earth and man, to forget the pains of the past year, and to throw off the world's ugliness.

In the Languedoc region of southern France, the carnival is the most important feast of the year, symbolizing the combined regeneration of man, nature, and time. A Carnival King (a "vagabond") is first celebrated, then judged and burned. The image of primative man, he represents chaos and disorder. This yearly sacrificial rite represents the laying of a foundation of a new order in the world. Likewise, in the "Aude" region, the stuffed "Pailhasse de Cournonterral," covered with wine dregs, represents primitive man.

At mid-Lent in the French city of Nantes, a fattened ox is paraded through town before being the object of a raffle. (This is a direct upshot of ancient Celtic practices.)

Christmas

The anniversary day of Christ's birth, Christmas replaces the pagan feast of the winter solstice. In Celtic and Germanic rites, the sacred Tree, a fir, was celebrated on this day.

In Alsace, December 24th is dedicated to Adam and Eve, because biblical legend presents Christ as the new Adam who was to save all humanity. You must abstain from eating apples on this day because you risk getting ulcers. In the same region, at 3:00 in the afternoon, the branches of trees that have not yet born fruit are cut. (Later in the year, the first fruits of these trees are given to children—they alone have the power to chase away evil spirits and therefore assure good crops.) On Christmas Eve, a girl who walks backward toward a pear tree, and then circles it nine times will see the image of her future husband. If she makes noise in a chicken coop and a hen answers her, she will remain single; if a rooster answers, she will find a husband. She can also scatter twelve sage leaves in the wind to have news of her future husband.

Witches and demons come out on Christmas night—they can be seen wandering outside the way they do on the summer solstice. It has been affirmed that phantoms disappear on this night, but it is best to leave the doors open at midnight so that the evil spirits can leave. It is a night of marvels, illustrated by the harmony between man and the plant and animal worlds. At midnight animals speak the language of men. In each haxel tree grows a golden bough; if you succeed in cutting it during the twelve strokes of midnight, you will always be rich, but if you don't do it during that time, you will join the dead. If a hole is dug in a cemetery at midnight, gold will be found there. Druidical stones begin turning over (some have seen the menhirs of Carnac go and drink by the side of the ocean).

Engraving extracted from the "Illustration," 19th c. (Bibl. des Arts Déco.)

If you go outside the church during the consecration at midnight Mass, you can see a procession of dead souls through town. In order to uncover witches at this Mass, cross two knives on the edge of a fountain or carry three kinds of wood. Whoever fasts on Christmas Eve, enters the church backward, and takes the holy water with his left hand, will know all those who will die within the year.

Linked to tree worship, the *yule log* is burned on Christmas Eve. (The French cake of the same name is eaten on that night.) As many logs as there are inhabitants of a house are placed in the hearth. The fire must not go out on this night under the penalty of disaster, and a person armed with a gun must always stay by the fire during midnight Mass. This fire must only be tended with your fingers—no iron instrument can go near it. If this fire makes a lot of sparks, the harvest will be plentiful the following summer. If it projects headless shadows onto the walls, some members of the family will die during the year. Its ashes must be carefully saved— they protect against storms, cure illnesses, and fertilize the earth. A log reserved for Christmas Eve must not be sat on—it will give you boils.

A *Christmas tree*, a fir, must be burned before the twelfth night after Christmas (January 6, the original Christmas Day). Those who neglect to do this risk having a death in the family.

Father Christmas or Santa Claus is our equivalent of the Germanic Saint Nicholas who, riding on a donkey, comes down from the sky on moonbeams on the night of December 5. Legend says that while visiting three nuns, this holy bishop tossed them some coins down the chimney. The money supposedly fell into the stockings that were drying. A protector of children, Saint Nicholas is often accompanied by a Bogyman, all covered with dirt and armed with rods and candlesticks.

Children born on Christmas night understand the language of birds.

In Anglo-Saxon countries, the plum pudding is stirred in the direction of the sun; a wish accompanying this gesture will be granted. This superstition goes back to ancient solar rites.

The decorations that adorn the tree and house on Christmas Day also serve as talismans against demons. Holly must be gathered before Christmas Eve; otherwise, there is a risk of being menaced by an enemy's ill thoughts in this world or the next.

In Northern England, a black man who enters a house on Christmas morning before anyone else brings luck. But a red-headed man or woman presages catastrophes. In addition, it is inadvisable to take something out of the house on this morning without first bringing something into it.

According to an ancient belief, the day of the week that Christmas falls on has a great importance because each god exercizes his influence: "Christmas comes on Monday and all is lost"; "When Christmas falls on Thursday, you can sell your carts and oxen. But if it falls on Friday, the wheat winds up in ashes." In general, the temperature on Christmas Day is considered to determine that of Easter Day: "Christmas at the pinion, Easter at the embers"; "Gnats at Christmas, icicles at Easter." The closer this feast is to a new moon, the better the crops.

Corpus Christi (Feast of)

Between May 21 and June 24, according to the date of Easter, the Feast of Corpus Christi or of the Holy Sacrament gives rise to many processions that remain, above all, religious. A few superstitions have, however, been grafted onto this Christian practice.

In the Provence region of France, successfully passing between the cross and the banner carried in the procession is believed to protect you from fevers for one year.

In the Cevenne region of France, it is inadvisable to shear woolen animals during the octave of Corpus Christi—they will die within the year.

No caterpillar can withstand rains during the Feast of Corpus Christi: "If it rains on Thursday of the Corpus Christi Feast, the wheat will pour forth but the caterpillars will die." The weather during the procession is of great importance: "As goes the consecration, so goes the threshing."

Days

The seven days of the week have varied significance according to their heirarchical order and in terms of the month to which each is related. Many beliefs attached to the days of the week originate from the worship of the pagan divinities to whom these days were dedicated. Altered by religious calendars, little by little the succession of days took on a new meaning. For a long time Sunday was considered the first day of the week, and certain superstitions are founded on this reality. Days are, in general, indexed in terms of their lucky or unlucky character for man.

The days of the week. Illustration by Halkett for "Rumpelstiltskin" by the Brothers Grimm. London, 1882.

MONDAY

First day of the week in the Christian calendar, Monday determines the weather and atmosphere of the days to come. A saying explains: "Nasty Monday, beautiful week." Placed under the sign of the moon, Monday is considered a rather unfavorable day, particularly in Alsace where it is believed that a wedding celebrated on this day produces an insane couple!

Three Mondays during the year are particularly unlucky: the first Monday in April, the day of Cain's birth; the second Monday in August, when Sodom and Gomorrha were destroyed; and the last Monday in December, the day of Judas's birth.

Finally, in Paris it is said that if you wear an emerald on a Monday, you won't be able to do anything right for the rest of the week.

TUESDAY

Placed under the sign of Mars, the god of war, Tuesday is the ideal day for combat in the West, but Arabs fear fighting on a Tuesday. On the commercial side, however, it is an auspicious day.

Tuesday is a wonderful day for getting married, but you musn't wear a flower in your buttonhole!

WEDNESDAY

Placed under the sign of Mercury, Wednesday is lucky for Moslems, who believe that God created light on the third day of the week. In the West, it favors business and trips; some say that sorcerers take a rest on this day.

You must neither get married nor wear gloves on a Wednesday.

When a new moon falls on a Wednesday, expect the worst: "Changing moon, bearded woman, and mossy meadow do not bring great returns"; "Wednesday moon, grumbling woman, twilight wind, once in a hundred years is too often."

THURSDAY

Arabs and Germanic tradition consider Thursday a lucky day. It is a favorable day for weddings and, in the Orient, for bringing a new bride under the conjugal roof.

Different traditions, however, maintain that you must not wear a ruby, work, eat chicken, or spin yarn on a Thursday.

This ideal day often makes people dream of a "week of four Thursdays."

FRIDAY

Placed under the sign of Venus, Friday is considered a bad day. It is said that Eve offered the apple to Adam on a Friday.

During the night between Friday and Saturday, devils and witches meet at the Sabbath. In England and the United States, it used to be a common practice to hang criminals on a Friday.

Nothing must be undertaken on this day. Neither cut out nor sew shirts on Fridays because they will be too tight and cause skin diseases. Bretons avoid burying their dead on a Friday because three members of the family will die before the end of the year.

A child born on a Friday will have visions and the gift of curing fevers. In Hungary, on the other hand, being born on a Friday is a bad omen, but the misfortune can be erased by placing a few drops of blood on a piece of cloth cut out of an old article of clothing and burning it. If you have a dream on Friday night, tell it to someone in your family the next morning—it will come true. Alsacians believed that if you cut your nails and hair on a Friday, you would have good sight and hearing.

According to a widespread belief, a direct relationship exists between the weather on Friday and that on Sunday: "As is the weather on Friday, so is the weather on Sunday!" but "Nasty Friday, beautiful Sunday" is said just as often. It is also affirmed: "Those who laugh on Friday will cry on Sunday."

Associated with the number thirteen, Friday is a particularly significant day, most often unlucky, except perhaps for games of chance. (See Holy Week.)

SATURDAY

The Jewish day begins and ends with the setting of the sun; the Sabbath, therefore, lasts from Friday evening to Saturday evening. All traditions dealing with the Witches' Sabbath are spread over the days of Friday and Saturday.

God created man on Saturday; on this day the sun always shines for at least a few hours. Sayings are often proof of this: "The preeminent sun on Saturdays takes its bow"; "In winter as in summer, never a Saturday passes without the sun sticking its nose into it." Bretons specify that it is the day when the Blessed Virgin dries her linens.

In Scotland, whoever is born on a Saturday has the ability to see phantoms.

In general it is considered bad luck to fill a Saturday with work. But it is a good day for going on trips and telling your dreams, because they might come true!

SUNDAY

Sunday is a very favorable day because it calls to mind Christ's resurrection and illustrates the sun—"Sun"day—the star of life. Children born on this day have a superior destiny.

Placed under the protection of God, Sunday's child wears his or her birthday like a talisman—he can make light of evil spirits and his or her work is always fruitful. Gifted with prophecy, he or she will see things in life that are unimaginable for others.

Sunday is, of course, the ideal day for a mother and her newborn who are leaving the bed after childbirth. It is also recommended that all medical treatments begin on this seventh day.

"Sunday Sanctification," image from a catechism of the 19th c.

Like the Christian God, man should rest on Sunday and limit his activities to cultural affairs. Consequently, it is ill-advised to undertake a project or conduct a transaction. In the United States, it is bad luck to put new sheets on a bed on this day. A choir singer who sings a wrong note in church will find a burned meal upon returning home.

Long considered the first day of the week, Sunday still governs the weather of the days to come: "Very often the week is bothered by Sunday-morning rain"; "Who cries on Sunday will not laugh on Friday."

In general, Tuesday, Wednesday, and Friday are hardly favorable for business and projects. You must especially not cut your nails or hair on these days (unless you're an Alsacian). Whoever cuts his nails on Friday lengthens the devil's horns. But if a young girl dares to cut her nails nine Fridays in a row, on the ninth Friday she will meet her future husband.

Table of Good and Bad Days

January
Lucky days: 4, 19, 27, 31
Unlucky days: 13, 23
   or 1, 2, 4, 5, 10, 15, 17, 29

February
Lucky days: 7, 8, 18
Unlucky days: 2, 10, 17, 21
   or 8, 10, 17

March
Lucky days: 3, 9, 12, 14, 16
Unlucky days: 13, 19, 23, 28
   or 16, 17, 20

April
Lucky days: 5, 27
Unlucky days: 10, 20, 29, 30
   or 16, 21

May
Lucky days: 1, 2, 4, 6, 9, 14
Unlucky days: 10, 17, 20
   or 7, 15, 20

June
Lucky days: 3, 5, 7, 9, 12, 23
Unlucky days: 4, 20
   or 4, 8

July
Lucky days: 2, 6, 10, 23, 30
Unlucky days: 5, 13, 27
   or 15, 21

August
Lucky days: 5, 7, 10, 14, 19
Unlucky days: 2, 13, 27, 31
   or 19, 20

September
Lucky days: 6, 10, 15, 18, 30
Unlucky days: 13, 16, 22, 24
   or 6, 7

October
Lucky days: 13, 16, 20, 31
Unlucky days: 3, 9, 27
   or 6

November
Lucky days: 3, 13, 23, 30
Unlucky days: 6, 25
   or 15, 20

December
Lucky days: 10, 20, 29
Unlucky days: 15, 28, 31
   or 6, 7, 9, 28

The first two lines, lucky days and unlucky days, correspond to a table of French origin. It was supposedly given to Adam by an angel and indicates the best days for farmers to carry out their planting. The second line of unlucky days is taken from a 16th century English table.

End of the World (Apocalypse)

This notion is based on various realities; Christians interpret it in terms of divine Creation and Christ's birth, and other interpretations are founded on cyclical and natural phenomena.

Because God created the world in six days, it is said that the world will last six thousand years. It is also believed that starting with the birth of Jesus Christ, the world will last as many years as there are verses in the Psalms. Medieval millennialists predicted that starting with the year one thousand, evil would dominate the world. They depended upon marvels for their predictions, such as comets (images of snakes in the sky) or earthquakes.

The idea of an annihilation of civilization by cosmic intervention accompanied by cataclysms also rests on a cyclical conception of time. Preceded by a demonic dark age, the end of the world will happen only after a series of catastrophes that date back to 9,000 or 10,000 B.C. Astrologers foresee a new world shock in the year 2,000.

Epiphany

Also called *adoration of the Magi*, Epiphany is one of the oldest church celebrations. For a long time it was confused with Christmas, particularly in the Orient. Every January 6th, Epiphany commemorates the arrival of the three Wise Men carrying gifts for the Baby Jesus. Dividing up among the family a Twelfth Night cake into which a bean has been slipped is a custom that is still alive and that gives rise to a certain number of superstitions.

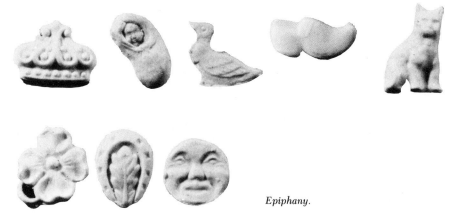

Epiphany.

In France, the cake is divided into an odd number of portions. The youngest of those present (innocent and pure) hides under the table and according to his heart, designates the order of the dividing up. The person who finds the bean receives a golden crown and chooses a male or female partner to whom he or she grants a kiss and a silver crown. The bean in this pastry is a reminder that the pastry was originally a bean cake.

In order to know the state of health of the absent relatives, you must put the portions of the cake reserved for them in a piece of furniture. The condition of the portions a few hours later gives a good indication of the health of those absent.

In order to protect themselves from fires and floods, some people in Germanic countries trace the initials of the wise men—Gaspar, Melchior, and Balthazar—on the doors of their homes.

According to an ancient belief, cold weather on the eve of the Adoration announces a good year; rain, on the contrary, brings misfortune.

On the other hand, "Rain on the Adoration, grain to the roof!" and "For the Adoration, a drop on the roof: a season of peas."

Holy Week

Holy Week is the week that precedes Easter, but the only truly significant days are Thursday, Friday, and Saturday, because in traditional rites this "week" only began on Thursday. The weather during these days has an important prophetic meaning.

Maunday Thursday, called green Thursday in eastern France, celebrates the ceremony of Holy Communion and inaugurates the cycle of rituals in memory of Christ's Passion. Spinach greens are eaten at lunch to avoid stomach ailments during the coming year and, in a more general way, to purify oneself of winter ailments. A few superstitions underline the role of the temperature on this day: "Frost on Maundy Thursday freezes the buckwheat"; "Good weather on Maunday Thursday lasts throughout the year."

The day of the Passion and death of Christ, *Good Friday* is the most inauspicious day of the year. It is a period of penitence and fasting that brings to mind the ancient blood rites present in many civilizations. All action undertaken on this day is destined to fail; restrictions are innumerable. Whoever climbs a tree risks taking a mortal fall. Whoever eats an egg will find a toad in it. Bread baked on Good Friday either molds immediately or stays fresh forever. A child must never be weaned on this day, because he or she will refuse to feed himself or herself. Good Friday is, however, favorable for certain activities, particularly those that are capable of purifying the environment or warding off evil spirits. It is the day for chasing flies out of the house for the year—simply hang a herring from the ceiling. Also, you can eliminate vermin from the henhouse and weeds from your garden. Eggs laid on this day bear hens that change their feathers at the same time every year or chickens with multicolored feathers. A rooster born on Good Friday will crow more often than other roosters in the mornings. It is believed that an egg laid on this day will never rot—it is kept on the mantel to ward off evil spirits, and it allows witches to be revealed on Christmas night. In addition, this egg facilitates teething in young children. An egg from Good Friday must not be confused with an Easter egg.

On this day, wine growers shake the wine and vinegar vats so that their contents don't turn into water.

Restrictions on work do not apply to certain agricultural labors. On the contrary, it is advisable to sow peas as well as potatoes at noon. A young boy who puts on his first pair of long pants on Good Friday will be happy in married life.

Being between the Crucifixion and the Resurrection, Easter Eve Day is an empty and silent day. Only the weather plays an essential role—in effect, the wind that blows on Easter Eve Day is the predominant wind for the year: "The wind blows for fifty whole days from where it blew on Easter Eve Day."

Holy Sunday is Easter, the day that commemorates Christ's Resurrection. It falls between March 22 and April 25. Children born on this day are particularly lucky. In the morning, winged bells, whose sounds ward off demons, return from Rome carrying eggs for children. They let their gifts fall in gardens and houses; then, the gifts must be looked for! This day is therefore a time of merrymaking. Hard boiled eggs, painted red in memory of Christ's blood, were given to children; thus began the custom of decorating Easter eggs. On Easter morning, the sun dances as it comes up over the horizon and a lamb appears in the sky. This day of feasting concludes the Lenten season. New clothes for the year are worn on this day. Holy water from Easter Sunday cures all illnesses.

Since Easter often falls in April, rain is often expected on this day: "A wet Easter makes for strong stalks"; "Rain on Easter fills the bins." In general, you must not wash, tend, or plant cabbage during Holy Week!

Hours of the Day

The cycle of light and darkness lays the foundation of most magical or superstitious beliefs and symbols. In many civilizations, darkness is associated with all the forces of Evil, whether they are pagan or Christian. In contrast, daylight corresponds to Good, God, and the sun.

It is advisable not to go out of your house until after the sun has risen and the cock has crowed, chasing away evil spirits. All gestures made at the time of awakening have an importance for the day. You must get out of bed on your fight foot and put your clothes on right side out. It is always best to cross yourself and spit on the ground three times. The first person or animal encountered sets the tone for the day.

The sun at its zenith marks the center of the day. It is a privileged moment for collecting your thoughts, preferably when the noon Angelus tolls. But beware of the noon demons or "Empusae" who appear in various forms: trees, oxen, vipers, or flies. They come out on the twelfth stroke of the clock, especially in summer. In Russia, the demons break the limbs of harvesters who don't have time to throw themselves face down on the ground when they catch sight of the demons.

When the sun sets, the forces of night are ushered in and all activity must come to an end. Night is, in effect, the domain of witches, ghosts, and the Devil. Whoever dies during the night goes directly to hell. Water must not be thrown outside after sunset. A person out walking at night can protect himself with signs of the cross and a small light.

At *midnight* witches and demons meet at the Sabbath. You must always cross yourself when the twelve strokes sound. In houses it is the privileged hour for phantoms. To hear birds sing at this hour announces an approaching death. It is also, of course, the prime hour for crime.

Months

JANUARY

The first month of the year, January is the month of wishes and vows. It plays an important role in determining the quality of the coming seasons. It incarnates winter more than does December. A peasant must therefore watch over his provisions ("In January be sure to calculate that you eat half of your stock") and remain prudent ("Save a whole crown for the month of January!"). It is even a bad omen if January is too mild: "January gift, February ingratitude"; "Greenery in January, summer will take pity." And in the Languedoc region of France: "January often makes mistakes that are reproached in March."

FEBRUARY

"Of all the months, February is the shortest and the slyest." On the old Roman calendar, February ended the year and was considered an unlucky month. Then Julius Caesar fixed an additional day, February 29th, onto the year every four years. As in January, farmers fear a February that is too warm: "It is better to see a rabid dog than a naked man in February."

In general, this capricious month must not be trusted: "February comes in like a lion, goes out like a lamb."

When the month lasts twenty-nine days, in the Saintonge region it is believed that: "A leap year is a sterile year." During leap years, February 29th is to be especially feared.

MARCH

The first month of spring on the Roman calendar, March inaugurated the new year after a military truce set from October to the end of February. The green woodpecker that is associated with March is a prophetic bird that announces rain and sudden showers. In Alsace, the nights from March 20 to 24, called "black nights," are unlucky, especially for births. The spirits of darkness that come with winter are said to sense spring's approach and stage one last battle before disappearing. On March 10, in memory of the four martyrs, you must spit on each fruit tree so that it will bear many fruits. True March weather is that of sudden showers, and its rains are impatiently awaited: "March with its hammers comes and knocks at our doors"; "When it has thundered in March, the cows' milk is drawn." Like February, it is a changing month: "March buys its mother's (winter) fur-lined coat and sells it three days later."

APRIL

This is the month of transition from the bad season to the good season, the month of renewal. Consequently, the return of winter is still feared: "In April, don't uncover yourself one stitch"; "If there were neither a lord nor the month of April on earth, there would never be famine or war."

Traditionally in Europe, April 1 is a day of pranks and jokes. This custom was born in France where, in 1564, the beginning of the year was changed to March 25. People then had the custom of giving each other gifts on this date to celebrate the first day of the new year. But when March 25 fell during Holy Week, the Church demanded that the holiday be moved up to April 1. When the beginning of the new year was changed to January, the French amused themselves by visiting their friends on April 1 to make them believe that it was again the first day of the year. In addition, the obligation of abstaining from meat during Holy Week is undoubtedly the origin of the famous French "April Fish" that you hang on your neighbor's back. In general, the game consists of making your victims believe the worst absurdities: "April makes the flower, May has the honor of it."

MAY

Being the foremost month of spring and germination, May symbolizes the joy of regeneration. It is dedicated to lovers who, little by little, get to know each other before becoming engaged. Young women and flowers are given the time to blossom. Marriage in May is strictly forbidden—the union will be unhappy, sterile, and stormy. Whoever marries in May marries poverty. This month, consequently, is consecrated to the Virgin Mary, the image of virginity.

The most widespread custom deals with amorous ritual. The young men of a village go in procession to gather leafy branches called "Maypoles" that they then attach to the doors of the houses where young women live. (The length of the branch depends on the girl's age.) In the Upper Vosges, the Maypole is decorated with colored ribbons or eggshells. The kind of branch used is symbolic: Bramble is injurious, hornbeam pleasant, and birch expresses virginity. This custom of "honoring" the girls on Mayday or the first Sunday of the month is often accompanied by quests and banquets.

Groups of boys serenade each house and the inhabitants, by their gifts, are assured of a good year. In Provence, "Mayos," little girls in white, crowned with flowers, try to prepare themselves for becoming good wives. In the evening, a banquet reunites the boys and girls. The girls put up a "Maypole" for auction (the right to carry a huge candle of 30 to 40 pounds during the Corpus Christi day procession). The elected boy becomes the May king and chooses some May maidens of honor. The quest is sometimes lead by a young man covered with foliage and moss who symbolizes spring. In Upper Savoy, it is a good omen if no one recognizes him in his costume.

On May 3, the Feast of the Finding of the True Cross, little crosses are made with hazelwood sticks, blessed at church, and planted in the middle of fields.

May is the month when donkeys mate.

Cats born in May do not hunt rats. A child born during this month will always be fragile.

In general, it is a month during which nothing must be undertaken.

Today's Labor Day in France (May 1) was originally, for Christians, the feast day of Saint Joseph the carpenter. In Germany, the night of May 1 (Walpurgis night from German paganism) corresponds to the great annual witches' Sabbath that takes place on the Blocksberg. This explains the frequency of storms on this date. On the night before Walpurgis night, all the houses in a village are sprinkled with holy water. In certain locations in Alsace, the bells are rung in the middle of the night. Children born on this night are considered birds of misfortune. Dew from the

morning of May 1 revives your skin color. In Franche-Comté, cows are
said to lose half of their milk when it rains on the first day of May. May 1 is
also the day for lilies of the valley, symbols of rebirth and purity that in
the 18th century were considered aphrodisiacs.

May is not a deceptive month like April: "In May, do what you like."

JUNE

In June summer settles in and barely inspires the superstitious who are
especially sensitive to periods of change. Only the Saint John feast on the
summer solstice consecrates the long patience of May.

June.

June rains have dangerous repercussions for the crops: "June rain
ruins the mill"; "If it rains in June, eat your fist." Belgians affirm: "A field
is really good-for-nothing when in June it produces nothing." Everyone
knows that "hay is made in June." It is said, however, that: "Year of hay,
year of nothing."

JULY

This seventh month of the year is one of intensive agricultural labors.
More than August, it symbolizes summer, and in Provence it is said:
"Whoever curses the summer, curses his father." It is harvest time in
many regions, and it is believed that: "One never knows if July is good
until after the harvest." Both the sun and the rain are welcome: "Beautiful
July, perfect love"; "July without storms, famine for the village."

AUGUST

For Alsacians, August 1 was the day of Lucifer's downfall. There must be no blood-letting on this day or a sick person will die very quickly. It is the hardest month of the summer for farmers. In effect, "Whoever sleeps in August sleeps at his own expense" and "Whoever sleeps in August will soon regret it."

September.

SEPTEMBER AND OCTOBER

These are the autumnal months of intermediate weather. Many foresee the extent of the cold weather to come from the behavior of migratory birds or animals.

"When the wild geese head away from the dry, cold, North wind, wrap yourself up good and warm in your sheets, little man."

Winter will be very rigorous if cats have a thick coat of fur, if hedgehogs construct their burrows facing south, or if anthills are high and the ants bury their nests very deeply.

Plants have the same prophetic value: "Thin-skinned garlic, short, beautiful winter"; "When onions have three skins, great coldness to come."

In September, grape harvest season, shooting stars supposedly have a favorable influence on the vineyards: "When there are many shooting stars in September, the vats will be too small in November."

October. Miniature from "Les Très Riches Heures" by Duc de Berry (Chantilly, Musée Condé).

NOVEMBER

November marks the arrival of winter and is associated with a feeling of sterility of the earth. The Druids made this date All Souls' Day and the first day of the year. Christianity made it All Saints' Day, a happy feast, but chose November 2 to celebrate the dead.

On the night of October 31, Americans celebrate Halloween: On this night, spirits of the dead have the right to one last escapade before winter. The Irish, who hear footsteps behind them at this time of year, avoid turning around—it is death following and to see it means you have already gone to be with it. Hollowed-out pumpkins carved with human faces and holding lighted candles are placed behind windows or in front of doors.

Many superstitions dealing with this period come from Celtic traditions.

A person must especially not go out on the night of All Saints' Day because all the souls of the dead are floating around freely. (But whoever has the courage to set foot outside can hear the souls talking.)

In southwestern France, a family has a nine course meal together on the evening of All Saints' Day; only members of the family who have died are spoken of. Once the dinner is over, lamps are left lit and the remains of the nine courses are left on the table for the dead souls.

A child born on the night of All Saints' Day is protected until his death and endowed with the gift of double vision.

On November 2, because the souls are always outside, a person must not go hunting because he risks wounding the souls.

November 11, the feast day of Saint Martin, patron of the vineyards, is a key day for determining winter weather. On this day it is useful to eat a fattened goose, because its wishbone has a prophetic value (if the wishbone is white, winter will be mild, if it is red, winter will be cold).

Since the 17th century, single young women who will reach the age of 25 during the year do something to please Saint Catherine on November 25. This saint has a great reputation as a provider of husbands.

In eastern France, Saint André, patron of single women, is celebrated on November 30. Young women toss melted lead in a tub of water; while drying, the lead takes the shape of the tool that characterizes the trade of her future husband: a shoe, pitchfork, saw, and so forth. Some women boil rags and see the faces of their future husbands in the steam.

DECEMBER

For the Church, December is the month of Advent, a time of penitence that precedes Christmas and begins on December 3 at the latest.

Each day between December 25 and December 31 has a significance for the coming year. If the wind blows on the night of the December 25, the next grape harvest will be plentiful. The weather during the day of December 27 foretells that of the month of March. If a tempest blows on the night of December 27, a great person in this world will die. The weather during the day on December 28 foretells the weather for April, but if a child dies on this day of the Holy Innocents, many newborns will lose their lives soon after. The weather on the day of December 29 foretells the weather for the beginning of summer and that on December 30 foretells the weather for the end of the summer. This belief comes from ancient Vedic texts from India that saw the image of the twelve months to come in the twelve days following the winter solstice. (See also Christmas and Year.)

Palm Sunday

Every year, the Romans cut olive or laurel branches to celebrate the return of spring. In memory of Christ's entry into Jerusalem, the Christian Church moved this celebration to Palm Sunday, which falls between March 15 and April 18. Christ was in fact acclaimed by the townspeople, who laid palm and olive branches under the feet of his donkey.

This Sunday is also called Flower Sunday and "Box Sunday." Palms and box tree branches blessed on this day protect against illness and ward off demons. They are placed in every bedroom above the bed, as well as in barns.

Some people planted one of these blessed branches in their garden; its rotting was a sign of happiness, but if it took root, it was a sign of death. In effect, box and rosemary are reputed to be abortive plants.

When new branches are put in a house, branches from the previous year must be burned, but never thrown away.

In some regions, various types of branches were burned; placed under a roof, ashes from this fire were a protection against lightning.

In general, it is accepted that the wind that blows on Palm Sunday will be the dominant one for the year; some specify that it is the wind that blows during the reading of the Gospel during the Palm Sunday service.

Pentecost

The word first designates the paschal time, then a precise date: the fiftieth day after Easter. The Pentecost commemorates the descent of the Holy Ghost to the Apostles in the form of tongues of flame. It coincides with ancient Jewish harvest feasts and German agricultural celebrations.

Holy water from Pentecost Sunday must be sprinkled at four corners of a house to ward off storms. On Monday of the Pentecost, in certain regions of Germany, young men cracked their whips in front of their financées' houses—the noise supposedly chased away evil spirits who had been there since winter.

When it rains on Saturday of the Pentecost, it will rain for the next seven weeks. The wind that blows on the eve of the Pentecost lasts for six weeks.

Rogations

These are the prayers recited during the three-day-long penitence procession started by Saint Mamertius, 5th century bishop of Vienna, after a series of catastrophes. They seek to attract God's blessings on the earth's bounty. Depending on the date of Easter, Rogation Days falls between April 27 and May 31. These three days must be consecrated to prayer—all work is forbidden.

Doing a wash during Rogation Days is risking death. Anything planted at this time will not grow.

The weather during the Rogation Days determines that of the agricultural seasons: If there is good weather on the first day, the sun will shine for the hay-making season; the second day will foretell the weather for the grain harvest; the third, the weather for the grape harvest.

Saints

Practices relating to saints intimately link religion and superstition. During the Medieval period, saint worship was a substitute for certain pagan practices. Here we will speak only of those saints who are remembered today.

ICE SAINTS

During April and May, the rebirth of the earth is still fragile; at this time, Romans held religious celebrations in order to reclaim the earth's protection. Then the Church replaced these rites by the invocation of Ice Saints. The most celebrated are Mamertius and Pancras, whose celebration announced the beginning of summer in the Medieval period. Saint George gathers the cherries, Saint Mark sells them. These saints are reputed to be either "hail makers or wine makers." Saint Mark also protects against fly bites. When it rains on Saint George's feast day, there will be neither plums or barley.

RAIN SAINTS

The most famous of these saints are Medard and Barnabas, enemy brothers who make rain and good weather. Saint Medard is responsible for the rains that fall on his feast day and that seem to never want to stop. He is nicknamed the "great pisser": "Saint Medard, great pisser, make it rain forty days later." But Saint Barnabas watches over the grain. It rains forty days later "unless Saint Barnabas lops off his foot, shortens his nose, or punches him in the mouth." Consequently: "When it rains on Saint Medard, take your hat without delay, but if there is good weather for Barnabas, your coat at home can stay."

SAINT ANNE

Every year, on July 26 and 27, crowds make a pilgrimage to Saint Anne of Auray in Brittany. This miracle working saint is also the patroness of the Bretons. People come to thank her for curing illnesses, extinguishing conflagrations, calming tempests, or causing favorable trials. Many leave a votive offering, a wax object, a cross, or a crutch hung on the chapel walls. Whoever goes up the parvis steps on his knees will see his wishes granted.

171

SAINT ANTHONY OF PADUA

He has the power to have lost or stolen objects found. It is customary to promise him a gift in case of a favorable result.

SAINT CHRISTOPHER

This former saint was the patron of travellers. It used to be popular to hang his medal in cars or planes. It is not certain that he existed, but some believe that the Church created him to replace legendary giants of popular beliefs.

SAINT "GLINGLIN"

This fictitious saint is associated with a date so far back in the distant past that it has become uncertain. Anything that has to do with Saint Glinglin will be realized when the moon is made of green cheese.

SAINT JOHN

On June 24, date of the summer solstice, the Nativity of Saint John the Baptist, Saint John's feast day, is celebrated. The customary Saint John fires that are jumped over by lovers today are part of the ancient cycle of fires that were lit at the solstices and equinoxes (a Christmas yule log goes back to this tradition).

Like Christmas night, Saint John's night is fertile for miracles and the Devil is muzzled for a time. Oaks blossom on this night and fade before dawn; no one has ever seen this flower. A young woman who holds a white sheet under an oak on this night, gathers the pollen from the flowers, and then places it under her pillow will see her future husband appear in a dream. In Austria, hidden treasures are said to be revealed by will-o'-the-wisps on the night of Saint John.

Black cats are burned in Saint John fires and whoever wants to get married during the year must jump over nine different fires or over the same fire nine times. Children less than one year old must be balanced over one of these fires nine times for strength and courage. Everywhere, embers from these fires are saved because they protect against storms.

On the morning of Saint John, the Italians collect a few drops of sap from an oak—it is miraculous and heals wounds. In Russia, dew gathered on this morning protects against evil spells, removes freckles, and cures eye ailments.

172

On June 24, it is best not to go to the wine cellar and treat the wine. In Germany, it is believed that a man can be struck dead by lightning on this day.

If a good crop is desired, a farmer must sleep on his manure on the night of Saint John.

SAINT "NITOUCHE"

This saint is also fictitious and noted for his smooth hypocracy. He is named after the French expression "N'y touche!" ("don't touch").

SAINT VALENTINE

This young priest was put to death for being opposed to a law that forbid marriage to soldiers. Lovers celebrate him on February 14, a day that in Greece was also dedicated to the gods of Woman and of marriage. Especially in Anglo-Saxon countries, men and women send each other cards. A yellow crocus is the symbol of this day, and a young girl who wears one in a buttonhole can hope to encounter the man of her life. In Great Britain and in the United States, the bird that a girl catches sight of on the morning of Saint Valentine is said to define the character of her future

The lovers. Anonymous wood engraving from the 16th c. (Bibl. Nat.)

husband. A blackbird announces a man of the Church, a sparrow a farmer, a yellow bird a rich man, and a robin a sailor. A green woodpecker, however, is a sign of celibacy.

By throwing melted lead into water on this day, a girl can see the silhouette of her future husband outlined.

Sometimes it happens that a person no longer knows which saint to devote himself to! In this case, take some ivy leaves and inscribe the name of a saint on each one, then throw them into a well. The first leaf that sinks into the water indicates the name of the saint whom you should acknowledge. Pieces of cloth dropped into a pitcher achieve the same result. As a last resort, call upon Robert, the common first name of the Devil.

Trinity Sunday

Trinity Sunday is the Sunday after the Pentecost; it has a reputation as sad as Saint Medard's.

If it rains on the Trinity, all the Sundays of the year will be muddy.

A person in a state of grace can see three suns rise on Trinity Sunday.

Year

In Rome the beginning of the year was on March 1 until the intervention of Caesar, who chose January 1. Before finally being fixed on this date, the first day of the year fluctuated many times: In France, under the Merovingians, the year began on March 1; under the Carolingians, it began on Christmas day. The Capetians preferred March 25. In the 11th century, the year was made to begin on Easter Day; finally Charles IX fixed the date of January 1 in 1564. This date remained unchanged except when the Republican calendar decided to make the year begin on the day of the spring equinox. It is easy to understand the doubts placed on all sayings having to do with the New Year that date back before the 15th century!

Whatever its place on the calendar, the first day of the year has always been celebrated as a hope for the twelve months to come.

SAINT SYLVESTER/NEW YEAR'S EVE

On this day, everyone hangs mistletoe on the ceiling or in doorways. When midnight sounds, families and friends kiss each other under the mistletoe while wishing each other a Happy New Year. This tradition comes from Celtic Druidism (see Mistletoe).

It brings misfortune if you let the fire go out on the night of Saint Sylvester.

If, on this night, the wind blows from the west, there will be great abundance of milk and fish, but a great person in this world will disappear. If it blows from the east, especially from the northeast, there is a danger of famine or some other calamity. If it blows from the north, it foretells cold and a tempest followed by abundance. If it blows from the south, the year will be warm and prosperous. If the night is clear and there is no wind, there will be an abundance of all goods.

NEW YEAR'S DAY

Upon waking up, you must toss your right shoe into the air. If it falls right side up, it is a sign that you will get married; if it is pointed toward the door, it leaves no hope regarding marriage. The first stranger encountered in a house or crossing the threshold is of the greatest importance. In general, encountering a woman is a bad omen; encountering a man is the sign of a good year ahead.

In general, all the events of this day risk dominating the months to come. If, for example, you have the misfortune of being penniless on this day, you will be poor all year long!

All wishes made for a loved one have a very good chance of being granted.

In Alsace, this day is particularly grave for young women. If the first person they encounter is a man, they will marry within the year; if it is a woman, they will remain single or have a quarrelsome mother-in-law to tolerate; if they find themselves in front of two men, they will have a lover in the year. In Scotland, if the first person to enter a house after the last stroke of midnight on New Year's Day is a black-haired man carrying a coal shovel, it will be a good year for the entire family. This belief is so widespread that in some regions a tall dark-haired man is recruited especially for the occasion.

In the last century in eastern France, peasants followed the custom of wishing trees a Happy New Year. Also molehills were destroyed in order to be rid of them for the year.

New Year's Day allows the weather of the future to be foreseen: "A calm and clear New Year's night gives enthusiasm for a good year"; "Mild, clear weather on New Year's Day assures good weather for the year"; "A bad year comes in swimming."

The Human Body

For a long time, the body served as a basis for interpretation of the universal and social orders: Each limb and organ became organized into a hierarchical and coherent system. This view of the human body rested both on a physiognomy that explained physical states in terms of the soul or mood, and an opposite idea that saw illness as a concretization of troubles of the spirit. Thus the words "love" and "heart" can be used indiscriminately, and the head, it can be affirmed, supplants the feet or legs. The superstitious mentality applies itself to deciphering the exterior aspect—the color of the eyes, the shape of the hand, an expression, or a gait. It uses these facts to define moral characters. Such judgments refer in part to social customs: In this way, messy hair or thin, tight lips allow a personality to be discerned. But, in general, the body is conceived only as a receptacle of exterior, sometimes supernatural forces. An illness is feared only in terms of its local manifestations, the body being the composite of organs and autonomous senses. Physical pain or the alteration of one of these parts results not from the action of a microbe or virus, but from the game of spiritual force that takes hold of the human body like the Devil takes hold of a witch. Therefore, the cure is not a matter of medical care, but of expelling spirits and warding off spells.

This "intellectual" view of the human body even comprises nourishment: Each ailment is an abstraction that influences not so much the body, as the character and spirit.

Ablutions

River, bath, or ocean waters appear to be more than a simple means of maintaining physical health; from the beginning, they were associated with purifying virtues for the soul or spirit. Immersion, such as the baptism of John the Baptist in the Jordan or the sacred bathing in the Ganges, remains a sacrament common to many religions. However, during the medieval period, the Christian Church condemned the warm bath as too sensual and accepted the cold bath only as a mortification. From ass's milk baths (dear to Cleopatra) to the rubbing-on of human blood, all recipes, whatever the price or cruelty, were tried for preserving the complexion's youthfulness and freshness.

A bath rids a person of heartaches. Yet it is not advisable to sing in the bath in the morning, for the evening could end badly. Welsh miners never wash themselves completely because they think that they would aggravate the risks of their profession. It is believed that washing the body in detail must be avoided because luck goes away with the dirt.

During the morning dressing, it is a good omen to sprinkle water around: It ushers in a good day and success at work. On the other hand, a girl who splashes her clothes while dressing will marry a drunkard. Washing also chases away worries: Two people mustn't use the same water because the second person will take on the troubles and misfortunes left there by the first. Formerly, in Greece, it was said that a man who bathed in the same water as a woman lost his virility.

One mustn't enter water with the feet before the head: The head is the most noble part of the body and must be respected.

Whoever takes a bath in the sea must wait until seven waves have rolled over the immersed head to escape drowning.

Abnormality

All physical differences are an insult to world order. Invalids, in the broad sense—this can simply be a redhead in a population of brown-haired people or a left-handed person—deserved their punishments; therefore, it is proper to be suspicious of them. But this difference can also be a sign of privileged contact with the forces of the world. Invalids have either the evil eye or the gift of double vision, sometimes both. The physical defect compensates for the exceptional psychic powers.

BLIND MAN

This traditional personage of legend, cut off from the visible world, is supposedly endowed with powers more extraordinary than the simple visual sense. He "sees," in spirit, supernatural elements of the universe; he knows the secrets hidden beneath a tangible appearance. He is therefore reputed to be wise and devine.

Whoever passes a blind man and smiles at him will have nothing to fear, but in general, it is a bad omen to encounter one.

Cataracts that have blinded a person can be cured by burning the head of a black cat. The remains are reduced to a powder, then blown into the ill person's eyes in order to make him recover his vision. If a pregnant woman closes the eyes of a dead person, she must cross herself on the stomach in order to avoid the risk of giving birth to a blind infant.

Whoever pulls up a mandrake root lacks respect for the plant and thereby goes blind.

"The Parable of the Blind" (detail), by Breugel the Elder (Naples, Musée de Capodimonte).

HUNCHBACK

Marked by nature, which forces them to live with their eyes lowered toward the ground, hunchbacks attract sorcery to themselves. They were used by royal courts since their presence protected the sacred person of the monarch.

Although this failing, which excludes him from the village group, still frightens those around him, a hunchback is often a very prized personage, for his hump is reputed to be beneficent. Today in casinos, it is common to encounter a hunchbacked employee. Race track gamblers are also familiar with the virtues of this deformity.

Whoever encounters a hunchback on his path, particularly in the morning, will live a happy day.

IDIOT

The "village idiot," far from being excluded from the group, plays an important and respected role. He brings happiness to the community undoubtedly because he brings together the weaknesses and defects that threaten all of the others. If he leaves the region, his troubles run the risk of spreading to all the inhabitants.

Encountering an idiot at the time of an important transaction is a very good omen. Fishermen think that this assures them of a happy and safe trip. Idiots are in fact called "God's proof." They were created and wanted by a superior divinity and, as such, can only bring good.

Parsley sown by an idiot will grow better than that of his neighbor.

LAME MAN

His infirmity, whatever its origin, confers a kind of supernatural power on him that compensates for the physical weakness. This belief is repeated for all visible deficiencies of the human body. The entourage supposes that the victims have an excess of spirit, even though they adopt a suspicious attitude. Vulcan, the crippled god, was also the most able of blacksmiths. Talleyrand, the "lame devil," incarnated finesse and subtle trickery.

In general, to encounter a lame man is a bad omen except in Anglo-Saxon countries, where to see one from behind foretells troubles.

If a funeral encounters a lame donkey, the dead person will go to hell.

LEFT-HANDED PERSON

Christ was seated at the right hand of God; ever since, all that comes from the left is considered evil. But the Romans were already using the word "sinister" to designate that side. Left-handed people are therefore marked by this condemnation. Whoever encounters a left-handed person on Tuesday can expect the worst of troubles, but on any other day of the week it is a good omen.

Left-handed people are contrary to nature and adapt poorly to social life. They are less gifted on the intellectual and physical plane than "normal" people.

Finally, it is believed that they see better from the left eye than from the right.

Aliments

Eating is a natural activity. More than any other, it is inscribed in the social rules that govern each civilization. In certain places it has such a sacred character that men and women eat together only once in their lives—the day of their marriage.

A popular saying affirms, "Better the forepart of a horse than the backside of a doctor." This assertion rests on the widespread idea that a cause and effect relationship exists between the quantity of food absorbed and good health. At any rate, the act of eating diminishes the risks of illness.

In Africa and in the Orient, cooking is a religious rite entailing numerous taboos. In Europe, where food preparation depends more on a social than on a religious code, it is however necessary to respect certain traditions relative to the dishes themselves and to the seasons.

Certain dishes should not be served at given times under any circumstances. A person who serves roots in April makes his guest itchy.

In May, the heads and feet of animals are reputedly impure and must be banished from the family table. Drinking water while fasting is also forbidden during this month. If out-of-season fruit is served, it makes indelible stains on clothes.

BLACK PUDDING

This aliment requires long, meticulous work that has long had an important social value—the putting to death of a pig was a great moment in peasant life. White pudding in particular remains a choice dish that must be treated with respect and upon which a quasi autonomous life is conferred.

Pudding proves to be capricious and sensitive: If someone jokes or laughs while it is cooking, it explodes noisily. If the number of pieces put in the saucepan are counted, the pudding will be inedible.

The black-pudding feast in Lower Brittany, end of the 19th c. (Bibl. des Arts Déco.)

BREAD

"All bakers are ordered, under the penalty of incarceration, to make only one kind of bread, the bread of Equality." (Article 3 of the Decree of 1793 signed by Fouché.)

Bread, wine, and meat are the three basic foods, those that are presumed to bring strength. Bread is made from flour, a white, holy, divinatory substance, and from wheat that is itself used in divination and that symbolizes the seed of life. Bread is the offering dedicated to the gods that pleases them and replaces human sacrifices. The holy bread of the Eucharist represents the body of Christ. In early Christian times, certain communities took bread in the form of a human body that symbolized Christ, and ate it together. This practice was not forbidden until the 6th century.

Sharing bread is to share friendship. This beneficent and holy substance must be respected. It must not be stuck with a fork or knife during baking. Bread must be broken rather than cut and the first break must never be made with a pointed object—that would wound a wandering soul. The sign of the cross must be made over it before first breaking it or it won't be digested and will settle immediately. Some say it must never be broken with the hands over a bare table. The following is a general superstition: A round loaf of bread must never be turned over! Some think that turning the bread over brings misfortune on the house, while others say that it makes the Blessed Virgin cry and it rains. This act is sacrilegious because it lacks respect for this holy aliment and for the person of Christ, which it represents. In the Middle Ages, the bread reserved for the hangman was placed aside and turned over. A woman who sets a round loaf upside down would be accused of earning her living lying on her back.

Bread should never be wasted or thrown out; otherwise, there is a risk of one day experiencing famine. Crumbs can, however, be given to the birds, the creatures of God Almighty. Whoever dares to burn bread attracts all the misfortunes of the earth.

Bread that overflows in baking or that bursts at that time is a presage of death. If it crumbles when you want to cut it, it announces family disputes. Making bread that gets a hole in the middle while baking or pulling out the soft part of the bread digs a grave for a near relative. Bread baked on Good Friday will fall immediately or be fresh all year. If baked on Christmas Eve, it will neither mold nor dry out.

On New Year's Day, a bread crust should be thrown into the well so that the well won't dry up. On Maundy Thursday it is necessary to hang a loaf of bread from the ceiling in order to keep illnesses away. A piece of bread is placed in a newborn's cradle to facilitate growth and near a man who had just died so that his soul can continue to sustain itself. A small piece of bread is also placed near an infant who is going to be baptized.

He who wants to be assured of not losing a knife he has just bought cuts a piece of bread and gives it to a dog. The person who dares to eat a slice of bread that another person has already taken a bit of, risks making enemies or catching rabies. It is said that if a piece is held under the armpit a little while, it will kill the dog to which it is given. Finally, bread is reputed to make the feathers fall off a goose that devours it and to make donkeys mate.

A slice of buttered bread remains a means of divination equal in popularity to that of "heads or tails" with a coin. When the slice falls on the buttered side, it is a bad omen, but a slice that falls by accident on the unbuttered side announces the imminent arrival of a visitor. A round loaf of bread topped with a blessed church candle and set on water will stop over drowned bodies. Some say it must first be ballasted with mercury, while others say that it is sufficient to stuff in it a piece of paper that bears the name of the person whose body is being looked for.

Whoever cuts unequal slices of bread reveals that he has been telling lies since he was old enough to eat at the table.

BROTH

To make a liquid boil is to ally opposites, water and fire. Drinking vegetable or beef broth purifies the body like an interior bath where vital forces taken from various aliments are concentrated.

Chicken broth is well known for bringing life back to a dying person. Artemisia broth is known for its great purifying virtues.

If you want to silence incessantly-croaking frogs, pour a broth made the first day of Lent into their pond. A decoction of beef broth sprinkled on the walls of a house keeps snakes away. The Devil hates boiled water and gets angry when it cools. In England it is said that water that has been on the fire must never be left in a bedroom—whoever drinks it or uses it for washing will be assailed with nightmares. Once this water has cooled, it becomes dangerous: "Boiled water saves lives, but after a while it kills people."

BUTTER

Butter has importance, especially as a product made from milk, a basic peasant alimentation for centuries. The making of butter has always been threatened by sorcerers who knew how to cast spells on the cattle and intervene in this somewhat mysterious labor. The Celtic people used butter, honey, and wax to bribe evil.

A churn must be made of hazelwood, because this wood terrorizes malevolent forces. In northern Scotland, a churn is dissembled when a stranger approaches. Nine pinches of salt must be thrown into the churn and nine into the fire before beginning the operation.

In Alsace, witches cast spells on cows in order to drink the milk. In order to keep witches away, thorns must be placed in the churn or the milk boiled with a sickle in it so that the witch rubs her skin off or gets cut stealing the milk or butter.

A peasant attaches a hemp rope to the left hind leg of his cow and guides it down a path where herds pass; the cow will thereby give as much butter as all the cows that passed that day.

In order to increase production, the bottom of the churn can be rubbed with cat fat.

"The Butter Churner," French engraving, 18th c. (Bibl. des Arts Déco.)

When a person dies of cancer, a pat of butter is placed near his bed, then covered with earth after the burial in order to annihilate the illness.

In England it is claimed that milk refuses to curdle when the tide is out-going; in France, on the other hand, the privileged moment for churning is at slack tide.

CAKE

Pastry, formerly an offertory to pagon gods, remains at the center of all festivities such as marriages, baptisms, and burials. As a necessary part of the birthday meal, it is decorated with a number of candles corresponding to the age of the person being celebrated.

Every July 29 in the Vosges, before the sun rises, a cake called "Saint-Wolf" is made. It is triangular in shape, and a pinch of blessed salt

The Twelfth Night Cake, beginning of the 19th c. (Musée des Arts et Traditions Populaires.)

is put in it. It must be given to a beggar in order to protect the house against sorcery.

A part of the Twelfth Night cake made for the Epiphany is kept for each absent member of the family. The state of conservation of the parts a few days later indicates the state of health of those absent.

Likewise, in Brittany, a piece is saved for the absent sailor when a Saint-Michael flan is eaten. On days when there is a tempest, look at what remains of the piece—it reveals the situation of the sailor.

Candlemas crepes bring luck and fortune if they are eaten before 8 P.M.; if not, they can have the opposite effect.

CHEWING GUM

This sweet is not liked by European parents, who affirm to their children that it sticks to the bowels. In the United States, a young man who, while contemplating a stick of chewing gum, thinks fervently about the girl he wants to love him, must offer it to her immediately; when she begins to chew it, she will no longer be able to resist him.

EGGS

See Chapter 4.

MILK

Milk, man's first food, offered without effort by generous animals, is a form of divine gift and therefore symbolizes spiritual food. Divine Speech has been compared to this precious elixir. By its white color and abundance, it illustrates purity and immortality. It is proper, therefore, to respect it—like oil—and whoever spills it exposes himself to great misfortunes.

It is particularly inadvisable to spill a few drops of milk on the threshold of the house. Fairies are attracted by this beverage and might pass through the door. For others, a drop of milk on the ground attracts seven days of misfortune during which nothing must be undertaken.

Peasants are careful to obtain the best milk from their herd. It is necessary to deposit in a bronze basin the milk from a cow being milked for the first time if it is hoped to obtain much in the future. When a cow is being sold, a few hairs should be pulled from the tail so that it will remain a good milker. In addition, at the first milking after a cow has calved, it is recommended that three drops from each udder be made to pass through a ring to purify the milk and avoid infections.

Whoever puts a foot in the milk bucket or throws this liquid in the fire dries up the udders of the cow forever. The same catastrophe happens when figwood is thrown into the fireplace. But whoever puts a glow worm in his house is assured that the milk will not dry up.

"The Milkmaid," by Vermeer, 1660 (Amsterdam, Rijskmuseum).

If it is thought that a cow has been sucked by a snake, its udders must be rubbed with Passion grass. In addition, a pinch of salt is put in milk that is sold so that no one can bewitch the cow from a distance by means of its milk. The liquid, therefore, even once drawn from the animal, remains physically linked to it.

A fire caused by lightning can be put out with cow's milk. If a person's shoes are whitewashed with milk he will be covered with fleas. Finally, a dog's and wolf's milk have multiple curative virtues.

Whoever wishes to steal cow's milk from a neighbor places a bucket in the fireplace and "milks" the pothook. To get revenge, all that is necessary is to give a bucket that is still wet a few blows with a knife—the robber will succumb.

A child brought up on goat's milk will be an idiot. It is known that bad mothers—like bewitched cows—nurse snakes in their breasts.

In order to make the mother's milk disappear after weaning, her husband's night bonnet, in which he has urinated, must be placed over her breasts. Others place two large shellfish there. Finally, she can put on a necklace of corks or wear a bunch of parsley in a pendant. (See Nursing.)

OIL

In Mediterranean countries, this fatty matter has long been at the base of daily alimentation. Therefore, it acquired a holy character: It was offered in sacrifice to Greek and Roman gods and it was adorned with certain magical virtues. It thus had the power to consecrate authority of kings and priests at the time of anointing rites.

Even in its more ordinary usage, oil remains a respected liquid: It must not be spilled—this clumsiness brings misery into the home.

Olive oil can double or triple in volume. It is sovereign against intoxication and cures sterility if a spoonful is taken every morning for nine days.

In order to know whether a man or animal is bewitched or not, put a drop of oil in a cup of water: If the drop remains compact, there is nothing to fear; if it breaks up, it's a sign of possession.

SALT

Born of the waters, salt, by its virtues, surpasses the simple role of condiment. In Europe it was a rare and dear commodity that alone somewhat raised the taste of a poor man's food. It lasts a long time and its reputation of incorruptability is a symbol of friendship and given promise.

But salt is also corrosive, therefore a destroyer of evil forces that fear it more than all others. Before being able to cast a spell, witches must count, one by one, the grains of salt in a house. They never finish in time (this is one of the reasons why salt has such a conjuratory value).

A small sachet of salt is worn around the neck to protect against evil spells. Some throw a little salt on the threshold of a new house and put a salt shaker on the table before bringing furniture in. Brides hide a few pinches of salt in their pockets. On April 1, some salt is put at the four corners of fields. Fearful people never go out at night without a few grains of salt in their hands. Salt is also laid on the body of a newborn to assure his or her happiness.

Since salt is a sign of friendship, it is inadvisable to salt one's own food—each fellow diner must take care of his neighbor. He who knocks over a salt shaker risks seeing a friendship break up. In Italy, the host never offers salt to a guest—it would bring bad luck.

To ward off a spell or protect a newborn, three grains of salt are put in the fire, at the windows, on brooms, and so forth. Three grains in milk keep it from souring.

Salt also has a prophetic power. If you are sick, take three grains of salt in your right hand. If they dissolve immediately, it's a sign that you are going to die; if they don't, it foretells recovery. On Christmas night, a small cup of salt must be left on the table. If the next morning it hasn't moved, it foretells a radiant future; if the salt is dispersed, Death prowls in the house.

Because salt is a holy aliment, spilling the salt shaker on the table brings misfortune. In Scandinavian countries, however, bad luck doesn't await you unless the salt gets wet. To ward off this spell, a pinch of salt is thrown over the shoulder. Tradition also links this belief to a blunder by Judas at the time of the Lord's Supper—he supposedly spilled salt on the holy table!

Salt, of course, is associated with tears and it is believed that each grain that falls corresponds to as many tears. To avoid such sadness, the grains must be picked up and put in the oven—the tears then dry up.

Finally, in Germany, a girl who forgets the salt shaker in setting the table admits that she has lost her virginity.

Asthma

It is said that these respiratory problems are provoked by a witch who, disguised as a cat, rests on the chest of the sick person. To cure asthma, it is therefore recommended that you eat raw cat meat. Others consume mule slaver or breathe the air from a stable. Also, a pipe can be smoked while fasting or poultices of cabbage leaves soaked in oil can be placed on the body for a few days.

Some place a slipper under their bolster each night to avoid attacks during the day.

Finally, it is believed that asthmatics live longer than those in perfect health.

Beard

A sign of virility, courage, and wisdom, beards have long been reserved for gods, priests, and soldiers. An enemy's beard was cut off to humiliate him.

Hair from the beard, like other hair and nails, matter both living and inert, is used by magicians in casting spells. A beard should not be shaved on Tuesday, Wednesday, or Friday, nor should any hair be left on the blade—a witch might get hold of the hair.

A beard is for men what menstruation is for women—it is born of secretions released by excesses of food that find no other way of leaving the body. But sometimes, certain women also have a few hairs around the mouth; it's a sign that they have a particularly languishing demeanor.

Men with a thin beard have a feminine temperament. On the other hand, a bushy beard indicates an amiable and conciliating character.

A man who hasn't got a beard isn't a man.

When the color of a beard is different from that of the hair on the head, it gives notice of a personality of little attraction.

So that the salsifies will have many branches, they must be sown by a bearded man.

Touching a man's beard brings good luck.

Beauty Mark

These benign skin tumors are more or less lucky, depending on their location, unlike freckles that are supposedly marks of the Devil.

Beauty marks are a sign of luck on the right hand, of bad luck on the left hand, elbow, or wrist, and of fortune on the forearm. A beauty mark brings prosperity when it is in the middle of the forehead; above the temple, it reveals a person who is wise and full of understanding. It is a good omen on the neck, but in Ireland it is believed that on the nape of the neck, it signifies that a person will be hanged. Finally, a beauty mark on a woman's left breast makes her irresistible.

Although these marks are reputed as esthetic, some seek to get rid of them. Rub them with pumpkin seeds, then avoid washing them. A child's mother or a dog(!) must lick the spots for a few days in order to lift them out.

It is believed that freckles result from the sun's action on a face covered with an invisible sieve. For others, the child must have received a fistfull of sand or seeds in the face. To make the spots disappear, they must be rubbed with dog's milk.

Belly

This somewhat despised part of the body is known for the pains it provokes, most often of uncertain origin—a belly-ache, like heartburn, can come from the stomach or liver, as well as from the intestines.

A fat belly is often sensual but scorned, whereas a wide belly indicates a taste for work and prudence. When hairy below the naval, it is a mark of boldness, a taste for learning, and a great need for friendship.

When the belly aches, it is "the worms (that) are pissing on your heart." Cow dung or a salve with brandy or incense are reputed to cure bellyaches, unless you prefer to drink some cider diluted with twelve ewe dung and four snails. Some motorists believe that letting a chain drag behind their vehicle protects against heartburn and bellyaches.

In order to get rid of worms, remedies must be administered at the changes of the moon because the worms "wax" and "wane" with the moon. Tuesdays and Fridays are the best days for carrying out this operation. Excellent remedies include crushed pumpkin seeds, water in which a piece of lead has been left to soak until the water is colored, or even roasted worms in flour. A cataplasm of brandy, garlic, or incense can also be made on the naval, suffocating the worms that breathe through it; some prefer filling their socks with earthworms.

When a stomach is upset, it must be corrected with a comb dipped in holy water, then left in a pot of wine. The comb must stay on the ill person's belly for twenty-four hours. This person must then drink a mouthful of the wine and throw away the rest.

Bites

One of the most widespread remedies for treating venomous reptile bites aims at making the poison go back into the animal itself. Thus, when a snake bites you, place its skin or head on the wound.

An aggressive viper is crushed and the sore rubbed with its blood. But the viper must not be killed by the person it attacked—the person would no longer be able to heal. The wounded person is also made to drink viper broth. Certain "venom stones" exist that are placed on the wound. Garlic, chopped and placed on the wound or consumed directly, is also an excellent treatment for viper bites.

To treat other snake bites, such as from an asp, lemon remains the only recourse. You can, however, eat a portion composed of two figs, two dried nuts, twenty rue leaves, and a crushed grain of salt every morning before breakfast.

Bites on the toes must be rubbed with plantain or sorrel or an ox-eye daisy placed on them.

Insect bites are treated with parsley or walnut leaves. Some rub them with three different herbs mixed with urine.

Whatever the origin, a bite is exorcised by saying, "May this bite become sweet like the milk of the Blessed Virgin Mary."

Blood

Symbol of fire, heat, and life, human or animal blood is a supreme gift that is ritually sacrificed to the most respected divinities. The blood that flows from the body corresponds both to a sacred gift and to a spiritual purification—man gains in spirit what he loses in substance. The traditional practice of blood-letting attempts to chase away "bad moods" in drawing out the overflow of blood. In certain civilizations, blood is also considered a vehicle of the soul: After a sacrifice, the bloodstains on the ground are wiped very carefully; they still contain some of the spirit. This vital substance still plays a role as a talisman: A sword wet with blood possesses superior virtues.

Blood can sometimes act as a love potion. A young man takes a few drops on the little finger of his right hand and discretely drips them into the wine glass of a young lady. With one drink, she will fall in love with him. But whoever bleeds, even from the nose, on All Saints' Day will not live much longer.

In spite of everything, bleeding, always of evil omen, can be stopped by tying a key around the ill person's neck or by slipping a wrought iron key in back of him. Ashes, spider webs, or snakeskins are also placed on the wound. Some cut a blade of grass in two, place it in a cross on the wound, and spit on it.

In order to close up a bleeding wound, urinate on it, then rub it with dung or earthworms. A snail is placed on the wound and a stone is applied to it, then replaced right side up where it was found. A little holy water will have the same effect.

If a person has a nose bleed, three drops of blood mixed with some water in a cup must be drunk or two sticks of straw crossed at the ill person's back without his knowledge.

When blood circulates poorly in the body, some walnut leaves gathered on June 24 before sunrise must be consumed.

The rite of exchanging blood from wrist to wrist, especially between men, is the most well-known and undoubtedly the most ancient form of allying spirits. It recalls to mind the traditional blood weddings begun in ancestral societies. Male or female friendship also had the function of assuring the cohesion and understanding of each group of the society, joined in a "natural" base.

Bone

Death dances and the representation of a skeleton in all the arts most often attempt to make the spectator feel the presence of death and the vanity of all things. But this representation can also preach the hedonistic message, "Enjoy quickly while there is still time." A skeleton is a representation of the durable part of man after death and, therefore, of his immortality. This bone full of virtue and firmness, yet with the ability to be broken, is in opposition to the marrow, a substance of life and knowledge.

Musical instruments made from human bones keep away evil forces by their sounds. A fragment of human bone worn in an amulet cures stomach disorders. Touching a femur or any other long bone taken from a cemetery cures fevers.

In Arabia it is believed that two bodies should not be buried in the same coffin because their bones run the risk of being intermixed or even stolen on Judgment Day.

Knucklebones, the origin of dice used by gamblers, were formerly very prized divinatory objects.

In case of an accident, it is good to take a "fall wine," made by mixing the white part of hen or cat droppings with white wine. But, if a bone is broken, the bone-setter must be called. He alone knows the gestures and formulas that allow fractures to be repaired and bones soldered together again.

Breath

Lovers and all those who live in society fear bad breath. However, certain groups in the Middle Ages saw the mark of intelligence in a strong and burning breath—solid and courageous animals, like the lion, have very strong breaths and are, besides, great drinkers. A short, light breath marks a tightness of the lungs and a corruption of the chest.

To counteract bad breath, before going to bed at night you must take a piece of myrrh the size of a hazelnut and let it melt slowly in your mouth.

Cancer

For superstitious spirits, this progressive and most often incurable sickness can only be the fruit of sorcery that must be exorcized. Cancer was personalized in the form of a crab or a worm that consumed a body and each day claimed its allowance of food.

All persons suffering from cancer must feed the "crabs" or tumors to keep from growing weak. Some raw meat should be placed by the sick person's bed or on the sore and replaced at regular intervals. In certain regions, it is preferable to use a toad that has soaked in olive oil or a black hen cut in two while it was alive.

It is possible to eliminate the illness by attracting the crab or worm causing it into a cataplasm of plants that is frequently renewed—in destroying this medicinal mass, the animal that burrowed into it to devour the bait is done away with. The most frequently used plants for attracting the cancer worm are houseleek, burdock, coltsfoot, violets, or female tobacco leaves soaked in oil. In Scandinavian regions, a frog is believed to be able to suck out the cancer; therefore, in order to be cured, the sick person must swallow a frog or small toad. Around the Mediterranean, it is preferable to eat a raw lizard.

An attempt to exorcize the tumor is also made by asking it to stop growing or bothering whomever is suffering. Certain formulas like "Vanish like Nicodemus took Our Lord Jesus Christ down from the cross!" or else "Don't continue to swell until the day when the Virgin Mary gives birth to another son!" were still being used in France at the turn of the century.

A spider that passes in front of a sleeping person's face is reputed to bring him cancer. In Brittany, when a person dies of this illness, a pat of butter is placed by the corpse. It must be thrown out after the burial because it has taken in evil forces that could attack other members of the family.

Cheek

The shape of cheeks on a face—their roundness, hollowness, their dimples—reveals a person's personality at first glance.

Plump cheeks are a sign of an unusual sensual appetite; gaunt cheeks indicate a much more reserved and rigid temperament. An emaciated face belongs to a melancholy person who has undoubtedly suffered; jowls are a sign of a more than mediocre intelligence. Full, round cheeks are a sign of a wise person full of spirit. When cheeks are hollow, they reveal meanness and jealousy. A man with prominent cheekbones will be sensitive and gentle, but wrinkles on the cheeks are marks of insanity.

For some, a dimple is God's fingerprint; for others it is the mark of the Devil's shoe! In general, a dimple is considered lucky.

If a person's cheeks begin to turn red, it is a sign that someone is talking about him or her.

Chilblains

Many recipes related to both ancient magical practices and popular medicine exist for curing or protecting against chilblains and chapping.

To protect the inhabitants of a house from these afflictions, it is a good idea to place a half-eaten Christmas cake under a bed. Water taken from the first snow and passed over your ears or hands allows chapping and chilblains to be avoided. Human urine and strawberry juice are reputed to have the same effect. In cold weather, shoes and gloves of wolfskin remain the most effective protection.

Getting up at 4 A.M. on May 1 cures chapping; if this method proves to be ineffective, on the morning of May 1st put your hands in manure, then beat them three times in a row with the lid to the breadbox.

On other dates, whoever suffers from these afflictions must walk around a mare three times while holding his shirt between his teeth. While remaining seated, a person with chapped feet crosses them, then strikes the afflicted areas with holly leaves that were gathered one by one.

Some put walnut oil on their chilblains, then lick it off, keeping it in their mouth for a while; little by little this mitigates the pain. Others light a candle and drip wax on the affected area. It is also possible to soak the area in water in which a slaughtered pig has been dipped.

More human in our eyes are the ointments of shoemakers' wax base or cataplasms of turnip pulp, hot ashes, or carpenters' glue. One of the most common processes for relieving the pain is to wash the skin with a bush-bean broth or else a mixture of soot and vinegar.

Chin

In general, women are attributed with receding chins, a sign of weakness, and men are attributed with protruding chins, a sign of will!

A pointed chin signals an active, quick mind that can be clever or generous. Traditionally, greed is incarnated in a hooked chin, whereas a dimpled chin on a man indicates a determined and judicious character.

A double chin that is a little flabby is not very well considered—it is a sign of excessive sensuality. But a flat chin indicates a cold and dry person. It is not much better to have a small chin, a sign of timidity, or a wide, heavy chin, a sign of inadmissible coarseness and violence. On the other hand, a round chin endowed with dimples reveals great kindness.

Colic

This most often benign indisposition is attributed to the influence of the moon. In order to combat it you must drink some aromatic wine in which have been soaked laurel berries that were gathered at the hour when Mars or Mercury, enemies of our satellite, was at its peak.

A simple touch of a moled hand is very effective for calming these pains. Your middle finger can also be pressed against the sick person's belly while saying, "Passion-Colic that is between my heart and liver, between my spleen and lung, stop. In the name of the Father, Son, and Holy Ghost, sick person, God has cured you. Amen."

Others prefer to eat buckshot or drink an infusion of herbs, sheep droppings, or horse dung. Viper broth or brandy in which a viper has been is also very effective.

Corn

This callosity that sometimes deforms toes announces, when it begins to ache, a change in the weather. In order to get rid of them, you must put as many lily of the valley roots in your pocket as you have corns on your feet; when the roots dry out, the corns have disappeared.

Making a corn bleed can be fatal, but cutting it off while the moon is waning allows you to be rid of it.

Some people apply a red onion cut in two to a corn, then put the onion back together and throw it out. A corn can also be rubbed with a garlic clove on a Friday of the first quarter of the moon.

Others recommend baths of vineshoot ashes mixed with water. You can also put ivy or houseleek leaves, yeast, or coarse salt on your corns.

Corpulence

Perhaps more than any other physical aspect, a person's size and weight characterize his true personality in popular thought or Medieval medicine. Corpulence is also governed by social rules that have set the canons of beauty for several decades—the French Renaissance of the 16th century exalted round chubby shapes, the 20th century West is prone to esthetic leanness. In poor countries today, plump bodies, especially feminine ones, are highly regarded, since an abundance of food plays a role in the social heirarchy. Wealthier countries value leanness undoubtedly linked to a social vision of the intellectual level attained by man. Height itself was at the base of racial ideologies that affirmed the "natural" superiority of a tall blond over a short brunette. Doctors in the Middle Ages identified a tall body with depth of insight by a relationship of cause and effect.

"When a donkey is lean, all the flies bite it." It is the center of jeers and laughs that do not bounce off the thickness of its body. A lean person has protruding, hard bones that exteriorize his moral narrowness and wickedness. An interior fire consumes him; his flesh is absorbed by his anxious, unstable spirit. He can eat incessantly without ever gaining weight. In addition, only sexual frigidity is in accordance with such an absence of flesh.

This leanness can go to the point of rickets, attributed to poor blood. To combat it, it is necessary to drink a small glass of fresh animal blood or chicken broth seasoned with couch grass. Place three gudgeons on the belly of a child suffering from rickets. When the fish dry out, throw them over your shoulder without turning around. It is also recommended that the child be made to eat, on a new plate, a raw egg from a black hen, or that you apply on the child a cataplasm of three fresh egg yolks from a black hen. Rusty water made by leaving some old nails to soak in a bucket for one night or nine days is an excellent remedy for undernourishment.

Whoever wishes to lose weight must have a Mass said in reverse in his or her name and have an odd number of candles lighted during the ceremony. In Italy, a glance from a monk is believed to have the same effect; if you want to keep your roundness, you must cross yourself three times or spit on the ground when you encounter a monk.

A thin person, on the contrary, enjoys a good reputation—his slimness is identified with beauty. Too much fragility is displeasing, though. Dainty feet and a slender body, at least in women, implies a certain trickery and a soul with perverse inclinations.

Although bulkiness is a sign of good health and authority in some countries, it evokes an image of gorging and laziness. Don't we say "fat as a pig"? An excess of fat paralyzes the body's movement, causing it to grow flabby in lust and apathetic immobility. Heavy people have a slow and dull mind in the image of their body; thought has a hard time circulating in the thick flesh. A fat man resembles a woman and has very little interest in love: "Fat flesh, cold flesh." The reverse is also said: A thin woman resembles a man. Heavy people die younger than others. They affirm themselves that "better to be envied than pitied."

Tall people supposedly have a natural authority, being built for dominating the world, but they sometimes lose their heads in the clouds. Their dimensions bother them in daily life; they are nonchalant and lazy. A proverb affirms: "Tall gent, vain gent; short gent, courageous gent." It is known that in order to grow you must eat your soup and stretch your limbs each morning. In addition, those who wear a ruby on their fingers appear to be larger than life.

By a compensatory phenomenon, short people are accorded the privilege of a big heart: "In small jars there are good ointments." They have quick and lively minds and rush with determination into life without hiding from difficulties. But, undoubtedly, these moral qualities reveal a certain mistrust for short bodies.

Corpulence is also analyzed in terms of the relationship between weight and height. A tall, thin man is reputedly vain, greedy, cruel, and sometimes unscrupulous. If he is of the same height but heavier, it reveals a rather coarse, two-faced, ungrateful personality.

A short, thin body, like that of an elf, belongs to an ingenious, prudent, secretive, and intelligent man. A short, heavy man is endowed with all the vices: jealousy, stupidity, stubbornness, and a dullness of mind.

A body that sags out in front is a sign that the person is carrying some kind of moral burden—money or work problems, anger, or dissatisfaction. If the body bends out in back, it reveals a person that is distracted and mediocre, but solid and obstinate.

Dance

Dance has long been a sacred language that established a contract between man and the gods. It is first of all an offering, a thanksgiving, but it is also a means for man to annihilate his terrestrial ego so that he can enter into direct contact with telluric and stellar forces. Dance is a parade of love and seduction that is practiced at the time of weddings and burials or in celebration of a harvest or return of a season. Carnival time is dedicated to dance, but it can also be a war dance.

St. Vitus' dance, lithography, 1823 (Bibl. de l'Ancienne Faculté de Médecine de Paris).

A dance floor is a magical place, often circular, where evil forces can be lying in wait. The Devil often takes on the form of a flute player or a fiddler. You should always cross yourself before beginning a dance.

At night at Carnac, goblins force a person out walking to dance around the menhirs until he dies of exhaustion.

Whoever wants to be cured of epilepsy must dance in a church on Assumption Day. But St. Vitus' dance, or chorea, is an illness that is difficult to treat. A person stricken with it was considered to be possessed by the Devil, and it was necessary to exorcize it. However, a mistletoe infusion passed for curing chorea. It was also possible to place a pigeon cut in two on the sick person's spinal column or else to hang a lead cross engraved with the initials of the three wise men, G, M, B, around his neck. A necklace of seven peony roots gathered during a waning moon or a crown of three rings of mistletoe laced together are also effective.

Drinks

COFFEE

> *Coffee is an ambiguous substance; undoubtedly it has a hand in the*
> *revolutionary glory, for its advent in the 18th century, brought*
> *critical lucidity, the black spark that destroyed the old dozing or-*
> *der. And yet, coffee, "sexual alibi," is but a part of that infernal*
> *trilogy (carelessness of love) of which tobacco and alcohol are the*
> *two other pieces.*
>
> Roland Barthes, Michelet

In Western countries, coffee is more well known as a drink than as a
plant. It is believed to have a prophetic value. Diviners interpreted the
figures left by coffee on the bottom of saucers—the liquid appeared to be
directly associated with its consumer. Others were interested in the bubbles that formed on the surface of a cup of coffee—if they floated in your
direction, it announced your coming into a large sum of money. But
problems can arise if they direct themselves in the opposite direction.

Chicory is believed to make whoever chews a few of its leaves
invisible. In any case, it brings luck, and explorers always took one of its
roots in their pockets because it opened bolts and destroyed obstacles.

WINE

Wine, a symbol of blood and born of the sun and the earth, regenerates
the human body. Along with bread and salt, it is a sacred aliment that
Christianity has taken up in the Eucharist.

"Good Wine!" Imagery by Épinal, c. 1840 (Bibl. Nat.).

Drinking wine restores your forces; it is said that "a glass of red wine in an old pot belly is like a new beam in a new barn." Red wine, like thick blood, nourishes the body and doesn't go to the head, whereas white wine makes you parched. In order to make a newborn stout, make him or her drink some wine in which the mother's wedding ring has been soaked. In certain winegrowing countries, a child is bathed in wine at birth. If nail clippings are mixed with wine, it immediately intoxicates whoever drinks it. Wine cures numerous illnesses—migraines, colds, and fevers in particular; it facilitates digestion. To cure rabies, the sick person must drink a glass of wine into which have been put a few hairs from the rabid dog that bit him. A sword that has been dipped in wine is reputed to cure all fevers.

Pouring a glass of wine in the sea calms a tempest, but spilling wine is a bad omen, especially if it falls on a shoe.

A bottle of wine must always be passed around a table in a clockwise direction—the wine risks turning if it is passed counterclockwise.

Ears

Ears make us attentive to the exterior world. Speech and sounds act like semen that penetrates the auditory cavities that some identify with the vagina—the auricles then correspond to a penis.

"When your ears ring, someone is talking about you." When it is only your left ear that rings, it indicates that someone is criticizing you; if it is only your right ear, someone is praising you. But this ringing can also be an alarm signal given by the body, unveiling considerable anger or hidden sadness. Finally, it can announce to you that death is near. When your left ear is ringing, it is best to bite your little finger—the person who is speaking ill of you will immediately bite his tongue.

People have their earlobes pierced and hang rings in them in order to have good eyesight. Sailors' earrings announced their engagement to the sea and so protected them from drowning.

Small ears are a mark of benevolence and kindness, but when they are hemmed, they announce insanity. When they are large, they represent generosity sometimes allied with conceit or stupidity. Flat ears reveal a coarse nature; square, they belong to a noble soul. Long ears are the dominant sign of wisdom and even immortality.

In order to cure earaches, plug the ears up with a deshelled snail or a slice of warm bacon; you can also pour some milk from a sow or wetnurse, warm oil, or sap from a male ash on them.

Otitis is treated by putting juice gathered from cracking a snail shell in the ear. The shell is then buried and as it decomposes, it brings recovery.

In treating mumps it is best to wear a rope from a black cow around

Dance macabre, engraved wood from the 15th c. (Bibl. des Arts Déco.)

your neck or a necklace of wool and hot laurel leaves. It is also possible to take some grandy in which a grass snake stripped of its skin has soaked and pour it in the ears. Putting cow urine in the ear cavities or drinking water from a bucket that a cat or horse has just drunk out of is also recommended.

You can attempt to cure deafness by putting a little cat urine in the ears, but it is preferable to try and prevent it. Two children of the same age who do not yet know how to walk must not kiss each other or else they will become deaf. Whoever indulges in masturbation will be destined to the same evil.

Elbow

One becomes conscious of this joint when the "funny bone" hits violently against an object. In addition, this pain is a very bad omen that must be conjured by hitting the other elbow with as much force as the first.

In the United States, it is believed that an itchy elbow announces that you will soon be sleeping in a stranger's bed—some specify that the person will be of the opposite sex. An old Welsh joke says that whoever wants to avenge himself of an enemy must bite his elbow—if he succeeds in making this gesture, his enemy will be struck dead.

Epidemics

Contagious illnesses that manifest themselves in murderous epidemics have always been considered as scourges sent by God to punish man for his sins.

In order to protect yourself from the contagion, it is necessary to eat garlic and wear around your neck a little sachet containing dead spiders. Plague and cholera immediately attack those who had the imprudence to eat in a cemetery.

In England, a piece of raw meat was believed to turn black in a few seconds when it came in contact with air from a house where cholera was going to strike. To treat this illness, it is recommended that you spend a night in a cemetery.

In France, people wore little talismans of red clay called "plague stones" on their chests in order to protect themselves from the plague. To cure this illness, it is necessary to apply a toad to the first part of the body afflicted and let the animal die on this spot. When it is thrown away, it will take the illness with it.

Epilepsy

This illness is indiscriminately called falling sickness or epilepsy, and its manifestations (fits, convulsions, and disorderly movements) are due not to the sick person but to some demonic force, introduced into his being, that is restless to get out. Epilepsy is supposedly a second language held by a supernatural double or opposite, but inside human skin. The most effective curative practice, then, is to exorcize the possessed.

A sick person can be seated on one side of a balance and his weight poured out in grain on the other side. When the scales tip to the side of the grain, it is a sign that the epileptic is cured. The epileptic also wears a small sachet on the stomach, containing blessed box leaves, fern, and juniper that are renewed every eight hours. For thirty-six days he or she recites four novenas every twenty-four hours while invoking Saint Vitus. Others implore Saint Barthelemy on his feast day (August 24) while dancing in a church.

"The Plague at Marseille in 1720," optical view from the 18th c. (Bouvet coll.)

An afflicted child is passed under the canopy of the Holy Sacrament Procession. Some advise secretly drinking well water in a dead person's skull at night. An infusion of mistletoe from an oak or a potion of linden mixed with three drops of cat's blood taken from under it tail will have the same effect. The sick person can also eat jelly made from live earthworms or raven's brain. An epileptic is cured if he or she consumes a lizard's back reduced to a powder, a mole's liver, bear's bile, or a child's excrement. Or perhaps he or she would prefer to swallow the powder from a woman's skull.

A crucifix nail hung on a sick person's arm calms sufferings. Epileptics also often wear a necklace of peonies gathered during a waning moon.

A magic ring protects you from falling sickness. This ring is silver with a piece of an elk's hoof mounted on it. Some Monday in spring, engrave a consecrated formula inside it: DABI, HABI, HABER, HABR. Then wear it every day on your index finger.

Eyes

Eyes, the organs of vision, are also a "mirror of the soul" and symbolize knowledge and supernatural perception. Curiously, a single eye illustrates gifts of clairvoyance and double vision—we speak of the "evil eye" and of "God's Eye." In addition, both eyes do not have the same value: the left, associated with the moon, incarnates passivity and the past; the right, linked to the sun—itself an eye of the sky—is supposedly the image of activity and the future. Undoubtedly for this reason, only the latter is endowed with extraordinary powers. For centuries, color variations of the iris have been a point of fascination and their interpretation, of course, defines not only moral values, but also esthetic qualities that in general are of little interest to the superstitious.

"Little eyes see far away, big eyes see up close"—in this way common reason reestablishes the equilibrium overlooked by nature. A small eye is supposedly a sign of vivacity and cleverness; if it is also round, it 203 indicates a man who is weak, stupid, and slow-minded. Big eyes, a little cow-like, reveal a lazy, jealous, narrow-minded personality. When it is of a medium size and a dark color, the eye is that of a poised, obliging, honest being. Deep-set eyes hide like from the soul—these people are therefore suspicious and wicked although intelligent. When eyes jut out and are a little globular, they rudely reveal a person who is both obliging and inconstant.

"Green eyes go to Hell, black eyes to Purgatory, gray eyes to Paradise, blue eyes to Heaven." This interpretation is also expressed in the formula: "Green eyes, vipers' eyes; blue eyes, lovers' eyes; brown eyes, pigs' eyes." Black signals a person full of strength and life, but often wicked and hard. Blue, on the contrary, is supposedly feminine and a sign of sensitivity and gentleness. If a woman wants her child to have black eyes, she must eat a mouse during her pregnancy.

Clear eyes are a sign of good health, whereas red eyes, bathed in tears, indicate an angry, hypocritical character like the famous medieval "sanguine nature." If the white of the eye leans toward yellow, it is a sign of lust and excessive violence.

A look, even more than the color of the iris, defines a man's hidden personality. Whoever stares at you with unblinking wide open eyes undoubtedly has something to hide. Whoever bats his or her eyes incessantly is not worth much, but is presumptuous and a traitor. A fleeting glance reveals pride, lust, and seduction. He who can never look you in the eye is a miser full of bad intentions. Lively eyes with a sharp look signal an angry, lymphatic character. A woman with big, rolling eyes is a public danger.

Whoever wishes to preserve his eyesight must eat three raw carrots every month or permanently wear an emerald ring. A gold ring in your left ear has the same virtue. Others wash their eyes with blueberry juice or rub them with rue. A child's first wet diaper also guarantees against vision troubles. You can also hang a lark's foot at your place of work or wash your eyes at a sacred fountain on the night of Saint John.

If your right eye stings, it is an excellent omen, but if it is your left, troubles are on their way. Whoever gets dust in his or her eye must rub it gently with a gold wedding band or any other small piece of gold. He or she also rubs the unaffected eye while spitting on the ground or touches the ear corresponding to the suffering eye with a knife. In order to combat cataracts, burn a cat's head, then blow the ashes in front of the sick person's eyes. Some people wash their eyes in rain water gathered on thistle leaves. On the other hand, swallow droppings on the face causes blindness.

The look of the devil . . . Detail from a scripture, Bourges Cathedral, 14th c.

To relieve sore eyes, some place two vervain leaves on the fist opposite the suffering eye, then attach them with a thread from a spider's web. Others take baths in assorted flowers the color of their eyes. They also bathe their eyes with the yolks from three eggs laid on a Thursday or with the white of an egg, from the same day, mixed with alum. Eye baths with your own urine are also recommended. Finally, you can rub your eyes with a four leaf clover or curdled milk. Some scrounge up nine grains of barley from nine different houses, then make the sign of the cross on their eyelids with each grain and toss it behind them without turning around. Onyx stones or agates are talismans against vision trouble.

Vine shoots reduced to a powder and applied in a lotion cure inflammation of the conjunctiva. People afflicted with this disorder also place a slice of cold veal on the eye.

Whoever suffers from a *sty* must rub the eye with a green garlic clove. Others prefer cow's urine. Some ring a person's doorbell, then run off in order to rid themselves of this ill. You can also rub the eye between 11 P.M. and midnight while saying, "Savage ill, sorcerer's ill, leave on behalf of God Almighty."

A person who squints is not well accepted; to encounter him is a very bad omen because he carries a symbol of the evil cross within him.

On the other hand, a one-eyed person, like most handicapped, supposedly has magical talents, in particular that of double vision.

One way witches can be recognized is that they never cry.

A girl who wants to be loved by a young man must wink at the biggest star she can see at night before going to bed.

If your left eye twitches, it is a sign that someone is in the process of betraying you.

Animals' eyes, in particular those of birds, sometimes have magical virtues. A lark's right eye hidden in a wolfskin makes you irresistible to the opposite sex. Dropped into a woman's glass, this eye transforms her drink into a love potion. A swallow's eye in a bed keeps a person from sleeping. A wolf's eye guarantees against fear and both its eyes assure a traveller of a troublefree trip if he puts the eyes in his walking stick.

If an *eyelash* on the right eye turns downward, it is a sign of luck for a man; of course the left eye has the opposite significance. These omens are opposite for women!

Eyelids are a part of a look in the highest degree. When they are arched, they signal a bold, extraordinary, congenial character. But if they sag and cover the eyes, it is a sign of greed and deceit. A man with thin, short eyelids will be timid and incredulous, but if they are thick and wide, on the contrary, he will be confident and daring. Narrow eyes reveal a certain silliness, but are very seductive. Finally, a few hairs on the eyelids indicate a great simplicity and a loving heart.

According to a very old belief, some people have "the evil eye" or "eye of the Devil," and with a single glance can inscribe misfortune on the destiny of those around them. Since the Devil has little, lively eyes, people having very narrow, deep set, somber eyes are especially charged with having the evil eye. In any case, whoever has two different-colored eyes is opposed to nature. In China, eyes that are too light in color have a similar reputation. Finally, spinsters usually have the evil eye—their menstrual blood, no longer having any purpose, infects their glance like a poison. If menopause resolves this problem, they still remain evil since the blood is enclosed in their bodies and makes them wicked and poisonous. The evil eye especially affects women who have just given birth, children, cows, dogs, flies, milk, and wheat. If this eye is cast upon a family, the family will go from disaster to catastrophe and all its members will be afflicted with colic. To protect yourself from this spell, you must always make the sign of the horns behind your back when someone looks at you for too long. Others wear nine betony leaves and nine grains of salt around their necks in little sachets. The most common talisman is a piece of iron—a key or a horseshoe. In the Orient, people wear something blue. Some plant a fig tree in front of their houses to protect themselves all their lives, or put a stag's horn in their pockets.

A child is very sensitive to the "evil eye," but certain practices allow him to be assured of immunity. He is made to drink some wine in which his mother's wedding band has soaked and he is spit on at birth. In oriental countries, it is believed that a child must be left dirty and in old clothes because the Devil only likes beauty.

A few techniques exist for conjuring this evil eye if prevention fails. Spit three times into the possessed person's eye or burn an animal that died at the hands of the enchanter (the enchanter will also die in the flames). Sometimes a simple sign of the cross is sufficient. Otherwise, a figurine can be made in the image of the person who bears the evil eye and pins stuck in it to remove the spell. When it is a matter of a child, he or she is bathed in a basin of water containing an old piece of silver. Also the child can be held upside down for a few minutes every morning.

Fertility

Beliefs about fertility have the essential aim of strangling any effective or potential sterility. Sterility is usually the result of sorcery and you must seek to conjure it. Formerly, fertility rites played a primordial role in the calendar of feasts, love having a value only as sanctioned by procreation.

Most of the practices deal with the adoration of phallic forms, such as stones, trees, or springs. In Brittany, naked lovers dance around the menhirs, the woman sometimes rubbing her belly against one. A person can also wash in spring water reputed to be fecundating or, if this manoeuver fails, eat a purée of red slugs the next morning. In Alsace, women touch Saint Ignace's gown.

To determine which partner is sterile, both the husband and wife must urinate in a pot filled with wheat, then the two pots must be buried for nine days. From the pot of a sterile husband, worms or a frog will come out; if the woman is sterile, the pot will be full of menstrual blood.

In order to conjure their misfortune, a couple can toss a handful of peas on the road in front of their house.

If a couple cannot have any children, the husband must wear a pair of pants belonging to a father of a numerous family.

Fevers

"Red dragon, blue dragon, white dragon, flying dragon; whatever kind you are, I summon you, I conjure you to go into the eye of the fattest toad you can find!" This conjuration, in the form of a lament, illustrates the traditional perspective that governs the interpretation of fevers called quartan, tertian, or "trembling" (malaria). They are considered to be illnesses within themselves although they are often only symptoms. All methods for getting rid of them treat them as illnesses—fevers are still as varied as there are regions and countries. Like most illnesses that are both well-known and benign and that often disappear without reason after a few days, fevers are warded off, limited, or strangled by an immense network of pragmatic or mystical superstitions.

To prevent a summer fever, it is advisable to eat a daisy at the beginning of spring or, on an empty stomach, to eat an egg laid on Good Friday without salt or bread. Others swallow three or nine live spiders or a mixture of chalk from a gravestone and white wine before eating. It is also possible to chew nine leaves from the first stalks of wheat for the season. A bone from a dead person worn as an amulet or a jasper stone stops fevers. Preventive treatment sometimes calls for the little finger on your left hand to be wrapped in the skin of a fried egg before you go to sleep or for carrying leaves from a blessed thistle in your armpit. To cure malaria, the sick person is advised to wear two eggshells in which, un-known to him, two live spiders have been hidden.

Once a fever has set in, it is a matter of making it leave or lessening the ill. The touch of a moled hand, although effective, sometimes proves to be insufficient. In this case, different cataplasms and pomades are applied according to the parts of the body being treated. The soles of the feet are rubbed with red onions or slugs. A magpie cut in two is placed on kidneys. The stomach is covered with a frog crushed between two nut-shells. A bandage of new cloth containing a mixture of salt, a spider's web, and onions is worn on the wrist for one day. A little sack of pomade made from brioche, camphor, and wine cooked together in a new earthen pot can also be attached. The chest is daubed with blessed earth and stale bread made from seasoned wheat and vinegar.

A fever can also be discretely transmitted to a plant or an unknown person. Some secretly go out at night and hang a ribbon on the branch of an aspen; others nail some hair or nail clippings into the trunk of the same tree. A piece of silver is placed in the middle of a crossroads: Whoever picks it up is seized with the illness. A hard-boiled egg dipped in the sick person's urine is placed on an anthill; the ants eat it, and the first person to walk by the anthill catches the fever. In the morning before sunrise, a sick person can tie his left arm to a tree trunk, then recite three Lord's Prayers and three Hail Marys, and walk away leaving the rope tied to the tree. He can also pull up some grass and throw it over his left shoulder without turning around. Others give a gift of bread or salt to a plant, like a mint, bow to it, and beg it to take the illness away.

A piece of wood can be taken and carved with as many notches as days that the fever has lasted, then thrown into a fire while you walk backward toward it saying, "The person who has a fever is X years old. I don't want him to have a fever; I don't want it and I burn it."

Various drinks also have the virtue of warding off this suffering. Some people swallow mice droppings, decoctions of snakeskin, or dog droppings infused in dry, white wine. The sick person's urine, absinthe, or saffron boiled in water will have the same effect. Others drink milk churned in nine different churns or swallow five or six live lice. A sick person can also go for a walk in the morning dew, barefooted and before eating, or eat a garlic clove under the same conditions. He turns up his shirt sleeves beginning with the left side while reciting his morning prayer. He may drink a bowl of warm milk that has been lapped by a dog. He wears a little paper around his neck on which is inscribed a magic formula (the number of words in it get fewer as the illness disappears). He goes to sleep in manure and lights three candles so that he will perspire. He can also be rubbed with viper, marmot, or chicken fat stretched out on a piece of greasy butcher paper.

Finally, it is affirmed that people born on a Friday have the power to cure fevers.

Foot

Feet, assuring a body's foundation on the ground, are especially important, in terms of their shape, in how they come in contact with the ground.

Flat feet are unlucky and even bring illness to all those around. Encountering on a Monday a person endowed with such feet brings misfortune. In contrast, whoever has six toes on one foot instead of five is marked by luck. A woman whose second toe is longer than her big toe wears the pants in the family. But in Scotland, a longer second toe is a sign of bad health for man.

Big feet signify a dullness and slowness of the mind: "Dumb like his feet." When feet are thin and agile, they reveal timidity and intelligent prudence. The lines of the sole are also revealing: Long, they indicate a sick and miserable man; short, they show a strong, subtle, solid being.

You must always get up on your right foot if you want it to be a good day, but walk in excrement with your left foot to bring happiness. Whoever puts a foot on someone else's shadow hurts the shadow.

When you feel your foot itching, it is a sign that you will soon take a trip to unknown lands. Whoever stumbles with the right foot in walking will soon encounter a new friend. The same clumsiness with the left foot announces problems.

Forehead

Tradition sees a forehead as a mirror of thought. A tilted head, the forehead resting on a hand, is the posture for deep meditation—it is the posture that Rodin gave to his "Thinker." This element of the face is essential in the eyes of physiognomists who see it as a parchment where serenity, joy or sorrow, ignorance, and wickedness are inscribed. We present two classification systems that are often confused and sometimes in opposition: the first is traditional, the second, inspired by Lavater, a Swiss philosophical poet of the 18th century, was very popular in the 19th century.

A convex, high forehead is a sign of liberalism and gaiety; when this is convex toward the upper part of the forehead and combined with a pointy chin, it announces simplicity and kindness, but its owner is usually unhappy and plays the role of the victim in social life. A large, wide, hairless forehead is that of a swindler and a liar often endowed with wit and not lacking in boldness. Big and fleshy, it is that of someone with a gift for quibbling. Fleshy temples accompanied by fat cheeks are characteristics of the angry and violent, but also of courageous heros. Protruding temples on a pointy forehead indicate pride, versatility, and weakness. A small forehead supposedly indicates a powerful mind with a daring and curious judgment, but also sometimes wickedness. A man with a cleft nose and a forehead divided in two by wrinkles is very kind, but he has no luck.

The more compact and tight the forehead, the more it is a sign of character; the more it is stretched out, the more it announces weakness. When a forehead is high and perched forward, it indicates irretrievable stupidity; when it is set back more, on the contrary, it indicates strength of dreams and imagination. When it is straight and peaked toward the top, it is the forehead of a philosopher gifted with reflection, but if there is no curvature, it is that of an idiot. When it is very prominent, it designates a

43

ſera pendu car il ſera uoleur

Illustration taken from the "Métoposcopie" by Cardan, 17th c.

narrow mind. A solid arch of eyebrows on a square forehead announces wisdom and courage, but if the forehead is short, wrinkled, and irregular, the person is dishonest. A smooth, stretched forehead with no wrinkles is that of a cold and pretentious person, with a gift for vengeance; a raised forehead in combination with a pointed chin indicates a feeble mind. Deep, slanting folds foretell stupidity and wickedness; when the folds are parallel and horizontal, this fortells wisdom and honesty.

The "ideal" forehead must be in proportion to the rest of the face, without permanent wrinkles. Wrinkles should only be outlined in a show of indignation, pain, or intense meditation. The brow ridge should be prominent because it is a sign of shrewdness and an enterprising spirit.

This forehead, lighter in color than the rest of the face, must "recede toward the top and come forward toward the bottom."

Gout

An illness of drinkers and gourmands, gout was fitting for notables and those fond of good living. It was usually treated by bleeding it, but some formulas cured it or at least lessened the pain.

In order to prevent attacks of gout, it is a good idea to always carry a hematite stone.

"Gout," lithography from 1823 (Bibl. de l'Ancienne Faculté de Médecine de Paris).

In order to cure it, Saint Como must be called upon or else black currant berries must be eaten from a previously blessed bush. The sovereign cure is a red gurnard's head burned and reduced to a powder that is then consumed in small quantities of water.

Hair

Whether it grows on the body or on the head, hair identifies with the individual. Sorcerers use it constantly to bewitch their victims. It also appears as an ornament that simple souls seek to rid themselves of. An ideal of deprivation is put into a concrete form in monks' caps and bald bronzes.

A woman's hair, this natural ornament, is still taboo in many civilizations, particularly Islamic, because it expresses the sexuality of women. It is hidden from all other men except the woman's husband. A man's hair, on the contrary, is exhibited with pride—it is supposedly a sign of strength and virility, undoubtedly by analogy with the animal world. Sampson, the invincible warrior, became weakened when Delilah cut his hair. For some years, however, Westerners have believed that long hair on a man is a mark of femininity.

A hairy chest indicates a particular sexual power, and hair on the arms and the back of the hands expresses a happy vitality and assured good fortune. In India it is believed that a man with a smooth chest can be only a thief.

If hair grows on a man's forehead and in front of his ears, it is a sign of longevity. But a woman whose hair grows low on her forehead will become a widow very quickly. In general, the way an individual's hair grows allows his character to be determined. A person with abundant hair that covers the forehead and temples is of a somewhat coarse, angry, vain nature—he cherishes luxury, but without hesitation accords his trust to those around him. A man with curly hair pushed away from the forehead is endowed with a simple and artistic soul.

If a woman with straight hair wakes up one morning with two curls on her forehead, it is a sign that her husband is going to die. Fine, straight hair corresponds to a timid, pacific, and easy-to-live-with temperament. A cowlick presages great activity and much luck during the day. Short, thick hair denotes a restless and fearless character, often deceitful and sometimes sensitive to beauty. Frizzy hair is that of a very simple and lucid man. But a frizzy mane reveals a lustful and wicked liar. Finally, a thick

"Young Woman 'à la Toilette'," Japanese print by Harunobu (Paris, private coll.).

head of hair can only belong to a negligent, distracted man, but one who is congenial and has a pleasant demeanor. A woman with curly hair is supposedly warm and friendly, but if her hair is thin and dull, she is a cunning wrong-doer.

A black head of hair draws its vitality from the earth, but red hair feeds from blood and fire. Blonds, on the contrary, lack blood and earth—they vampirize their red-headed or brunette partners. The myth of the femme fatale or so-called vamp, was undoubtedly born from this belief. In general, very blond hair denotes a malleable man, greedy for honor and glory. A black mane, on the contrary, characterizes a persevering, hardworking, obliging person. A redhead (Judas was one) bears the evil eye and is considered diabolical. In Alsace, red-headed children are said to be little devils. A head of red hair makes a man deceitful, slanderous, jealous, and perverse. But he is also reputed to have a quick mind and agile body. A white mane, of course, reveals someone who is full of opinions and experience, but who is fearful and weak. If white hairs appear early, it is a sign that a man is fickle and a braggart. In addition, it is said to be useless to pull out a gray or white hair because ten will grow back in its place. In order to color your hair, you need only soak a few hairs in a decoction of gold powder boiled in water. In general, the most esteemed man, endowed with an honest and tranquil nature, will have a head of hair that is not very thick and of an undecided color.

Whoever stands in the rain with his head uncovered will never be bald. But whoever cuts his hair during a waning moon or does not burn the cut hair immediately will certainly lose his head of hair. To cure baldness, a person's skull must be shaved completely and the fallen hair singed so that it doesn't lose its fluid. The skin can also be rubbed with onion juice or goose droppings. Still, touching a bald head brings good luck.

Hair becomes dull and thin if it is cut during a waxing moon. It is preferable to carry out this operation on a Tuesday if you wish to live a long time or on a Thursday, the luckiest day. But whoever cuts hair on a Friday will never be rich—a Monday or a Sunday attract bad luck. In addition, it is not advisable to cut your own hair, because you become unlucky for those around you. In Germany, a child's hair is not cut until he or she is one year old. In Southern Italy, a coin must be put in the hand of a child whose hair is being cut for the first time. Relatives assist in this ceremony because the child is very vulnerable to evil influences at that time. If a sailor has his hair cut on board ship before a tempest, he will meet with great happiness in returning home. Cut hair must either be burned or saved because all sorts of powers can take hold of it. A bird that steals a hair from a woman to build its nest gives the woman migraines.

If someone's hair does catch fire in the fireplace, it is a sign that he or she will die from drowning; if the hair catches fire quickly, it is a sign of longevity. You must never comb your hair at night because the hair left in the comb will attract nocturnal forces. If you let your comb fall when you are combing your hair, it foretells an approaching deception. Whoever suddenly loses a lot of hair also loses health and fortune.

Hair is used by spell casters: Sourcerers make chains of them that imprison their victims. Sorcerers can also make themselves a wig from your hair; they dip the wig in owl's blood and become invincible. In order to become invisible, this wig must be made of a hanged man's hair. A husband who wants to assure himself of his wife's fidelity burns a lock of his hair and places three pinches of it in the conjugal bed. When your hair tingles, it is a sign that a devil is passing.

Whoever combs his hair risks losing his memory; some eastern European students avoid combing their hair before an exam.

If you find a hair on your shoulder, it announces the arrival of an important letter during the day.

Hairpins also play a role in this hair affair. Finding one presages a new friendship; losing one, hostility near at hand. But if it falls to the ground from your hair and you pick it up, it is a sign that someone is thinking of you (except in Germany where it is believed that this is a sign of a love that is broken).

When a part unintentionally forms in a woman's wet hair, it is a sign that she will soon be a widow.

Hand

A hand gives and takes, hits and caresses. It is a direct extention of the human heart and ambivalent like the heart is.

The opposition between the right and left hand is very pronounced: The former, the hand of God, is used to take oaths; the other, that of the Devil, serves to cast spells and conjure them. A person can cross or join his hands, but a fiancée must avoid touching her right hand with her left until her wedding, otherwise she risks being unhappy. An itchy right hand announces the near arrival of money or good news; a left hand that itches announces that you will soon have to pay for something. In order to ward off the spell, it is best to immediately rub your left hand on wood. Greeting a person by extending your left hand always brings misfortune.

A child's hands must never be washed until he has attained the age of one year, because he risks being poor all his life. Two people who wash their hands in the same water must toss it out immediately, because they risk getting into a quarrel. Washing your hands in urine protects you from sorcery.

In order to keep your hands from perspiring, suffocate a green frog

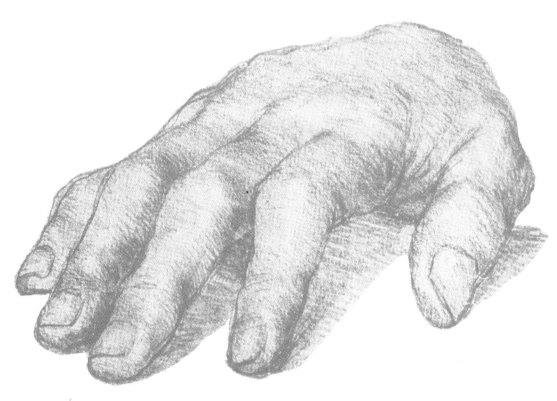

"Study of a Hand," by Holbein the Younger (Musée du Louvre).

in your hands (the same effect can be obtained by dipping your hands in the holy water basin of a church you are entering for the first time).

If three people hold out their hands at the same time to say hello to one another, all three will be assured of encountering luck. Four people must not cross their hands in order to greet one another, but if there are two couples, this gesture presages an unforeseen wedding.

The lustful and liars have fat fingers and hands covered with hair. Long, fat hands reveal a peaceful and obliging person who is kind to all and agreeable to visit. But if the hands are short and fat, they foretell a homely, hard-working character, sometimes deceitful and vain although without a spirit of spite. Long, fine hands are a mark of intelligence and sociability, but also of a taste for secrecy and vengeance. Clammy hands let us know that someone is in love; cold hands indicate a very warm temperament.

At the time of the Jewish New Year, whoever looks at his shadow and does not see the outline of his right hand risks losing a son within the year; if the left hand remains invisible, the person will lose a daughter; if only one of the fingers is hidden, a friend will die.

FINGERS

Whoever is born with more than five fingers on one hand is a child cherished by the gods and will have many powers. Flat or webbed fingers indicate a sorcerer. In general, pointing at something is dangerous, especially in the direction of a ship about to set sail—it will go down during its crossing. Whoever points at a rainbow will see a flower or a caterpillar grow from the end of his finger. Pointing at a person causes him or her to have the evil eye; this person must exorcize it immediately by making the sign of the horns pointed downward. These same horns (made with the index and little fingers) pointed upward are the sign of the Devil and sorcerers. The index and middle fingers can also be crossed to exorcize the evil eye. (This same gesture can be made hypocritically behind your back when you lie.)

The *thumb*, consecrated to Venus, incarnates power. It was by turning his thumb toward the ground that Caesar condemned a gladiator. A numbness of the left thumb presages nothing good.

The *index* is Jupiter's finger, sometimes called "poisonous finger" or "finger of the evil eye"; this finger must not be used for applying ointments. When this finger of judgment is longer than the middle finger, it is a sign of dishonesty.

The *middle finger*, consecrated to Saturn, is the finger of wisdom and personality.

The *ring finger*, linked to the sun, is in direct contact with the heart and sexuality. The left ring finger, the one a wedding band is worn on, is very beneficent and endowed with healing powers. It is with this finger that certain illnesses can be exorcized.

The *little finger*, consecrated to Mercury, is the finger of esoterism and divination. It is the one that reveals to us secrets that we should have ignored: "My little finger told me!" If the finger is curved but not hooked, it is a sign of good health.

A child born with long hands is predisposed to art, but money will flow between his fingers.

He who draws in his fingers and noisily cracks his knuckles is assured that someone loves him.

A one-handed person, like a one-eyed or one-legged person, compensates for the loss of his physical integrity with a gift for clairvoyance and divination. But, deprived of a creative hand, he lives on the outside of the times.

217

A moled hand is reputed to have great virtues for curing illnesses. In order to possess one, you need only suffocate a mole in your hand.

THE HAND OF GLORY

When it is lit, all the inhabitants of a house fall into a deep sleep. It was very useful to robbers who used it to pillage houses. Take a hanged man's hand and press it against his shroud to give him back his last bit of blood. Then let the hand lie in a container containing saltpeter powder, salt, and a pepper. Fifteen days later dry the hand in the sunlight or even in an oven that is fed with vervain and ferns. This hand serves as a candlestick to a torch composed of the hanged man's fat, pure beeswax, and sesame from Lapland. To protect yourself against the effects of this sorcery and thereby against robbers, you must coat the doorways and windows of your house with a mixture of fat from a white chicken, screech owl's blood, and a gall from a black cat. In order to be effective, this must be carried out during the height of the summer.

Head

A face is only the exterior, the appearance of an individual. The head is the most important part of the human body: It is the head that supports the feet. It supplants physical strength, but in compensation, "He who hasn't got a good head must have good legs." The Egyptians never ate an animal's head because it represented a mystery that was not good to approach.

The shape of a head is the best way of knowing the character of the person you are approaching. When it is small and soft looking, it belongs to a scientist and indicates a tendency toward sadness, whereas if it is big and round, it announces prudence, constancy, and fidelity. If it is long and deformed, it characterizes an envious person, but the person whose head is fat and ugly is full of wisdom and intelligence. A man who is bold to the point of being violent or imprudent has a fat, wide head, whereas miserly prudence and distrust are marked by the weight of a bowed head. A head that does not cease to move in every direction announces insanity and a taste for gossiping. People with fat heads are reputed to harvest very fat pumpkins and enormous turnips.

In order to avoid *headaches* you must keep a horse chestnut in your pocket or slip it under your pillow that is preferably made of dried ferns. It is also possible to put a bandage on your forehead containing a mixture of salt, cumin, bread, and mashed up juniper berries; when this unguent becomes dry, the bandage must be buried—it will take the ill with it.

"The Headache," lithography from the 1840s (Musée Carnavalet).

Other recipes exist that allow migraines to be avoided: Attach a sardine under each one of your heels or place a plucked magpie cut in two on your face. Carrying an odd number of little potatoes in your pocket or having a rubdown with earthworm oil also prevents headaches. Children's heads should be covered with pigeon droppings.

Whoever suffers from migraines can crown his or her head with braided ivy or make a bonnet of cabbage leaves dipped in butter. Some prefer firmly pressing the roofs of their mouths with their thumbs, and others prefer to sniff smelling salts or tobacco or else to wrap a piece of cloth soaked in vinegar around their foreheads; still others make themselves bandages of grated potatoes. Headaches can also be chased away by tying a hangman's rope around the forehead or, for men, a ribbon that belonged to a woman. No one believes that it is enough to simply sweep your bedroom floor against the grain. To cure a child's migraine, simply place a male moleskin on his skull.

When a person is assassinated, after a little time has passed his corpse must be unearthed and a sample taken from the moss growing on his skull—this moss was born of vital force that the person didn't have time to use and helps to make excellent love potions and cure all kinds of headaches. In addition, placed in a pigeon house, a man's skull attracts all the neighboring pigeons.

Heart

The ancients saw this organ as the seat of intelligence and the soul. Later on, it was considered the seat of the passions and the moods that determine our behavior. Romantics and Christians made it a symbol of love and charity.

A heart beats the way a clock ticks—to the rhythm of the earth. Sudden palpitations announce betrayal by a friend.

Despite its name, heartburn is usually a stomach ailment that is

Playing card, Germany, 16th c. (Bibl. des Arts Déco.)

revealed by vomiting. To combat it, drinking an infusion of St. John's wort gathered at dawn on Saint John's Day is very effective; some people in southern France prefer to swallow a powder made from toenail clippings. A pregnant woman's nausea is attributed to her baby's hair tickling her stomach.

To "hook up" someone's heart again, on a moonless night it is necessary to catch a live mole, cut off its feet in such a way that its nails are eliminated, then cut the animal in two and place the pieces on the person's heart while he or she is still warm; the mole will take away the bad fat and must be thrown far away. Lily of the valley and primula infusions are also reputed to strengthen weak hearts.

Garlic hung around the sick person's neck helps to destroy the worm gnawing at his heart. When this organ is "swimming in fat," an infusion of hawthorn, wild thyme, box tree cuttings, marsh mallow flowers, or walnut leaves helps to soothe it.

When a witch is suspected of provoking death in an animal by her sorcery, she can be transpierced by sticking the animal's heart with needles in the form of a cross.

Hernia

This rather frequent affliction makes those who suffer from it unfit for certain labors. What is important is putting the organs back in place, which explains the intervention of the tree, easily regenerated, in superstitions concerning this illness.

To prevent a child from contracting a hernia, take a fresh egg from Ascension Day and keep only the yolk. Then make the child urinate in the shell. Whoever carries out this rite three years in a row will never suffer from this ill.

To cure a child who suffers from a hernia, dig a corridor under a walnut tree root and pass the sick child through this tunnel three times: When the hole is filled in, the ill will be cured. Also a young, stout oak can be found and its trunk cut in such a way as to make a fork through which the child is passed. The two parts of the fork must then be bound back together. The recovery of the child will follow that of the tree. But if the tree dies or refuses to close up, the child will not be well. Let us note that this procedure is used for other illnesses.

An adult who wants to be cured of a hernia must embrace a stout oak in order to impregnate himself with its substance or else jump over three Saint John fires.

Hiccups

This little contraction that comes back at regular intervals is rather comical for those watching, but when it persists, it quickly becomes unpleasant for the person affected by it. It is strange to note that hiccups, evoking drunkenness, are sometimes reputed to promote a fresh complexion.

In Mediterranean regions, hiccups are attributed to the action of someone who speaks ill of you. In order to stop these hiccups, it is necessary to find or say the name of this enemy. In northern Europe, it is believed that a loved one is thinking of you.

To free a person from hiccups, place a cold key behind his back or else surprize or scare him suddenly. If a passionate discussion is provoked, whoever has the hiccups will forget the disorder. If these methods remain ineffective, pinch the person's little finger so hard that the pain cuts his breath.

To get rid of hiccups, you must swallow a mouthful of cold water in nine gulps or drink seven mouthfuls at a stretch. Drinking a glass of water upside down is also recommended (lean your head over in such a way that the rim of the glass is applied to your upper lip). Some recommend turning an object upside down, whether it be a glass or a hat. Others approve of counting to one hundred while holding their breaths.

Certain conjuratory formulas can also be effective if repeated three or seven times: "I have the hiccups, who made them? It was Jesus, I have them no more"; or else, "Let's go cuckoo, let's go to bed."

Central Europeans prescribe cutting a piece of paper in the shape of a cross, wetting it, and sticking it to your forehead to be freed from hiccups immediately.

Hospital

To many people a hospital appears to be a cursed enclosure marked by death. Anyone who enters its doors, whether in good health or not, was sure to fall ill and rub shoulders with death.

Whoever sleeps in the bed of someone who has died is assured of suffering the same fate.

Red and white flowers, symbols of death, are forbidden in hospitals.

Red- or pink-colored medicines are well received because they bring to mind the lifegiving blood and ruddy complexion of those in good health. But, no matter what color pills you take, it is inadvisable to leave a hospital on a Saturday—you run the risk of returning there soon.

If a nurse accidentally hits herself while sitting in a chair, it is a sign that a new patient is going to arrive. If her belt gets tangled up when she is sitting down, there is a strong possibility that she will be obliged to get up again very quickly.

"Ludicrous Surgical Operation," Holland, 16th c. (Madrid, Musée du Prado)

When a nurse puts the blankets on a chair when making a bed, she lets the patient know he or she hasn't got much longer to live. This belief is linked to an ancient custom that the dead should be rolled up in blankets before being put in their coffins.

The first patient to see a doctor in a new hospital is sure to be cured. But this and following patients must not become well to quickly—fate would be tempted by this presupposed recovery and very quickly bring the patients back to the same place. It is a bad omen to call on a doctor on a Friday.

Impotence

A multitude of talismans and magico-religious potions exist against this greatly feared weakness.

Marrow from a wolf's left foot mixed with ambergris is known for its curative virtues. A man or woman can coat his or her big toe on the left foot and back with a pomade having a chive and oil from St. John's wort base. He or she should also consume a stew of male goose testicles and hare intestines. Finally, a man can live chastely for six days, eat some spicy food on the morning of the seventh day, and then stare at his wife for ten seconds.

A periwinkle flower mixed with earthworms in some meat has an aphrodisiac influence just like spices or vervain. An oyster, the animal that begat Venus from the few drops of seawater it concealed, has the power to restore a man's virility. But it must be eaten in the morning so that it has time to be digested. In certain Mediterranean countries, the custom of having seashells in the morning instead of coffee with milk still stands.

The truffle, which appears mysteriously since it has neither a stem nor root and remains hidden from most people, is also adorned with these splendid virtues. It must be underlined, however, that it is always consumed with pepper.

Popular thought has never accepted impotence, form of masculine castration, as a natural phenomenon. On the contrary, it is supposedly the result of sorcery, set in motion by a sorcerer or an enemy, against two married people. This sorcery consists of "tying" the husband's codpiece to keep him from undoing his pants.

To prevent the codpiece from being tied, an engaged couple passes in front of a crucifix, without bowing to it, a few days before their wedding. On the morning of the ceremony, the bride puts on an article of clothing, preferably a stocking, inside out. The groom urinates three times in the wedding band given to him. He puts salt in his pockets and some coins in his shoes. The bride puts a ring in each of her shoes. During the ceremony, the bride holds a packet of little images placed upside down in her hand, and the groom hides a piece of a paschal candle in his jacket on his stomach. It is also desirable that the parish priest recite the Mass backwards. Those attending the wedding must make a lot of noise and beat the couple's feet when they are kneeling. When it is time for the wedding bands to be exchanged, the bride lets hers fall on the ground, the groom picks it up, and then pretends to be able to get the ring only halfway on her finger. When it is time for the benediction, the groom ties a knot in a leather shoestring while saying in a low, but still intelligible voice, "Hobal, Mibal, Varnabi." In general, it is more prudent to wear a ring set with a weasel's right eye on the little finger of the right hand.

Several methods are possible for satisfying a person's vengeance and tying the codpiece. This person can take the penis from a freshly-killed wolf, then go to the house of the future husband. At this place, he calls the groom by his name and when he answers, ties the penis with a white

The codpiece tier, end of the 19th c. (Bibl. Nat.)

shoelace. Some prefer to knot a silk, leather, or wool cord while saying the groom's name in a low voice when the wedding bands are exchanged. Others tie three knots in a rope while standing near a grave or consecrated place. A few recite a verse from the "Miserere mei" psalm backwards, make the sign of the cross three times in the air, and tie three knots in the codpiece while saying, "Ribald, Nobal, Barnabi." Finally, a shoestring can be tied and thrown into a flask of water.

Couples who are victims of this sorcery scratch and bite one another instead of getting to know one another, and the Devil, in the form of a phantom, comes between their bodies.

A couple whose wedding night has been so ruined resorts to multiple rites and attempts in order to escape their enemy. In the evening, the unfortunate couple is brought a broth or "bride's pie." They are advised to eat houseleeks or to rub each other with a raven's gall. A roasted green woodpecker seasoned with blessed salt is also recommended against this sorcery. The couple can also undress; the man then kisses the big toe on his wife's left foot and she kisses the big toe on her husband's right foot. Then they both make the sign of the cross, first with their hands and then with their heels. If this strategy fails, a hole is poked into a white wine vat and the first drops that escape are made to fall through the bride's wedding band.

A husband also has the possibility of pissing through the parish church keyhole. If a couple inhales smoke from a dead person's burning tooth or puts a straw filled with quicksilver near their bed, there is still some hope of their marriage being consummated.

Influenza

This illness, today well under control, for a long time appeared in the form of hard-hitting, fatal epidemics. The sudden rise in temperature and physical weakness that characterize influenza struck the imaginations of the superstitious who attempted to prevent it or slow it down.

Rusty water and fresh animal blood are traditional remedies for this type of illness. Other treatments concern themselves with influenza in a preventive way. A person must always carry a sachet of camphor or eat some fat slugs and dog droppings on an empty stomach. Some have a piece of cake baked in a new oven.

At the time of influenza epidemics, a spoonful of holy water was put in the evening soup. In order to cure the sick person, a cataplasm of sheep tallow melted with or without linseed oil and fennel seeds was applied to the chest for six hours. This was also wrapped in a warm, bloody lambskin or rabbitskin. Others put a pigeon that was quartered live on the painful area or a hot brick rubbed with garlic and wet with vinegar. Cow dung in a cataplasm or a dead hen or rooster had the same effect.

A person with influenza should drink a potion of milk and wine mixed with boiled dog droppings or oysters dissolved in milk. He or she should also swallow an egg yolk containing five or six live lice, urine from a seven-year-old girl, or soot from a chimney where only wood split in milk has burned. Snail syrup or three drops of blood taken from a cat's right ear and put in red wine are also advised. Others prefer drinking nine drops of he-goat blood boiled in white wine. Stones gathered from where a funeral procession has passed can also be boiled in water or milk. In general, spitting in a fire, then throwing some eggshells or cabbage cores in it lessen the illness.

Finally, take four small ferns and a chicory root and place them in four pots of boiling water. Then add a spoonful of honey and a licorice stick. The potion is to be consumed between meals.

Insanity

> *"What ho! What ho! this fellow is dancing mad; He hath been bitten by the Tarantula."*
>
> *Edgar Allan Poe*, The Gold Bug

Insanity was most often considered a demoniacal possession that it was necessary to exorcize. But in everyday life, a madman, as long as he isn't dangerous or raging, is an admissible personage, one who is even sought after. A simple person or someone whose mind is deranged is in direct contact with the gods. For a king he is a conjuratory double who has the right to say anything, but who can also be insulted without being hurt. Insanity is often a misunderstood wisdom that intelligence alone cannot grasp.

Encountering a madman is always a good omen, especially when he is seen singing out in the middle of a field. His presence in a house brings luck and wards off evil spells. Curiously, in Brittany, madmen are reputed to never drown. Making fun of madmen is always dangerous—a god can always be hiding under their human appearance.

Certain scenes, such as those that reveal truths forbidden to man, provoke insanity in those who witness them. Whoever remains in a cemetery on the night of All Saints' Day will learn the names of those who will die in the year to come, but he pays for this knowledge in general by a loss of reason. This will also happen to someone who accidentally learns the secrets of fairies or goblins or who attends a witches' Sabbath even if he or she didn't want to. Whoever clips his nails at night meets with the same fate.

In the Orient it is said that a person whose hair has caught fire will lose his or her reason. Ingesting a nightingale's heart or a magpie's brain will also lead to insanity, especially if the wind begins to change at the moment of the act. In Brittany, it is said: "Singing at the table and bedwetting are a sign of insanity." This saying reveals a certain connection between constant singing and a deranged mind; in the same region, it is believed that a young girl who sings at the table will have an insane husband.

Chrysolite is reputed to protect against insanity. So that it has all of its conjuratory power, it must be offered in September. Hellebore and fennel seeds have the power to cure insanity. In France, if someone tells you to "go find some fennel," it is the equivalent of "you have a screw loose."

In Brittany, children who were victims of anguish or sudden frights were made to wear a starfish around their necks: it supposedly protected them from spells, gave them back strength and courage, and especially kept them from going crazy. Nervous depression—even though this term sounds like an invention of our century—was combatted by making the sick person drink a broth of woodlice. It was very important to put in an odd number of these little animals. Against true insanity, the only recourse was in exorcism; certain pilgrimages were, however, beneficial for conjuring it. Whoever he was, an incurable or dangerous madman usually finished his days in an asylum where he died slowly.

In order to calm a madman, it is necessary to hang around his neck a talisman made from a hazelnut with a hole burrowed by an insect: Stick a peacock feather in the hole, then drip some mercury into it before plugging it with wax. When the madman has calmed down, the talisman must be thrown into a stream or river that will carry away the insanity.

Intoxication

There exist as many techniques for disgusting a drinker with alcohol as for making him drink without getting drunk!

In general, a more-or-less nauseating product is mixed into a drunkard's favorite drink. Some put a live eel into it; others mix some of the drunkard's fresh blood in some red wine. A crushed owl's egg will have the same effect whether it is consumed in wine or in an omelet. Some also use a powder made from a dead man's bone stolen from a cemetery by the full moon.

In order to sober up a drunk man, roll him in manure and make him drink some olive oil. Then he smells his own urine and wraps his genitals in a vinegar-soaked linen. A woman places the same cloth on her breasts.

Certain precautions allow a person to drink to his heart's content without becoming drunk. The Welsh eat roasted pig's lungs, assuring them immunity for twenty-four hours. It is also possible to take two spoonfuls of betony water and one of olive oil. A person must especially not drink from a glass that smells of savory or burned fingernails.

Itches

Like shivers and blinking, itches have no specific origin and are a sign of coming events.

As a general rule, all itches on the right side of the body announce that a person loves you or is thinking of you; on the left side, that a person is slandering you at the moment.

A tickling on the head is always a good omen. If your nose itches, you will soon have some small worry or someone will kiss you.

A slight irritation on the right hand announces the arrival of money or good news; on the left hand, you will soon make an unexpected expenditure. Likewise, scratching your right hip is a sign of money to come; your left hip, an expenditure near at hand. An itching of the knees is a sign of jealousy on your part or else announces that you will soon have to kneel in a strange place. Itchy feet presage a difficult voyage.

Jaundice

The color taken on by a person afflicted with this illness has caused people to look for remedies in yellow-colored foods, such as carrots, egg yolks, or else in urine itself that in the sick person is heavily colored by biliary pigments. It is important that "our" bile, yellow and secreted by the liver, is not confused with that of the ancients, an ill humor born in the spleen that provoked habitual bitterness, hatred, and acrimony.

Against excess of bile, it is recommended that a person urinate on some nettle nine times in a row at dawn or wear, around the neck or in an armpit, a sachet containing a crushed, hard-boiled egg (sometimes only the yolk is kept).

Capillary and hornbeam or borage wood infusions prevent the stopping up of the liver. Cow dung cataplasms or the consumption of dried hen droppings in white wine are also recommended. It is always a good idea to call upon Saint Sebastian or, if the sick person prefers, drink a young boy's urine every day on an empty stomach.

To hasten recovery from jaundice, hang a clump of mistletoe that grew over a bramble bush from the pothook on the hearth—the troubles disappear when the mistletoe balls dry out. A container that has never been used must be filled with vinegar and placed under the sick person's bed. Eating a tench is reputed to cure hepatitis, but the fish can also be placed on the sick person's belly. When the jaundice first breaks out, an egg must immediately be broken over an anthill—the ants will bury the illness with the egg.

In order to exorcize jaundice, take a coin in your right hand and make three circles with it around the suffering person's face while saying, "I beseech you and I command you, in the name of the living God, Emmanuel, and Abraham to leave this body."

The sick person can urinate and then make a dog drink the urine, but it is preferable for him to spit on a piece of pork or calf's liver and mix it with a black dog's food, or piss on a slice of sheep and make a dog eat it.

One of the most commonly used recipes consists of hollowing out a fat carrot, then filling it with the sick person's urine. This carrot can be left to rot or it can be hung in a fireplace so that the urine evaporates, then the person who is suffering must eat it raw or cooked.

Kiss

Giving a kiss or kissing is a sign of communion and spiritual union. A divine kiss is a breath that gives back live; a father kisses a son, to bring him benediction or forgiveness. Two enemies seal the end of hostilities with a kiss of peace. A kiss can also be a homage—someone asking protection kisses a sovereign's or lord's feet. Kissing is also a sign of communion and sharing—after a burial everyone kisses the widow to let her know that they share in her sorrow. Newlyweds are kissed in order to get a taste of their happiness. In contrast, kissing newborns or young children can be unlucky for them. A kiss is, of course, a symbol of love—an exchange of breaths signifies the communion of the souls and bodies. In modern French, the verb "baiser," to kiss, has taken on the specific meaning of "to make love."

"The Kiss of Judas" (detail), by Giotto, 1305 (Padua, Scrovegni Chapel).

A person must never be kissed on the nose, because it will attract discord. In Brittany, people greet each other by kissing each other's cheeks three times, twice on the left and once on the right.

Two children who have not yet learned to talk must not kiss each other. This act will make them deaf and dumb forever and keep their bodies and spirits from growing.

A young woman who is unexpectedly kissed by a tawny man will soon be proposed to. A young virgin girl who lets herself be kissed on the mouth will become pregnant. If she kisses a man with a moustache and does not let a hair from the moustache stick to her lips, she will be an old maid.

A person must never be kissed over his or her shoulder, because this gesture warns of an approaching breakup. It evokes Judas's kiss. Anyone who puts himself behind your back to kiss you risks betraying you very soon. Racine defined this kiss very well: "If I kiss my rival, it is to better stifle him!"

Knees

Knees are supposedly the principal seat of body strength and of an individual's authority: Knees are bent as a sign of humiliation or alligence; a person goes down on his knees to pray to gods or kings.

Fat knees indicate a timid, lazy character. When knees are thin or skinny, they indicate a solid, bold, secretive person.

Leg

"To pull someone's leg" is an expression still used today that shows the importance of this part of the body for our ancestors. During the period when men wore hose, a man with well-proportioned legs beamed with

"The Beggars," by Breugel the Elder (Musée du Louvre).

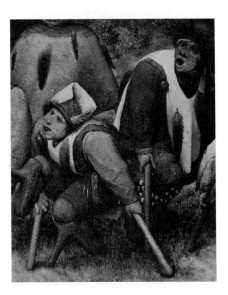

pride. (Here, the thigh is also included in the term "leg.") A dandy who wanted to be noticed at a lawn tennis match returned balls "under his leg."

When a person crosses himself or makes the sign of the horns, it is a good idea for him to cross his legs also, reinforcing the conjuration of evil forces. But a person who crosses his legs at a gambling table risks warding off luck. Whoever doesn't want goblins to spoil his sleep must cross his legs in bed.

For physiognomists, thin thighs are a sign of intelligence and honesty; short, fat thighs are a sign of a frustrated nature. Smooth, hairless legs in a man indicate fear, weakness, reserve, and a taste for chastity. Hairy legs are generally accompanied by a hairy body and signify lust, infidelity, strength, and wickedness. Big bones and thick hair indicate people who are full of strength and who combine prudence with a taste for secrecy, but they can also be a little slow-witted. Small bones and little hair indicate weakness, timidity, kindness, and some taste for the trivial.

Touching a handicapped man's wooden leg brings luck and happiness.

Lips

Lips are linked to the idea of sensuality, especially feminine, as opposed to the nose that more precisely defines male sexuality. Even when they are closed, lips are eloquent by their shape, betraying the character and feelings of their possessor.

The upper lip announces tastes for and tendencies toward sensual pleasure—anger and pride make it curve, goodness makes it full and round, and intellectual pleasure makes it fine. The lower lip usually only plays a support role, but if, with the teeth, it is larger than half the width of the mouth when seen in profile, it is a sign of absolute stupidity, greed, and wickedness. If one lip is bigger than the other, it is a sign of simplicity and a dullness of the mind. If the upper lip is larger, it is a sign of goodness—a prominent lower lip announces a certain coldness.

Lips that are fat and curve in the middle are a sign of uprightness, but also a certain tendency toward sensual pleasure, but if they are too fat they announce a sordid sensuality, even brutal wickedness. On the whole, fleshy, fat, protruding lips combine a great robustness with a taste for laziness and lust. On the other hand, when lips are thin and protruding, you can expect discretion, respect, prudence, and a taste for mind games from their possessors. When lips are short and thick, they are a sign of stinginess.

From tight lips whose edges are not apparent you can expect a taste for order combined with cold-bloodedness and exactitude, but little lips that hide a smile announce wickedness. A small, narrow mouth under a small nose is a sign of the fearful. A strongly traced middle line on a mouth with no apparent lips indicates greed, cunning, coldness, toughness, and a taste for flattery.

When the corners of the mouth turn up, they signify vanity and frivolity; if they slant downward, they reveal insensitivity and a tendency toward mistrust.

Well-shaped, pink lips belong to a person with a good temperament, but whoever has a mouth twice as large as one eye is an idiot.

If your lips itch, they announce that you are soon going to receive a kiss; smacking the lips is also an invitation to a kiss.

Medicine

In a sense, medicine itself is sometimes a superstition—a person thinks it is sufficient to take a pill or potion from a pharmacy in order to be cured of any illness. The use of a "placebo"—medicine that contains no active ingredient—is proof of the deep-rootedness of this belief. However, a miraculous medicine that guards against all illnesses does exist. When the sun (symbol of life) is at its zenith, gather four rue branches, nine juniper berries, and a walnut; toss in a dried fig and a little salt. This potion should be consumed several times on an empty stomach.

Nails

"No dead man should be wrapped in his shroud without someone cutting his nails. Whoever forgets to do this hastens the completion of the Naglfar ship, feared by gods and man alike."

This text from the *Snorra Edda* that Borges cites in his "Essay on Ancient Germanic Literature" sums up the spirit of superstitions dealing with nails. The Naglfar ship, the ship of the dead (the German word "nagel" means "nail"), is made with dead people's nails.

Horns, ivory, hair, and nails are insensitive matter, similar to death, and yet they are produced by living beings and are capable of growing and regenerating. A biblical legend has it that Adam and Eve had a garment of a horny matter, like a turtle or insect shell, then lost it when God chased them from terrestrial Paradise. Nails are vestiges of this ancient protection. Likewise, Siegfried and Achilles had skins insensitive to wounds, but they both had a weak point.

It is essential that you not be dispossessed of this strange and intimate part of yourself—witches who get hold of your nails have power over you. As is often true in the spirit of superstition, the same matter that allows a person to be bewitched is also used in exorcizing spells and illnesses—burned nails bring recovery.

"Se Repulen." Engraving taken from "Caprices" by Goya (Bibl. Nat.).

Nail clippings mixed in a drink make a violent potion that provokes death (this is a general belief). In some countries it is said that a pregnant woman who walks on bits of nails will immediately abort. For many people who fear or exorcize illnesses, all illnesses leave by the nails; they, therefore, advise scratching the hands and toes before undertaking all treatments. Clippings deposited at a crossroads are reputed to bring a fever down, and whoever cuts his nails on Good Friday—a frightening act, however—will cure himself of his toothaches. A girl who clips her nails nine Fridays in a row will see the man promised to her in a dream. In Spain, if a child's nails are clipped behind the front door of the house, he or she will have every chance of becoming an eminent singer.

As a general rule, cutting your nails on a Friday is unlucky and dangerous—in Brittany, a person who carries out this act is said to lengthen the Devil's horns. Some believe, however, that this spell can be conjured by first clipping the thumbnail, then that of the middle finger, little finger, index, and finally the ring finger. It is often said that Tuesdays, Wednesdays, and Fridays are unlucky days for carrying out this operation—for the English, Sunday is also a bad day.

The Romans never clipped their nails on a boat. This act was not supposed to be carried out during a religious service or at night, either—whoever had such audacity went insane. In Ireland, it is not advisable to face toward the north when you cut your nails. In the Orient, as well as in the West, it is thought that a child's nails should not be clipped. Whoever takes this action before a child is one year old will make the child a robber. But it is usually believed that biting a newborn's nails off for the first time is sufficient to conjure this spell; whoever forgets to do this will see an idiot or a robber grow up. This does not keep parents from telling their children "Don't bite your nails!" (The superstitious mind is not above contradiction.) In Spain it is believed that whoever cuts a child's nails on a Monday risks ruining the child's teeth. In Sicily, when a child's nails have just been clipped for the first time, a coin placed in his or her hand prevents him or her from becoming a robber.

Nail clippings should never be left on the spot or thrown out without first taking the precaution of spitting on them three times or cutting them again, one by one, into three pieces. Some believe that it is preferable to burn them; others, on the contrary, believe this act makes you go crazy. The Scandinavians prefer to bury them deep in the ground to keep elves from getting hold of them.

Hooked nails are a well-known sign of cupidity; if nails are convex, it is a sign that the person will die young.

White spots on nails are the object of various beliefs. In Germany, they announce the number of years left to live; in Spain they are the marks left by falsehoods a person has committed or the number of women a person is loved by—not a contradiction. In England, they are generally signs of gifts, but a more precise code exists: A spot on the thumbnail announces a gift; on the index, a new friendship; on the middle fingernail, a betrayal; on the ring fingernail, a success in love or business; and on the little fingernail, an approaching voyage. White spots are a good omen for children, but it is also said that a white spot appears on a finger that attemps to count the stars. Yellow or black spots presage illness or death. The sudden appearance of a white spot on the middle fingernail of your left hand foretells that an enemy will soon try to hand you a trap.

A *half-moon*, the semicircular whitish part at the base of a nail, is a good omen. If it is absent from all the fingernails, it is a very bad omen. Large, high half-moons reveal great generosity; if they are small or absent, meanness and dishonesty; very pale or white, a propensity for lust; too colored, fragility. For some they are a sign of longevity—the bigger they are, the longer their owner will live.

In order to protect a child from numbness of the fingers from the cold, his hands must be placed in ice water at the time of his birth.

Neck

The neck is a part of both the head and throat, intellect and sentiment.

It is a vulnerable part of the body that women adorn with necklaces or men with ties. These circular objects originally had a value as talismans. An executioner, knowing the fragility of the head's support, broke or cut off the neck in corporal punishments such as hanging, garroting, or decapitating.

In Holland, a pain in the neck or a stiff neck presage that a person will end up hanged.

A head that is carried high on a slender neck is a sign of pride and vanity. A long, delicate neck combined with slender feet present a deli-

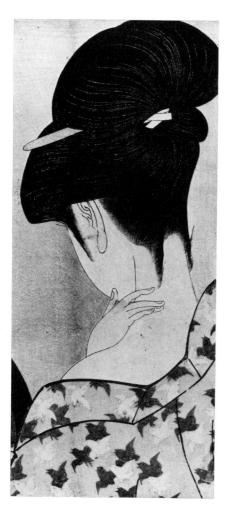

Japanese print from the 18th c. (Musée du Louvre)

cate, timid nature like a deer, but are sometimes a sign of versatility, lying, and ignorance.

The short, thick neck of a bull sometimes announces prudence and discretion, but more often indicates a propensity toward anger, greed, and a taste for authority.

In order to cure a stiff neck, wrap the neck in a wool stocking that has already been used but not washed. The neck can also be rubbed with cotton wet with olive oil in which the top of a poppy has soaked. You can also put a towel containing warm laurel leaves around the neck.

In the last century, a goiter was an affliction commonly treated with rock salt, ashes, or fig bark. To cure it, the sick person needed to wear the following salve in a linen around his neck for fifteen days: twelve red slugs mixed with bean flour and ground linseeds, then mixed with a decoction of sea sponge, wine dregs, and vine shoots, then put in the oven until it had "an unctuous consistancy."

Nose

"It is a rock! It is a peak!
It is a cape!
What am I saying, it is a cape?
It is a peninsula!"

(Edmond Rostand, *Cyrano de Bergerac*)

A nose "in the middle of the face," more than eyes that are usually big and beautiful, illustrates the perfection of the human body. A beautiful nose is so rare that it has a reputation of its own. Only Italians and the kings of France were said to have a truly perfect appendage. Roman noses were supposedly monopolized by noble-blooded families. In addition, nostrils correspond directly to the sexual organs: If they are thick and vibrant, they reveal large testicles, whereas a straight, long, thin nose foretells large sexual organs in a woman. Many expressions characterize the shapes of a nose—a trumpet nose, pug nose, potato nose, and hooked nose. They are witness to the attentive interest that this strange growth gives rise to.

A large nose is generally welcomed: "A big nose doesn't spoil the face"; without any doubt it belongs to a peaceful, faithful, gentle man. But if the nostrils are also very large, the person is quarrelsome and a vain liar.

In France it is said, "short nose, lazy nose," even though such a nose is often considered amusing and roguish. When it is pointed, it reveals a cranky, mean person, but one endowed with a good memory. A turned-up nose is a sign of lust and boldness. A long nose signals courage and pride, and when the tip is a little fat, it announces, in addition, prudence, fidelity, and honesty. A long round nose shows both a versatile hypocrite and a miser. A bump in the middle of the nose is a sign of inconstancy and coarseness. A flat nose is that of a credulous liar; hooked, that of a mischievous miser.

Those who have noses that are excessively colored are undoubtedly not very intelligent, but fond of good living. Thick hairs in the nose and on its bridge indicate a tranquil but versatile temperament.

A mother who pulls the hairs out of her child's nose every morning will make him a happy man. So that a child stays in good health, make the sign of the cross on his body and pull his nose before dressing him.

An itchy nose announces a dispute, a letter, or an undeclared lover. When your nose itches, do not resist and make a wish.

"The Princess of Trebizonde" (detail), by Pisanello (Verona, Santa-Anastasia).

A bloody nose is a bad omen unless only one drop falls from the left nostril—in this case it announces a coming fortune. If the blood flows from the right side, a family member will fall seriously ill. This will happen also if three drops fall one after the other. If a man's or a woman's nose bleeds in the presence of someone of the opposite sex, it is an admission of love.

Putting a key behind your back or on the nape of your neck is the most common treatment for bloody noses. The tip of a cat's tail or a little piece of newspaper can also be put in the afflicted nostril. Some plug their noses with spider webs filled with dust and flour. They also eat pigeon droppings or put a coin in a white handkerchief on the middle of their foreheads. Others write the initials INRI on their foreheads with their own blood. They wrap the little finger corresponding to the bloody nostril in a red string or wear a toad cut in two in a little sack around their necks.

Nostrils that are also closed belong to a quarrelsome, demented liar. If they are narrow and thin, they reveal a scornful character that usually masks sexual impotence.

Saliva

This liquid that some identify with semen has always had great magical power. It was with saliva that Jesus cured a blind man, but it was by spitting on Jesus's face that the crowd expressed its contempt for the condemned man.

Spitting while taking an oath authenticates the gesture as if it had been sworn on a Bible or a cross. The ritual formula of English schoolboys: "Finger wet, finger dry, cut my throat if I tell a lie!" is equivalent to the French phrase, "Wooden cross, iron cross, if I lie, I go to Hell!"

Spitting in your hands hardens the skin and fortifies whoever is going to undertake a new or difficult task, but this gesture can also ease the pain of or prevent contagion. A man who has involuntarily wounded another salivates on his guilty limb to keep his victim from suffering. Sicilian wet-nurses coat their breasts with saliva before letting a nursling feed. Spitting on a mosquito or wasp bite is reputed to soothe it.

But above all, saliva, like salt and the sign of the cross, is a means of conjuring the evil eye or sorcery. When a person finds himself confronted by evil forces, he must spit on the ground three times to protect himself against their influences. This gesture is always executed on hair that falls out or nail clippings to keep sorcerers from using them in their spells. When a monk, hunchback, or any other person suspected of having the evil eye is encountered, you must spit on the ground as soon as the person has passed. Doing this in front of the adversary might provoke him. When a child is born, the midwife spits on the newborn to protect him, and while he is still young, his mother must spit each time a compliment is paid to him. This custom is still very much observed in certain Mediterranean regions—all praises are followed by the formula "God protect him" or "God bless him!" and spitting.

A farmer knows that he must spit on the spot in the field where he is going to begin reaping. Likewise, it is a good idea to wet all new clothing with a little saliva. All unusual things must be greeted with spitting; this protects against possible complicating factors, such as a crossroads, a black cat, a cow that has just calved, a spring from which you are going to drink, a stone that has hurt an animal, a horseshoe, and even a fire—but only when it crackles in an abnormal way.

In Scandinavian countries, in order to bring luck to a hunter, you must spit on a broom and toss it after him when he leaves; to attract fish, a fisherman wets the maggot he has just put on his hook with saliva. A person setting out on foot spits on his right shoe before undertaking any journey, and a gambler calls on luck by spitting on the ceiling.

The Bretons know that they must spit in a fountain when they are not sure of the purity of its water: If the saliva dissolves or breaks up, the water is potable; if the saliva remains compact, it is preferable to abstain from drinking the water.

Sailors say that it is necessary to spit with the wind; otherwise, a tempest will be unleashed. Only old seadogs who have been around Cape Horn several times have the privilege of spitting into the wind without insulting the gods.

If you spit on a viper before eating, you will kill the viper immediately. Spitting into the open mouth of a frog frees you from nagging coughs.

Shiver

This sudden, involuntary tremble, when it is not a fever symptom, is a bad omen. In certain regions, a shiver announces that someone is seeking to harm you, but the most widespread belief is that it indicates Death is passing near by. For the Bretons, a shiver is a well-known sign of an approaching death. Shivering can also tell you that someone is walking on the site of your future grave.

A long shiver when you wake up in the morning or when you cross the doorway to your house is a sign of a bad day, but in the evening before going to bed, it announces, on the contrary, an excellent night, rich in pleasant dreams.

Skin

"A skin disorder is healthy for the sickly," according to the French saying. It expresses the general idea according to which skin afflictions are more a sign of recovery than of illness—they are a sign that the illness is trying to escape the body. The recommended formulas, therefore, aim at hastening this process.

Some, however, try to avoid these less-than-flattering lesions by never wearing furs on a Friday.

In general, in order to make a skin disorder disappear, a person must eat a lizard or roll in the grass on the morning of Saint John's day. For scabies, a pomade of crushed slate mixed with pepper and vinegar is recommended. Others roll completely nude in a field of oats.

Itches are treated with saliva unctions. They can also be treated by putting a frog on them every night.

In order to cure dermatoses, the sick person's blood must be purified—he or she should drink an infusion of walnut leaves gathered before dawn on June 24. Sometimes, a boxwood crown is placed on the head for a few hours, then the crown is hung on the ceiling—when the wood rots, the illness has disappeared. Children suffering from this type of sickness should not have their nails clipped or their condition will grow worse. It is, on the other hand, advisable to coat their nails with lard or to fix their hair with a bonnet of cabbage leaves. In addition, children should be washed with holy water. Finally, some hold up a child to a gray donkey eight days in a row.

Shingles are supposedly poisonous creatures that wrap themselves around a body to better suffocate the sick person. Only someone who has already been cured of this illness can exorcize this spell.

In order to cure nettle rash, take thirteen new pins and pass them around the lesions, one by one, for thirteen days. Then the sick person must toss them over his or her shoulder without turning around. This ceremony must take place before sunrise and be repeated a second time beginning on a major feast day.

The malicious breath of a sorcerer causes scurf. The breath of a person sick with a contagious disease is also evil, so he must not be kissed. Certain conjuratory methods are recommended for curing the disease. The sick person says: "9 scales reduced to 8, from 8 to 7, from 7 to 6, and so forth." The illness must be greeted every morning and evening. Others chew on a myrtle leaf and a grain of salt in the morning, then rub their skins with this lotion. Dissolved salt is put in the patient's mouth, or else he swallows some cooked and oiled holly leaves. He also rubs himself with the steam that forms on hot iron. In addition, he urinates on the staircase landings every morning. Also, take a few hairs from the left side of the head, cut them with a knife, then put them in a bud on a hazel tree. If the operation fails, try again with hair from the right side. Whoever washes on an empty stomach in water from the Loire or Vienna rivers will be rid of dermatoses. Finally, a bundle of sticks can be put under your pillow before you go to bed!

Dew, especially collected on the morning of May 1, is reputed to make skin supple and lustrous. In the eyes of the Germans, drinking cold coffee often has the same effect.

A woman who passes a halcyon feather over her face is sure to preserve her beauty. She must eat a peony twelve days in a row in order to have a rosy complexion. Her face will keep all its freshness if she rubs her skin with a baby's first wet diaper.

Certain unguents are excellent for rejuvenating the skin: Crush some sheep's and calf's bone, then boil them for three hours in a pot that has never been used (the grease that floats to the top must be collected with a silver spoon). Another pomade can be obtained by boiling oil, alum, and fat from a young goat in white wine.

Sleep

Many divinatory systems are founded on man's sleep. A horseshoe, feather, leaf, or key placed under a sleeping person's pillow will cause him or her to dream of the future. But a sleeper is also the ideal prey of nocturnal forces, particularly of sorcerers and fairies who only manifest themselves at night. This vulnerability is explained in part by the still-tenacious ignorance of science regarding sleep. A person can therefore imagine, without being contradicted, that the human soul takes flight toward some more-or-less beneficent beyond during sleep.

The head's orientation during sleep determines an individual's future. Directed toward the north, it announces a very short life; toward the south, a long life; toward the east, an assured fortune; and toward the west, astonishing voyages.

She who falls asleep while working will marry a widower. In order to conjure this spell, in Germany it is said that she must take off her shoes and put them in front of her face.

The first person of a newlywed couple to fall asleep on their wedding night will die before the other.

Insomniacs rub their temples with cat fat or eat chicken feet with cooked milkweed. Others smoke a mixture of black tobacco, toad powder, and honey. It is also possible to chew on ten hemp grains that have marinated in alcohol for ten days.

When a blackbird's right wing is hung from a red string in the middle of the main room of a house, it keeps the inhabitants from sleeping. A swallow's eye in a bed will have the same disastrous consequences.

A sleepwalker is believed to have been ill-baptized and the ceremony must be done again. For others, this person is someone who is both too imaginative and too fearful; he accomplishes at night what he doesn't dare to undertake during the day.

Sneeze

Demons tickle a man's nose to make him sneeze and thereby expel his soul. Italians respond to this spell with "God be with you," so that God will help the spirit return back inside the body immediately. The popular formula, "God bless you," was perhaps originally an expression of sympathy or despair because not too long ago, a sneeze signified an illness most often fatal, like plague or bronchitis. Isn't it still believed that a sneeze is contagious even when it is unexpected?

For some, however, a sneeze is a sign of good health, and a simple expression of pleasure. In general, a sneeze is supposedly lucky between noon and midnight when the moon is waning and unlucky at all other times. It brings luck in the morning, but misfortune in the evening. Before breakfast, a sneeze announces a present during the week. A sneeze at the moment when you undertake a new task is a sign of coming failure. In Wales, it simply brings bad luck. Others vary this judgment according to the days of the week:

> Sneezing on Monday keeps away danger,
> Sneezing on Tuesday, kiss a stranger,
> Sneezing on Wednesday, receive mail,
> Sneezing on Thursday, such is the best,
> Sneezing on Friday attracts misfortune,
> Sneezing on Saturday announces a lover,
> Sneezing on Sunday, the Devil for the week.

Whoever sneezes while talking reveals that he or she is not lying. At the table, you will have a new friend before the end of the meal. But Jewish tradition affirms that sneezing when you are speaking of a dead person bring misfortune. In order to conjure this spell, you must touch your earlobes and say: "They are in their world, we are in ours."

In China, sneezing on New Year's Day is believed to presage a disastrous year. Sneezing brings luck when it is from the right nostril and attracts bad luck when it is from the left.

A single sneeze grants a wish, two announce a kiss, and three, a radiant future. The Japanese think that a single sneeze is a sign that someone is saying something nice about you; two, that he is crushing you with insults.

Two people who sneeze at the same time bring great fortune on themselves.

Whoever feels like sneezing but doesn't can be assured that someone loves him or her, but doesn't dare to admit it.

A newborn remains in the hands of fairies until he or she sneezes.

Splinter

This little affliction is often painful and risks becoming infected.

Some gamblers believe, however, that a thorn or sliver of wood in the left foot must be left there for seven days in a row in order to win at gambling seven Sundays in a row.

In general, it is sufficient to apply rabbit fat on the splinter to make it come out on its own. If it doesn't, use a compress with urine or else place a salve on it made of hare fat, herring milt, pig's gall, gladiolus pulp, hawthorn roots, and so forth.

When you remove a thorn from your foot, you must suck the drop of blood that forms, make the sign of the cross, and offer this suffering to Christ who wore the crown of thorns.

So that a sore doesn't get infected, it is a good idea to blow on it three times, then place two little pieces of linen on it in a cross, and then say these words: "Point by point, my God, heal this sore like Saint Como and Saint Damien healed the five wounds of Our Lord Jesus Christ."

Sprain

Popular medicine easily confuses sprains and twists. When these injuries are serious, a bone setter is called in.

In order to heal twists, the person in pain must apply two rings of braided reed on the twist. He or she can ease the pain by coating the area with an unguent made of equal parts of boiled red wine and that year's honey. For nine days in a row he or she must recite the following formula: "Three angels on the sea who twist and untwist; Our Lord who twists again; good Saint Damien puts them in their joints, and good Saint Leu puts them in knots."

Bone setters are able to heal with the help of conjurations and magic formulas that mix Christianity and Paganism. They press on the pain with their left thumb or trace a circle around the joint with the same finger. These practices, of course, necessitate making signs of the cross and reciting the Lord's Prayer and the Hail Mary. In France, the two most used conjuratory formulas for healing sprains, twists, and dislocations are: "Sprain I defeat you, sprain I cross you, sprain I dress you" or else "Twist, be gone, the blow that God made is made; that which God did is undone, that it be done." In Alsace and eastern France, a healer can also say: "A stag struck against a stone. Our Lord Jesus Christ spared it. He rubbed lard and fat on it and it could walk again."

If the suffering person does not call on a bone setter, he can tie an eelskin, three strings soaked in holy water, or a string from a flour sack around the painful joint. Near the North Sea area, it is preferable to apply to the area a herring split in two. A twisted ankle can also be bathed in the water under a mill wheel. An unguent with a bran, vinegar, and olive and juniper oil base also activates healing.

Stitch or Sideache

This shooting pain is attributed to a temporary illness of the spleen. To avoid suffering from it, a person must suck on a pebble while running.

If a stitch crops up during a run, pick up a stone, spit on it, and put it back in the same place, the wet side facing the ground.

It is also possible to jog around a church, then bend over and touch the ground, keeping your legs straight and close together.

Some grill seven grains of oats, then toss them in a spring. Others boil a decoction of soot in milk. Finally, it is possible to soak three wheat grains in holy water and say three times, "Stitch of stitches. I command you to leave the body of . . ."

Throat

This word defined the internal part of the neck, but was also used to modestly designate the chest. Throat ailments include afflictions deep in the mouth, anginas, and nagging coughs as well as voice losses.

If a wolf sees you at sunrise, you risk it communicating its hoarseness to you. In order to get your voice back, you must call upon Saint Blaise and Saint John and make the sign of the cross on your neck and chest.

In order to prevent coughs and sore throats, it is a good idea to hang a plum tree branch in the fireplace.

Many recipes for syrups, gargles, and cataplasms exist for treating anginas, hoarseness, and other throat afflictions. Usually these treatments must be placed on the throat while they are hot. A sock full of hot ashes, mashed potatoes, or cow dung can be wrapped around the sick person's neck. A broth made of rye flour to which two crushed white lily bulbs have been added constitutes an excellent cataplasm. A catskin worn like a scarf also cures these ailments.

You can cure throat illnesses by rubbing the soles of your feet with an unguent made of garlic cooked in lard, but some prefer spitting in a frog's mouth! In Lorrain, the sick person pulls a lock of hair from the top of the head and makes a pad with it—this action raises the uvula up again and aids in the recovery.

Tongue

Since Aesop, people have known that a tongue is both the best and the worst thing in the world. Above all, it signifies speech. An intelligent and discreet person must above all know how to hold his or her tongue. The organ in itself "guards a stale smell of obscenity": it is shown only to a doctor and children stick it out to express their scorn for something. Only lovers intimately intermingle their tongues.

A tongue's color betrays illness: Red and filled with blood, it announces vigor; white or yellow, it shows the presence of unhealthy moods; black, it is the sign of plague.

Whoever bites his or her tongue while eating is being punished for a recent lie.

Physiognomists drew much information from this tongue that was both an organ and a deliverer of words. A tongue that wags indicates an instable, credulous character that you must be careful of. A tongue that trips or stutters is a sign of great pride, but also versatility, great goodness, but a tendency toward anger. If it is fat and rude, it belongs to someone who is impious, timid, and scornful, but not without ingenuity. Prudent, naive, impressionable people have a polite, chattering tongue.

Tooth

An ivory tooth, animal or human, still today has value as a talisman: An elephant's tusk, in particular, is highly sought after in Africa, where it is used to make grisgris, as well as in Europe, where ivory jewelry remains highly prized. In the Orient, working with this material is a true sculptural art. Due to its white color, which symbolizes all forms of purity, and to its hardness, which makes it an object reputed to be both eternal and incorruptable, a tooth, though common, appears as a precious commodity. In addition, like hair and nails, it takes root in the body—therefore the soul—of an individual and feeds from his life like a plant feeds from the earth. Its course follows that of the body: A child's first teeth illustrate his introduction into the social group as much as his first steps; his baby teeth fall out with age, then his "permanent" teeth grow in only to disappear over the years until finally, an old man, he has a toothless smile. In addition, medical misunderstanding regarding dental matters, incarnated by the traditional figure of a public tooth puller, provoked a myriad of recipes and practices in order to get rid of the toothaches that poisoned daily life in past centuries.

A tooth that falls out still signifies a loss of the vital energy linked to youth, and a sort of inevitable castration.

246

According to their shape and usage, teeth are linked to a diverse scale of moral values. It is affirmed that the ambitious have long teeth and that the lucky have widely spaced upper incisors ("lucky teeth"). These incisors that shine in the mouth's foreground and are revealed in every smile represent fame and celebrity. Canines, teeth that tear food with their pointed ends, are the image of strenuous work and hatred. Molars, more discreet but inalterable, incarnate endurance and tenacity. When the molars are large, a person is believed to be obstinate and hard-working. If the teeth situated at the back of the jaw are widely spaced, it is a sign that their owner must abandon his town or native country if he wishes to succeed in life.

Whoever has a complete and well-arranged set of teeth will have a

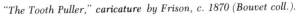

"The Tooth Puller," caricature by Frison, c. 1870 (Bouvet coll.).

long life even though he is greedy, lustful, and rash. An odd number of poorly-placed teeth indicate an intelligent and prudent character, but one that is envious and versatile. When they are small, fragile, and not very numerous, they reveal a honest, delicate, faithful, and timid man. He whose teeth are big and wide will be boastful, lewd, a little simple-minded, and a liar. But if the teeth are also solid and thick, he will have a long life, great courage, and a curious mind. Long, pointed incisors belong to a suspicious, unfaithful, shameless gourmand. Finally, yellow teeth evoke a slightly crazy, coarse, mischievous person.

According to diverse traditions, a child born with one or two teeth will be happy or unlucky. All agree, however, that if the first tooth pushes through the upper gum, the child will die young; if it pushes through the lower gum, he or she will be intelligent. If a baby cuts a tooth too soon, it is a sign that the mother will soon have another child. In addition, the number of teeth a child has at his or her first birthday indicates the number of brothers or sisters to come.

Teething rings facilitate the cutting of baby teeth. They are made of thirty-two peony grains soaked in holy water for twenty-four hours and strung on a red silk string with a new needle. It is also possible to rub the gums with marsh mallow or archangel roots. Ashwood has the same virtues. Others make a child sleep on a bed of ferns or put a necklace on him or her with a viper's head on it. In addition, the father's sweat-soaked shirt is put on the child's face or else a horseshoe is placed under the pillow.

Dreaming that you lose a tooth announces the death of a relative. The sharper the pain, the more imminent the death. A tooth that falls out continues to belong to the body and can therefore be used by all evil powers. In order to protect a child, hide a baby tooth that falls out in a mouse hole or bury it in a cemetery. A child can also place the tooth under his or her pillow at night, and a little mouse will come and take it and leave a coin in exchange. In Anglo-Saxon countries, this tooth is placed on a plate with some salt near the bed, and a fairy comes by at night and takes it. It is believed that if the tooth is not taken away before midnight, the child will be the prey of evil spirits attracted by this living matter. A woman loses a tooth with the delivery of each child.

Shameful to all but very widespread, toothaches unleash superstitious imagination. Certain rules allow them to be avoided forever. The most popular of these rules recommends wearing a mole's head and hind feet in a small leather sack as a pendant. Others hide a walnut or rabbit's foot offered by their godfather in the sack. A dead person's tooth also prevents this terrible pain. It is also possible to chew garlic on the morning of May 1 before sunrise or to permanently wear a hare's left foot under your left armpit. Some bite on a piece of iron when the bells sound on

Easter Eve. You are sure to have toothaches if you eat something at the moment when the bells sound for a burial.

If all these precepts fail, others exist for lessening the pain or getting rid of it. A moled hand (a hand that has slowly choked a mole) is reputed to be all-powerful against this type of problem. It need only be placed on the tooth or gum for a few minutes. People also seek to get rid of the pain by transmitting it to another living body, either directly or indirectly by the use of a key. Some bite an olive branch three times, then toss it in water. It is also possible to get up secretly at night, kneel under a hawthorn, hang a new ribbon on it, and then return to bed after having recited five Lord's Prayers or five Hail Marys. Or take a new key, push it into the aching gum in such a way that it becomes covered with blood, and then plant it in a place inaccessible to sunlight or moonlight. You can also nail a few locks of the sick person's hair and nail clippings into the trunk of an oak. Others simply plant a nail in a tree or wall. Rubbing an aching tooth against a gold piece can undoubtedly be explained in a similar way—the pain is communicated to the metal like a soul that is being exorcized. Some bite on the bones or teeth of a hanged man.

Certain potions or cataplasms sometimes replace this magical transfer of the pain. Apply a warmed laurel or cabbage leaf on the cheek. A few people rinse their mouths with wine in which a hare was boiled or with tobacco juice that was stolen a few hours earlier. Others go to a well very early in the morning and fill a bucket with water or swallow grape skins. The ear opposite the aching tooth is plugged with a garlic clove. Certain talismans are recommended: an old, holed tooth suspended on a red silk string or a pierced bean.

In order to make a tooth fall out, you must suck on a dried asparagus root.

For treating cavities, it is recommended that a grain of incense or mustard be put in the hollow tooth. A hot garlic clove can also be placed on it. If the pain is intolerable, put the clove in the corresponding ear and not on the tooth. Finally, it is always possible to write prayers on little pieces of paper, then hold them near the swollen cheek for a few hours.

Umbilical Cord

In most civilizations, a *navel* symbolizes a divine center—God is supposedly the navel of the earth and the North Star is the navel of the sky. The navel, however, inspires few superstitions. An umbilical cord, on the contrary, more mysterious and dangerous, is surrounded by beliefs and interdictions.

In a certain way this cord remains linked to a baby: It must not be burned (the child will die in a fire) nor thrown in water (the child will die from drowning). It is buried under a white rose bush so that the baby will have a light complexion, under a pink one so that he or she will have a ruddy complexion, or under a red one so that the baby will have rosy cheeks. In any case, this rose bush assures him or her of a pleasant voice. Those who wish to have a son that is fond of good living should bury his umbilical cord at the foot of a grapevine!

This cord is also believed to be a root. If it doesn't fall off on its own after seven days—the model time of creation—a man will not really be perfect.

A pregnant woman neither spins nor sews—her baby risks being strangled by the umbilical cord. For the same reason, she tucks necklaces and pendants inside her dress.

Set in a ring, an umbilical cord has the value of a talisman against bellyaches. If a child wears a small piece of it in a sack around his neck, it assures him of good luck. Finally, a piece of a baby's umbilical cord soaked in water along with a few of his first cut hairs can cure him of all illnesses. Others mix a piece of the cord with seed to be planted—it guarantees an excellent crop.

Urine

Urine is matter and poisons that the body refuses. It is therefore lucky and permits the healing of numerous illnesses. In general, washing your hands in urine protects against sorcery and the evil eye. Rubbing a newborn's first wet diaper on your face guarantees a ruddy complexion.

When drunk or applied to a sore, urine heals snake bites, tinea, or ulcerations of the ears. When a person is struck with high fevers, his urine is saved and nettle leaves are put in it: If the leaves remain green, the person will survive; if they dry out rapidly, there is no longer any hope.

So that a child does not suffer from urinary problems, the godfather must piss facing the sun on the morning of the child's baptism. Jade protects against all bladder afflictions. To treat water retention, you must wash your hands with cold water or place some crushed leek on your belly.

Many recipes exist for "curing" children of bed-wetting. A crushed maybug worn as a pendant, rat or mole droppings, and slugs roasted in an oven are all reputed to be effective. Water in which a dead person's bones have soaked or a milk soup in which a mouse has soaked also cure bed-wetting. A child can simply be put to bed on a mattress of ferns, broom, juniper, vine shoots, or ashes.

All sailors know that they must never piss against the wind, because it will provoke the Devil who could take revenge by sending a tempest.

Virginity

This is an absolute and sacred commodity that for a long time was a woman's only marketable value. Once she was deflowered, she could no longer get married. Virginity is also exalted by the great religions that put it in opposition to the carnal act that limits men and women to their animal reality.

Virginity confers supernatural powers on women. Snakes, dragons, and especially unicorns accept food only from the hand of a virgin. They kill her if she attempts to fool them.

A virgin puts out a candle with her first breath and lights it again with her second breath.

In the Orient, she is believed to be able to fertilize the earth with a bouquet of iris in her hand. Only a virgin can go through a swarm of wasps without being stung. In Great Britain, only a virgin can stare into the sun. In Poland, she has the power to make balls of water.

If a girl forgets to put salt on the table when she is setting it, it is a sign that she has lost her virginity. In Russia, it is believed that her chest develops suddenly when she loses her virginity.

A man who has physical relations with a virgin other than his wife risks catching a venereal disease.

Man has always sought to unlock the secrets of a woman's virginity. A potion of coal powder can be administered to a girl; if she is no longer a virgin, she will immediately have the urge to urinate. In general, a girl's urine is an excellent informer. The urine of virgins is light in color, sometimes white or green; that of women is darker in color. It is also possible to take a white string and measure the size of a girl's neck with it, double the measure, and then put each end of the string in her mouth. Then she tries to put her head through the ring formed by the string. If she manages this operation without any problem, she has certainly been with a man. If she cannot get her head through the ring, it is a sign of virginity. Loose stones refuse to budge if a deflowered woman touches them with her finger.

In Central Europe, a woman who has given birth to seven illegitimate children is believed to gain back her virginity.

It has long been maintained that a man can only really lose his virginity with a prostitute. A virgin girl who puts on a prostitute's blouse is destined for the streets.

Wart

Warts are not really an illness, but a spell that it is important to conjure by giving them to another person, water, or the earth.

You can attempt to get rid of them by rubbing them with vine sap,

"Old Man and Child," by Domenico Ghirlandajo, Italy, 15th c. (Musée du Louvre)

fig milk, menstrual blood, or a roasted scraped pigskin, or covering them with spider webs or cataplasms of houseleek, but anointing them with oil from a funeral chamber lamp seems to be the most effective.

A red or black string must be tied around the wart and then tossed into the grave of someone about to be buried. It is also possible to tie a string around the wart and then throw it into a fire, or else to cut an apple in two and rub the wart with it. Put the two halves back together and, as the apple rots, it will take the wart along with it. Some rub the wart with a scraped pigskin that they then hide under a stone at night by the light of a full moon—when the pigskin rots, the wart will fall off. A person can also rub the wart with a red slug that is then stuck through with a pin or thrown into a shaft.

In order to get rid of their warts, some put a piece of silver and some stones in a little sack and abandon it on a road—the person who picks up the sack will take on the warts. It is also possible to dip your hands in a holy water basin five times and each time recite five Lord's Prayers and five Hail Marys: The next person to take some of the holy water will take on the warts. It is also said that it is sufficient to wash your hands in the only water basin of a church you are entering for the first time. Some are content to rub a wart with a genista stem that they then toss over their shoulders.

In the evening during a full moon, whoever takes away an empty dish and pretends to wash it loses his warts immediately. He can also touch each wart with a green pea and then throw it in a well. A dead mole that is rubbed on warts and then thrown into the water has the same effect. It is more complicated, but also more effective, if a person stands at a crossroads near a stream and washes his or her hands in the stream when a funeral passes. It is simpler if you dip your hands in warm ox blood or, better still, wash your hands in a bucket that belongs to a neighbor.

Whoever puts a hand in water that was used to hard-boil eggs will see it become covered with warts.

Whooping Cough

The hoarse cough of a person suffering from this affliction brings to mind the cock's crow from the family poultry yard (the French word for this illness is "coqueluche"). In order to be cured then, all that is necessary is that you eat a roasted chicken for breakfast.

Some recommend daily consumption of buttered toast with crushed slugs. Crushed snails in sugar have the same curative value. The sick person can also consume raw garlic in order to stop the coughing fits. Decoctions of mistletoe or vervain leaves and wine that has stood in a goblet carved from an ivy trunk are reputed to be excellent remedies.

Other people make the sick person drink from a bucket that a cat, horse, or mule has drunk from or give him or her dog or mare's milk. It is also possible to cross a stream without getting wet and then to walk in a pine forest. A he-goat's hair sewn on a piece of cloth in the form of a cross and worn on the chest suffocates the cough.

In Picardie, at dawn the sick person stands in the middle of a crossroad and lights a candle on the axis of the road from which he came. Then, kneeling, he or she recites three Lord's Prayers and three Hail Marys for Saint Blaise. In addition, he or she must recite five Lord's Prayers and five Hail Marys for the next nine days.

Yawn

Social code demands that you cover your mouth when yawning. This custom rests on a very ancient belief that affirms that the Devil, always on the watch, is trying to get into a human body. It is essential to bar up his route. In other regions, three or four signs of the cross have the same effectiveness.

The Arabs think that if the Devil enters through the mouth, you can simply sneeze to make him come back out through the nose. The Turks believe that the soul escapes when a person yawns, so they close their mouths as quickly as possible. In South America, yawning signifies that Death is calling you; you must snap your fingers to drive it away.

Yawning is contagious—the first one to open his mouth drags all those around him in his path. In addition, whoever forgets to close his mouth risks swallowing a fly.

Study of a nude man, by Verrocchio, 15th c.

The Great Stages
of Life

All civilizations are equal before Life and Death. Everywhere, beliefs are perpetuated—secret and magical practices are transmitted from generation to generation to make this domain a universal superstition.

Fear of the beyond, ignorance of the mysteries of pregnancy and creation, and the slow path of man from infancy to old age—all pose many distressing questions and give birth to more superstitions than the regular renewal of the earth and inexplicable atmospheric conditions.

Therefore, in an instinctive reflex of defense, we try to master the great stages of life through a celebration or some extraordinary event. To this end, the great religions and all societies have established their own festive or commemorative cycles.

On the initial canvas of human life, religions embroidered parallel designs that little by little mixed with the originals. The spiritual aspirations of the Christians expressed themselves less in birth itself than in baptism, which alone leads the way to true life. In Medieval times, dead infants were sometimes resuscitated by some miracle so that they could be brought to the baptismal font. Almost everywhere in the world, the formation of states, identified by territorial masses and governed by a self-same law, transformed activities such as education and military service into what are today essential stages in life.

Agony

Despite the spiritual influence of religions, this painful period remains the morbid equivalent of childbirth, especially to superstitious minds. Every possible way is sought to assist in delivering the soul from the body.

All sharp objects must be removed, because the soul of the dying person risks hurting itself on them. Likewise, all containers holding water are emptied so that the soul avoids drowning; windows are also opened and sometimes a tile or slate is taken off of the roof. In Alsace, it is necessary to walk around a bed three times while jingling blessed hand bells so that the evil spirits will not hold back the dying person's soul. As a general rule, salt is thrown into the hearth.

"Death and the Aristocrat," engraving from the 18th c. (Musée Carnavalet.)

In order to shorten agony, the dying person's pillows are taken away and he or she is left to lie flat. In Brittany, clogs filled with dirt are put on the dying person to symbolize the return to nature. In order to prolong agony, a duck or pigeon feather must be placed under the person's pillow. If a dying person holds on until low tide, that person will live another six hours.

Three little thumps heard in a sick person's room announce imminent death. At the end of the agony, dogs and cows who hear, smell, or see death arrive, stir and begin to cry out. The sound of a cart drawn by a black horse, both symbols of death, also signals the dying person's last hour.

Baptism

Baptism, the official birth of a child for the Church and entrance into the religious community, is the substitute for ancient immersion rites. The salt and water are supposed to cleanse the child of original impurities.

An unbaptized child who dies could not have commited any fault other than that of original sin; it takes wing toward limbo and becomes a will-o'-the-wisp, angel, or phantom. Some affirm that an unbaptized child cannot die. A child who died before being baptized was buried and rain-water was believed to replace the baptismal water.

In any case, it is proper to baptize a child as soon as possible because he or she is at the mercy of all evil spirits. The Devil can attempt to take the child's place. A child can be protected until baptism by being covered with an article of clothing from the father or by hanging herbs, bread, salt, or a piece of metal over the cradle. Also, a candle is lit at the time of birth and put out only upon returning from the baptismal ceremony. Some fire gunshots and bang on pans before the baptism to drive away demons.

Parents often believe that their child's first name plays a direct role in the development of the child's personality. They sometimes name him or her after celebrities or great people in history.The good fortune of Jesus and Mohammed is known, and at the time of the French Revolution, many children were given the names of Liberty and Equality. In general, the oldest boy carries his grandfather's first name to continue the lineage and his middle name is that of the godfather or godmother. The more given names, the happier the child will be. In general, a family choses one of the names of the twelve Apostles. The name of an illegitimate child is chosen by a priest.

A child must never be named after a dead child, nor should he or she bear the name of a dog or cat in the house—the child and the animal would die. Also, a child's given name mustn't be revealed before baptism. The parents must avoid letting the child's initials form a word, because it is a bad omen for the child. In the midlands of France, all people named Agnes are believed to be crazy, and in Great Britain, it is believed that people named George are never hanged.

On the way to the church, the person who carries the child must take the shortest path and under no circumstances turn around even if someone calls him or her. The bells must ring a full peal; otherwise the child will be deaf and sing off key.

Two children must not be baptized with the same water—the second will die, because the first has taken all the "fluid" and left its sin in the water. In Germany, it is said that the same water must not be used for a girl and a boy, because the girl would then grow a beard. The baby's face mustn't be wiped, but left to dry on its own. If the baby doesn't cry, it is a sign that the evil spirit wasn't exorcized by the holy water and the child will be mischievous and disobediant. The baptismal water must be kept and given to the child to drink later—it will make the child an excellent singer.

If a child arrives at the baptismal font before the priest, the child will be endowed with second sight. If the priest makes a mistake in reciting the "credo," the child will stutter. The baby must be held high over the baptismal font if he or she is to grow quickly. A bonnet called a "chrism cloth," annointed with holy oil, is put on the child at the time of baptism. On the mother's churching day, a woman takes the bonnet back to the church and slips a coin in it. All the chrism clothes are burned together to make the ashes used on Ash Wednesday.

In Northern England, a child shouldn't be the first one baptized in a new church because of the custom of burying a child or man under the foundations of new churches. Baptism mustn't take place after a burial, but if it is held after a wedding, the child is assured of a happy life. The idea that baptism transforms a child's spirit and body is very widespread; it is believed that from weak he becomes strong, from slow to lively, and from sad to happy.

A piece of bread that was placed in the baby's sleeve must be given to the first person encountered as you are coming out of the church. The path taken coming to church mustn't be taken when you are leaving.

Choosing the godfather and godmother must be done with caution. In general, you mustn't ask for their assistance at the child's engagement party, because the child will never marry. You must never choose a godfather or godmother who has already lost a godchild. Preferably, the godmother is a young girl or a woman without a child, but she should never be a pregnant woman, because one of the two children will die within a year unless the godmother is expecting twins. In addition, the people chosen don't have the right to refuse or else they will be excluded from Heaven. If they have to refuse, they can redeem themselves by offering a fine gift to the mother.

If the baptismal candle remains lit until the ceremony, the godfather and godmother will marry shortly.

The godfather must begin his day by pissing, so that the child will not have any problems in this regard. He must wear a clean, new shirt. If the godfather makes an error in reciting the "credo," the child will be in contact with the invisible. If the godparents look into the baptismal font during the ceremony, the child will grow to look like them. If the child cries at the time of the sacrament, it means that the godparents didn't accept their role wholeheartedly.

The godparents must embrace upon returning from the baptism to keep the child from becoming bratty. The godfather must offer a meal to the entire gathering, particularly to the midwife, who holds the place of honor. In addition, he offers candied almonds, clothing, or an engraved metal cup or mug that is sometimes put in a little chest with the umbilical cord. All these expenditures are made to assure the baby, who possesses nothing, of future, material security.

A child must not be called by its name before it is baptized.

Birth

The moment when a child is born has prophetic significance for his or her future. Certain rites can ward off evil spirits that could profit from the child's weakness.

A baby born at noon or between 11 P.M. and midnight will be unhappy; one born at exactly midnight is the prey of infernal powers, but also has the power to converse with ghosts. One who comes into the world during the morning hours will always be hungry.

Sunday is a particularly favorable birthday since it is both the sun's day and the day of Christ's Resurrection. Friday, the day of Christ's death, is the most inauspicious, except in Anglo-Saxon countries where children born on this day are believed to be loving and generous. Children born on Wednesday will have a melancholy life, those born on Thursday, a glorious future, and those born on Monday and Tuesday will be endowed with great physical charms.

When birth takes place during a full moon, the child will have much luck in life. In general, the periods of Advent and Lent are unlucky for a newborn, but he or she will be given supernatural powers, such as the ability to see ghosts and spirits. Christmas is an excellent birthdate.

The following birthdates are reputed to be unlucky in eastern France (a child born on one of these dates will die very young or live a miserable life): January 1, 2, 6, 11, 17, and 18; February 8, 16, and 17; March 1, 12, 12, and 15; April 3, 15, 17, and 18; May 8, 10, 17, and 30; June 1 and 7; July 1, 5, and 6; August 1, 3, 18, and 20; September 15, 18, and 20; October 15 and 17; November 1, 7, and 11; December 1, 7, and 11.

A child born with a blue vein, or "death artery," on his or her forehead will not live to be old. Strawberry marks result from frights, dreams, and unsatisfied desires of the mother during pregnancy. The mother is believed to be able to remove these spots with her saliva if she licks them several days in a row.

A child born with teeth will die suddenly. A newborn with forceps marks on his or her head will travel a lot and live on at least two continents. A baby born with a caul will make a great orator and will be immune to shipwrecks and drowning. A redheaded child is possessed by Satan.

When the child is born, soak the mother's wedding ring in a glass of wine and then give the child a few drops to drink—this liquid protects the child against illnesses and the evil eye. So that a child has a ruddy complexion and good health, wash his face with his first wet diaper and then immediately put him into the arms of a young girl. So that he grows well, carry him to the top of the stairway in the house. In certain regions, a child is bathed in wine as a protection against intoxication and the wind.

In Normandy, a child's hands and feet are put in ice, so that he or she will never have numbness from the cold. In order to insure success with the opposite sex, a girl's or boy's nightshirt is slipped on the baby, or the baby is covered with some of its mother's clothes (if it's a boy) or father's clothes (if it's a girl).

At the moment of birth, throw coins out of the window in order to distract evil spirits. If, at that moment, the clouds form a lamb or sheep, it is an excellent omen.

A baby must not be complimented for its beauty. Those who go against this rule must either spit on the baby or verbally retract their compliments. It is an equally bad omen to kiss a baby. A child who refuses to take a breast is said to be bewitched. A boy will be happy in life if, when he pisses for the first time, he does so over his shoulder. Tradition has it that the bells toll either three or nine times for a boy and either two or eleven times for a girl. If a baby's navel doesn't heal, take a plowshare, bury it, and recite five Our Fathers.

In most countries, a tree is planted when a child is born, because the growth of the child is imagined to follow that of the tree. The Hebrews choose a cedar for boys and a pine for girls.

A cradle must be protected from all evil spirits, devils, and goblins. A necklace of garlic and a few onions or medallions is placed there. In Alsace, the medallions have tulips on them, a symbol of happiness. These amulets keep away goblins and elves who seek to replace the baby with their own monstrous offspring. Some hang brooms upside down in doorways, drive away all the cats, or tie three knots in the cord that connects the conjugal bed to the cradle. In general, a lit candle is left near the cradle until the child is baptized.

Avoid leaving a child alone on foggy days until he has his first tooth. It is not a good idea to put too many accessories in a cradle—the baby will have bellyaches. Preparing and rocking a cradle in a house before a child's birth are dangerous games because they are attempts to foretell destiny.

The mother's placenta must not be exposed to the moon, the sun, a dog, or a cat. It is usually buried under the cellar stairway.

In certain regions of the United States, it is believed that it is best to first have a girl, then a boy. When a child is born during a waxing moon, the next baby will be of the same sex. If on a mother's churching day she first encounters a male, her next child will be a boy. The first child will have a brother or sister depending on whether it says "papa" or "mama" first. If the hair on the nape of a newborn's neck grows straight out, the next child will be of the same sex, but if the hair lies flat, the next child will be of the opposite sex.

The seventh boy of a family of seven boys has healing powers and bears a mark in the shape of an ivy leaf on the bottom of his feet.

In antiquity, the birth of twins was always considered a mark of intervention by the gods. Twins are the fruit of relations between a mortel and a god—they are endowed with extended magical powers. Today twins are still attributed with the gifts of second sight and healing powers. Being

Illustration for Rueff's "De Generatione Homini." Frankfort, 1580.

in constant connection with one another, they can even communicate from afar and share all their sensations. When one of the two dies, the other is forewarned and takes the other's vital force. (These faculties only concern identical twins—when they don't resemble each other, they will be different and in opposition on all points; one will be honest, the other damned.)

Twins symbolize the duality of the world: sky and earth, God and Devil. In some countries twins were killed; in others, they were adored.

A general superstition says that all women who eat a twinned fruit during pregnancy will give birth to twins. In the south of Africa, it is even believed that if a man eats a double banana, his wife will have twins.

When a woman is expecting twins, she should go to see an old man who will wrap some black and white thread around her left wrist in order to unite the twins and avoid their being in opposition to each other.

Twins protect those around them from illnesses and they protect navigators from tempests. They have the power to restore youth to the aged, to give men their virile power.

Celibacy

Although they are well known in popular literature, old maids, bachelors, and unmarried mothers have inspired few superstitions.

It is especially important for a young girl to know the fatal omens of celibacy. If, by various means, she seeks to make the face of her future husband appear and only the image of a coffin forms, she has no more hope of marrying. The same is true if the first person she encounters on New Year's Day is a female. A young girl who doesn't look toward the north the first time she goes outside in the mornings will always remain single. She who for no reason reads the wedding sermon will know the same fate. Finally, it is inadvisable for a young girl to sit down while talking to her sweetheart—she will no longer be able to marry him. A man who has been refused three times will never marry.

The unmarried mother, long time excluded from the community, runs the risk of propagating evil. An unmarried mother was made to wear a straw crown on her head, so that she could be recognized. She could not be a godmother.

Childbirth

Rites and superstitions that refer to this fundamental moment are, for the most part, linked to the idea of danger—danger for the mother who can lose her life and for the newborn, an easy prey for evil forces.

In a house where a woman is going to give birth, all openings by which evil spirits could enter—chimneys, doors, and windows—must be protected.

To this end, the sign of the cross or the seal of Solomon is made in front of each one of these places. A knife is also placed in front of the bedroom door, because it will stop witches from crossing. Some people throw salt in the hearth, turn brooms upside down, and chase off the cats.

The mother's bed is surrounded with all sorts of protective signs, such as a lit candle from the Candlemas, a talisman in the shape of a toad, some parsley and garlic, or the very rare stone from an eagle's nest. If the Jericho rose opens when placed in this bedroom, the birthing will go well and the child will be happy.

A future mother must put on her husband's shirt, preferably the one he wore the day of their wedding. His nightcap has the same value. She takes off all her jewelry except, of course, her wedding band. A snake-skin gathered around her neck facilitates delivery.

Before a childbirth, untie everything that is tied, such as laces, cords, and buckles. Leave no lock or door shut.

All visitors must undo knots and buckles on their clothes. To assure an easy childbirth, the woman remains seated during the reading of the Gospel at Mass. She also strings her husband's socks and shoes together.

It is dangerous to go for the midwife alone, especially at night, and forget to cross yourself.

At the moment of childbirth, the biggest bell of the church is sounded three times if you have hung a belt there belonging to the woman in labor. If the woman suffers very much, an arrow must be shot through the roof of the house or a hole made in the roof with an axe. These weapons must already have been used for killing. If the woman doesn't cry out, the child will be of good character.

In Great Britain, a child born by Caesarean section is believed to have the power to communicate with the beyond and discover hidden treasures. In addition, a child whose mother dies during childbirth is endowed with an original force that it lends to the sick with a "kiss of life." A breech baby risks dying within a short time if its legs are not rubbed with ivy leaves. But a breech baby has a gift for healing, especially muscular afflictions like sprains.

A child born with a caul will have much luck in life. This superstition was so strong that it was customary to buy the "cauls" of these newborns with gold and save them as talismans. A child born with teeth will be selfish.

After the umbilical cord is cut, it has the value of a talisman, but be careful, because witches and sorcerers use them to make potions and cast spells. It is often preferable to bury the caul under a rosebush so that the child will have a ruddy complexion and good health. Do not burn it or the child will perish with the fire.

In Alsace, the midwife lets the cord dry out, then strings eggs on it and ties the ends together. If, at the age of five, the child can undo the knot, it is a promise of a brilliant future.

After childbirth, the first man who enters into the room must put the pothook from the hearth around his neck. All men are more or less welcome, but must in any case leave their hats outside the room. In Great Britain, a woman who has just given birth must go nowhere else but to church. If she visits a female friend, the friend is assured of having a baby within a year. A new mother must rest for nine days, during which time she is advised not to eat. Also a pile of sheets is placed on her belly to make the organs go back in.

A mother who dies in childbirth comes back each night to give her breast to her baby. A pair of new shoes must be put at the foot of the mother's coffin. This woman will be accepted into Heaven without any problem.

It brings luck to embrace a newborn. But, if the first object seized by a baby is taken with the left hand, his life will be unhappy. It also brings bad luck to weigh a newborn, because it is a way of verifying the quality of God's gift.

Childhood

You must never stride over a baby, or else it will not grow. A child who passes between the spokes of a wheel or under a car will not grow either. Also, the child must eat soup! It is proper to toss the baby's first bathwater under a tree so that the baby will become a handsome adult. The feet are inferior to the head; therefore, they must be dressed before all other parts of the body, in order for a child to have good health.

Jewish tradition says that the Devil threatens a child if you call the child handsome or charming. This tradition adds that a sleeping child must never be washed, because this is a practice for the dead.

In the United States, you should never throw a baby into the air, because he will become an idiot; but if he is bald, he will be a brilliant student. In addition, if this baby urinates in the fireplace, he will be neat and well brought up.

It brings bad luck to dress a child in black, because it is a sign that he or she will not live long. In Louisiana, a Bible, a card game, and a coin are placed within the baby's reach: If he chooses the Bible he will be happy; if it's the cards, he will be a gambler; the coin indicates that he will be successful in business.

A child must be lulled to sleep on your left shoulder or else he or she will be left-handed. Finally, it is best not to let an old diaper touch a baby or the baby will become a thief.

A small child must not look in the mirror before the age of six months, because he or she will die within the year or become an epileptic before the age of one. These dangers can be avoided by making the sign of the cross on the mirror.

Cutting a baby's fingernails or toenails before the age of one will make him or her a thief. The mother must chew off the nails rather than cut them with scissors.

Two children must not kiss each other before knowing how to talk or they will become mutes.

A child must be swung nine times over the first Saint John fire that follows the birth to assure strength and health.

Teeth, signs of growth, are the object of numerous superstitions. If they first push through the lower gum, the child will be full of spirit; if they are late in cutting through, the child is bewitched. To protect this child, hang a mole's feet around the child's neck in a little sack. Large incisors foretell a glorious future; long canines, unrestrained ambition; big molars, calmness and strength, but also stubborness. The two central incisors on the upper gum are called "lucky teeth" when they are long and far apart.

In Alsace, a father wears the front feet of a male or female mole, according to the baby's sex, around his neck to hasten the appearance of the baby's teeth. A holy relic can also be put on the baby's chest. In addition, each Friday during the first quarter of the moon, a wisp of the child's hair must be cut to fortify his or her head of hair.

A child's first seven years of life are the most dangerous—evil spirits are always ready to act. In certain regions, in order to protect a child, blotters in the effigy of saints are put in his food. A child is said to attain the age of reason at seven. When he is old enough to understand what is shown to him, make him a present of bread, salt, one egg, money, and a few matches; these symbolize food, intelligence, friendship, health, and light, all appropriate for guiding him toward Heaven. In Japan, it is believed that a child who carries a gun under his arm or over his head will not grow. The same problem occurs if he covers his head with a basket.

In order to cure a child of a mouth disease, pass a straw drawn out of manure under his tongue. In general, to protect a child from all illnesses, all that is necessary is to put two crossed sickles at the foot of the bed.

Conception

In general, conception is placed under the sign of the moon, which represents celestial seed and is a symbol of fertility in India.

If a woman undresses under moonbeams, she will very likely conceive. Formerly, a bed was surrounded by curtains to guard against the light from this star that supposedly begat insane children. If a man drinks river water in which the moon was reflected, he risks becoming pregnant. In any case, it is preferable, if a child is wished for, to practice the art of love during a waxing moon. There will also be a chance of conceiving a boy at this time; if the moon is waning, the child will undoubtedly be a girl.

The entire sky presides over this crucial moment: Saturn is believed to govern conception and Jupiter to organize the matter. Mars creates the head and limbs, the sun creates the heart and soul, and Venus creates the sex. Mercury adds on the voice, eyes, hair, and nails. Finally, the moon completes the work by filling in the gaps.

Various practices allow conception to be controlled. If sexual relations take place at noon, the child will be intelligent. In order to conceive a boy, the woman must eat hare intestines or wear a belt of she-goat hair soaked in ass's milk. If the sexual relations are far apart, a girl will be born. To be sure of conceiving, the couple must consume some pig-testicle powder.

Certain signs allow a woman to determine her future. She knows she has conceived if, at the moment of the act of love, she feels a pain in her thighs, has a red face, or has unusual cravings for earth, charcoal, apples, mulberries, or cherries. She can also be given milk and honey to drink. If she suffers navel pains the next day, it is a sign that she is pregnant. Finally, if the man has a toothache, his wife is undoubtedly expecting a baby.

A man is believed to go through the phases of conception as much as a woman; therefore, if a young girl is pregnant and doesn't know who the father of her future child is, you need only look in the neighborhood for the man who is ill or confined to his bed.

Contraception

This modern practice, at least in its known forms, is tarnished by superstitions founded both on "respect for life" and still unknown aspects of certain methods.

The most widespread beliefs refer to "the pill," the most effective chemical means of contraception. It makes the women who use it insane, frigid, or sterile. Their hair and teeth fall out and their natural growth stops. They have neither a chest nor hips. The pill is ineffective for young girls who wear contacts. Finally, a child born of a mother taking the pill will be mutilated, abnormal, or mentally retarded.

Some more traditional practices can sometimes have the same outcome, but they are most often abortive. If a pregnant woman looks at herself in a mirror, weighs herself, touchs cold animal meat, enters a dead person's house, or bears false witness, a child will not be born.

Old women often put another more-or-less magical practice to work to rid a mother of a child; these old women were called "angel makers." It was believed, in fact, that stillborn, unbaptized children became angels.

Death

This third and final stage of life always awakens in man an uncontrolled fear of the unknown, a fear capitalized on by religions and societies. Death, represented by the image of a spectre with a scythe or incarnated in numerous forms, manifests its presence every day through prophetic signs that all should know how to recognize.

"The Death and a Young Girl," by Hans Baldung Grien, 1517 (Musée de Bâle).

Animals and insects can see or smell approaching death and announce it by their cries or behavior. The hooting of screech owls and wood owls in the proximity of a house, a hen that crows in front of a rooster or like a rooster, or a dog that howls without reason are all bad omens. A horse that whinnies in front of a house, the strange noise of a fish boiling, and the grating sound of furniture gnawed on by woodworms are all called "death clocks" and signal the presence of the spectre lying in wait. If a weasel crosses your path, a bird gets into the house or taps at the window, a mole digs under the house, or you encounter a moth or white hare, death will come knocking shortly. The same is true if a hen lays an egg with two yolks. (Sometimes objects crack or move themselves without reason; bells toll or glasses break on their own or trees blossom out of season.)

All objects that are involuntarily crossed, such as knives, forks, or sticks of straw, also presage death. Persons who squint or cross their arms when greeted announce death. If you see a scythe in a field, you must cross yourself. If you dream that you lose a tooth or eat rotten eggs or fish, death is at hand. If there are thirteen people for dinner, if three lamps on the table are lit at the same time, if three cigarettes are lit with the same flame, if someone does a wash on Good Friday or during Rogation Days, or if a sheet dropped in water only goes in halfway or comes out partly dry, one of the persons present is condemned to death within the year.

Some signs warn in a more precise way and announce the more-or-less imminent death of someone close, such as a relative, friend, or neighbor. When these signs manifest themselves in the morning, the death will take place shortly; when the signs are in the evening, death leaves a respite. It is known that the mothers or wives of sailors always have an intuition of danger that threatens their sons or husbands. Night is propitious for certain visions, such as a laundress washing a shroud by the side of a pond, a funeral passing in silence, invisible rowers plowing the waves in cadence, or a wife losing her wedding band. If you feel your eyes fill with tears for no reason, it's a sign that you will soon have a reason to cry. A chilling shiver indicates that death is brushing past you. Sometimes a chariot drawn by a hack horse or twelve little pigs is heard in the distance.

Death must never be simulated, because you risk its taking you at your word! You can, however, attempt to foresee the hour and cause of your passage. Some place a cross of willow twigs on a consecrated fountain—if it floats, it is a sign of approaching death. The quicker it sinks, the further away the death date. The night of May 1, at midnight, some lean over the water in a fountain—if a skeleton is reflected, the person will die shortly. On New Year's Day in Brittany, the father of a family tosses slices of buttered bread into the air while naming the members of the family one by one. The slices that fall on the buttered side indicate those who will die in the twelve months to come. On the night of the Epiphany, you can also write the names of the Wise Men on your forehead with your own blood, then look in the mirror. It will reflect both your time of death and the circumstances.

A husband and wife must add the number of letters in their given names in order to know which of the two will die first. If the letters add up to an even number, the husband will depart first; if it's an odd number, it will be the wife.

Some know how to "vow" a relative to death by means of dolls stuck through with pins. Or, under the bed of their victim, they place earth from the cemetery, coffin nails, salt, or nail clippings mixed with bones. These people can also go to Sunday Mass before eating and slip a silver coin with a hole in it into the pocket of the person whose death they desire.

At the moment of death, the clock in the house must be stopped. In addition, all mirrors are veiled to keep the deceased from seeing into his destiny in the beyond. Some believe that the dead person's soul risks getting lost in the mirror or that dead souls might come through this window to visit their new friend. For various reasons, water in buckets and all other containers absolutely must be thrown out after a death—the dead person's soul could drown itself or simply wash itself of its sins, passing them on to the living. It is also believed that a soul passes through water or milk to get to heaven; saving these liquids, therefore, slows down the soul's taking wing.

In Jewish tradition, Death was supposedly a spirit armed with a sword dipped in three drops of poison: The first blow from this weapon kills a sick person, the second makes him a pale and deformed creature, and the third makes him a repugnant corpse. Therefore, water in a house is thrown out after a death because Death perhaps dipped its sword in it.

This volatile soul can, however, present itself to the living in the form of a fly, gnat, white mouse, bee, or hummingbird. Consequently, it is best to avoid sweeping or dusting the house.

The news must be announced to the bees and fruit trees that might take offence at being neglected or wait in vain for the deceased.

When a dead person keeps his eyes open, he is waiting for someone to join him. Formerly, the eyes of a condemned person on top of a funeral pyre were opened so that he might see the sky.

A dead person's laundry must be done separately so that death doesn't spread in the family. Also, a table setting is kept for the evening of the death so that the deceased can regain strength before taking wing toward the beyond. The Bretons leave a pitcher of milk near the body to "whitewash" it of its sins before Judgment Day.

If the flowers in the death chamber wither immediately, the dead person's soul is damned. But, if upon leaving the cemetery, you shout the deceased's name three times and hear only one echo, the deceased is in Heaven. Any money buried by the deceased must be uncovered; otherwise, he or she will never have a tranquil soul. Likewise, the family must uphold its promises and carry out the deceased's plans. At the moment when the body is lowered into the grave, the priest is informed of the dead soul's destiny by an unknown sign, but he isn't allowed to reveal the information. Some of the men present can burn the deceased's mattress at a crossroads—if the smoke goes up vertically, the soul is already in Heaven. On the other hand, the smoke might point toward the house that will next be touched by death. In any case, the deceased's finger must be rubbed against a mirror to liberate his soul.

In Brittany, children kiss the corpse, so that they will have good health. This kiss keeps you from being troubled by an untimely return of the deceased. For the same reason, the shroud and socks of the deceased are sewn together.

VIOLENT DEATHS

If, at the precise moment of birth, the clouds surround the moon, the child will end up drowned or hanged. In general, the soul of anyone who dies a violent death wanders on earth until the date arranged by destiny. These souls in torment take the form of ectoplasms, phantoms, or spirits.

A murder victim remains on earth until the guilty person is expiated or buried wearing the shoes he wore at the time of the crime.

A cross is erected at the scene of the crime; passersby toss a stone at

"The Triumph of Death" (detail), by Breugel the Elder (Madrid, Musée du Prado).

the foot of it to ward off demons. If the assassin enters the room where his victim's body is being viewed, the victim's wound reopens and begins to bleed. An instrument used in a crime wounds all who try to use it afterward. When a farmer cuts his hand with his sythe, he often thinks that it once armed the hand of a criminal.

Hanged persons remain suspended between heaven and hell forever, but those who hang themselves do not go to hell. As is his custom, the Devil waits near a dying person's mouth for his last breath, ready to seize his soul. But a hanged person's soul comes in contact with the rope and seeks another exit. Mandrake grows under the gallows; it is born of a hanged virgin's semen. After a hanging, the rope is not untied but cut—it is a highly sought-after talisman. A hanged man's fat and right hand are used by sorcerers. A wig made of this person's hair can make you invisible.

When someone drowns, he stays in the same place until someone comes to take his place. In a tempest, drowned souls can be heard groaning—they are trying to catch hold of the sides of the boat. Drowned women let their hair trail behind them; the hair gets tangled up in propellers and oars. It is believed that a person cannot drown without first coming to the surface three times. In addition, a drowned corpse reappears seven to nine days after the accident. You must never help a person who is drowning because it defies the nautical gods who are claiming a death. He must be left to their mercy. Sailors do not hoist a drowned body on board, but let it trail behind the boat; if the body pulls up alongside the planking, one of the members of the crew will die shortly. Drowned men float on their bellies, but drowned women float on their backs.

Souls in torment sometimes wander on phantom vessels that navigate with all black sails and are identified by the cries of crew members who moan and call out for help. No one has been able to approach these vessels; in general, they announce a tempest or bad weather.

In China, it is believed that the dead come back once a year on the last night of the year. A door must be left open for them and a bed, food, and water prepared for them. Unsatisfied dead persons track down negligent living people. (See All Saints' Day.)

Engagement

Formerly this religious ceremony had as much value as a wedding ceremony; an engaged man could not marry another without being accused of bigamy. This exchange of promises, made concrete by a ring offered to the young woman, must not be broken.

Before the exchange of promises, the man must let his hat fall on the ground and touch the young woman's left hand with his right hand.

There is but one engagement. If a man or woman gets engaged two times, he or she goes to hell; a third time the Devil seizes the soul.

In Brittany, a young man who wishes to get engaged must take part in a ritual: On the night of May 1 he hangs a hawthorn branch on the door of the one he loves; if the young woman refuses him, she substitutes cauliflower for the hawthorn.

A young man never asks for a girl's hand in marriage in person; he sends one or several representatives to the girl's family (preferably one is a good speaker: a taylor, miller, or tavern keeper). If these people are drawn back by some invisible force, stumble, sneeze, or have ears that ring during their mission, they can immediately abandon all hope, because these are signs that a marriage will be unhappy. This is also true if they encounter a monk, priest, lame man, blind man, hunchback, virgin, an entangled woman, a pregnant woman, dog, cat, horse, lizard, stag, roe deer, wild boar, or magpie. On the other hand, if these people hear thunder rumbling in the distance or have a left ear that rings and a bleeding left nostril, it is an excellent omen. The marriage will be even happier if on their way they come across a courtesan, wolf, she-goat, cicada, pigeon, toad, or spider.

A young woman must hide when a parson or notary arrives, so that her lover is obligated to look for her and offer her more gifts.

Finally, two people who are engaged bury their past life by breaking plates and glasses. This should assure them of a prosperous future.

If a family refuses a fiance, they stand up some embers in the fireplace or place a frying pan upside down in the fireplace. The girl's mother receiving the guests with a flat cake is also a sign of refusal.

Once a contract is sealed, the two young people close their fists, lock their little fingers together, drink from the same glass, and cut the bread together with the same knife.

If a member of the parish dies during the engagement period, the marriage will be unhappy. During this period, people must also abstain from killing.

On the eve of a wedding, the dowry is taken to the fiance's family who must pretend to refuse it. But sometimes the rite ends in fighting.

Before the official engagement, lovers consult each other in various ways: They rub their hips together, squeeze each other's hands, tap on each other's knees, hold hands during a ball, or pinch or touch hands through a holed stone. A young man can also signal his desire for a young woman by offering her a cake in a phallic shape, a ring, or a basket. If she accepts opening a ball with a man by going under the umbrella there, it is a definite engagement.

Funeral

This social and religious ceremony seeks to assure a dead soul's bliss and facilitate its passage toward the beyond. It is also a last homage given to the deceased by the living who do, however, organize everything so that the deceased cannot come back and bother them. In addition, it is known that, especially in Western countries today, funerals mask the reality of death. Various death practices, such as cannibalism, embalming, and cremation, are not dealt with as much here as the burial itself, which is at the origin of most of our superstitions.

During preparation for a funeral, a house must not be swept or dusted because there is a risk of hitting or even chasing away the dead soul. No one must work in the house—it would insult the deceased.

A watch beside a dead person begins with a eulogy. The deceased must never be left alone, because the Devil could seize his soul. A glass of wine or thirteen candles are set around the bed; in the case of the glass of wine, each family member clinks glasses with the deceased and wishes him a good journey. The watch ends at midnight and the assistants are then authorized to eat, but they must leave a little pot of honey near the

A poor man's funeral procession, lithography from the 19th c. (Bibl. des Arts Déco.)

bed in case the deceased's spirit decides to escape in the form of a fly (it must be nourished before its final flight toward the beyond).

A coffin must leave a house head first. The pallbearers have the same trade as the deceased or are in the same position—bachelors are pallbearers for bachelors, sailors for other sailors. The house must never be left empty during the burial, otherwise the dead soul remains to watch after it. Also, at least one door is left open, otherwise in returning from the cemetery, a terrible dispute will break out in the family.

It is inadvisable to postpone a burial, especially for an entire weekend. In effect, the body would remain exposed on a Sunday and Death, unsatisfied, would begin to look for someone else. Since Christ died on a Friday, it is a taboo day for burials. Finally, no one should attend a funeral without being invited—it would be a fatal risk.

A funeral procession must never be discontinuous or stopped, because it would then be possible for the deceased's soul to escape and transform itself into a phantom, hostile toward those gathered. On the other hand, if the horses that draw the hearse stop on their own, they must not be whipped; wait until they decide to go again. Whoever drives the hearse walks beside the horses, but never gets on them. When a procession is on its way to a church, the participants must mark each crossroad with a cross so that the deceased can find his way on Judgment Day or if he wants to return. When it passes near a calvary, it is a good idea to touch the head of the coffin to the foot of the cross. The head of the coffin should also touch a wall of the church. The attendants stop singing when they cross over a bridge. If, when the deceased is taken back to his house for the watch, the hearse crosses a bridge, the attendants avoid following the same route. In any case, they never cross over the same bridge twice. The pallbearers often put a rosemary branch in their mouths because this plant is a symbol of life.

Those who see a funeral procession pass must kneel or bow their heads; it is an insult to the dead person to stay at a window or in a doorway. Men take off their hats—if they leave them on and follow the procession a few minutes, they can be certain of dying in the next few days. Counting the number of vehicles in a cortege brings misfortune, since it corresponds to the number of years you have to live. In Scotland, it is believed that sunlight that rests on the face of one of the participants designates him as the next to die.

Coming across an empty hearse brings luck, but turning around to watch it drive away brings misfortune.

A grave must not be dug on a Sunday, a day when all activity is forbidden. Throwing a rose in the grave is a bad omen for the deceased, unless a stranger is present; otherwise, the deceased's soul will never know peace. In addition, gravediggers are known to always be intoxicated. In the United States, it is believed that those who do rubbings of gravestones in old cemeteries risk losing their memories.

Upon returning from the burial, everyone must wash his or her hands in front of the deceased's house; then the towel or cloth must be thrown over the roof of the house. It is also possible for the last person to wipe his hands to put the towel on a windowsill and say the Lord's Prayer and one Hail Mary every day until the wind carries off the towel. If you cry too much for the deceased, you will insult him and show that you believe that he is damned; if he is already in Purgatory, it will slow down his salvation. There should be a tone of gaiety, even drunkenness, during the funeral meal.

In some countries, people wear black clothes to a funeral in order to deceive the Devil (he reputedly cannot see the color black). In the same spirit, aboriginal populations of Australia paint their bodies white to make themselves invisible to evil spirits.

When a sailor dies and his body cannot be found, an imaginary funeral is held. During the watch, two towels are laid in a cross on a table and a picture of the deceased or an object belonging to him, as well as a little wax cross, is laid on top of the towels. All of this is taken to the church and placed on the catafalque. The wax cross, representing the body, is kept at the church and taken to the cemetery once a year.

Love (Encounter With)

In the more prosaic superstitions, this grand poetical idea is confused with the popular belief that a shoe exists for every foot and a lid for every pot. Love, very quickly linked to marriage, is perceived in a rather utilitarian perspective—it is a matter of provoking, maintaining, or controlling it.

First it is a matter of finding out if a person will be loved. A young girl takes a holly leaf and touches its points one by one saying, "Daughter, wife, widow, nun," the last point indicating her destiny. In order to know who the man is who will love her, she can call upon her star exclaiming, "Beautiful star, tell me if someone loves me." After she gathers three wild herbs and places them under her pillow, her star will show her the man of her life in a dream. She can also pick out of a crowd the man who loves her. For this, everyone must be brought together around a round table. A bottle is placed in the middle of the table and spun around, and the bottle-neck will point toward the sweetheart.

If a young girl holds a mirror over a well, she will see the image of the man who loves her. If she sleeps with a mirror under her pillow, she will dream of this man. A girl who encounters two men in a row on New Year's morning will have a suitor within the year.

In the United States, a girl who wants to meet the man of her life must stand by her house and count ten red cars, see a redheaded girl dressed in mauve, and see a man with a green tie. The man who follows this last person will be the man in question! A man need only eat the last piece of bread at a meal and wait for the first girl to come along.

Certain signs confirm that a person is loved. A fluttering left eyebrow, a lamp that flickers, or a fire that crackles all let you know that a heart burns for you from afar. A girl whose dress gets caught in brambles knows that a man is looking for her. A man who finds a white thread on his shirt collar knows that he is loved by a blond woman.

After an apple seed is shaken in a hat, the pointed end indicates in which direction the loved one lives.

In order to measure the intensity of love, it is best to apply the most widespread method: Pick off the petals of a daisy one by one saying, "I love you, a little, a lot, passionately, to distraction." The flower itself defines the situation. It is also possible to flick a cherry pit into the air with the thumb and index finger—the higher it goes, the deeper the love. Some snap their fingers and measure the intensity of love by the noise that is made.

If all these formulas are ineffective, others, fortunately, exist for provoking love in an unknown person or in a loved one. Powder from a Spanish fly or a crushed hippomanes (a black piece of flesh that adorns a foal's forehead at birth) is to be consumed by the candidate of your choice. A drop of your blood taken on a Good Friday, then dried and mixed with a hare's genitals and a dove's liver, is enough to make the person who consumes it fall madly in love with you. You can also sprinkle a rosebush with your blood, then make the person you want to attract sniff one of the roses. In Great Britain, blood taken from a man's finger on his left hand must be poured into the beverage belonging to the woman he wants to seduce. A woman, on the other hand, can make a man eat some bread impregnated with a few drops of menstral blood. In order to make herself loved, a girl must take a few hairs from the man she likes, offer them at the alter three times, then mix them with her own hair. She also has the possibility of boiling the hairs and lint found on one of this man's dirty shirts.

A bashful lover sometimes hides a hair from a wolf's tail in the food of the person who is the object of his dreams. Also, a ring that has been in a swallow's nest for nine days can be slipped on a loved one's finger. The white stone from a cock's head has the same virtue: Before taking the stone, you must stab the cock four times, then put it in a stew pan and bury it in an anthill for five days. Fingernail clippings secretly stolen from a girl can be mixed into her food. In addition, a loved one can be made to drink a liquid into which a few pinches of bone powder from someone recently deceased have been slipped. In order to conjure love potions, a man has only one recourse: taking off his shirt and pissing first on the collar then on the right sleeve. A few pieces of nutmeg that are swallowed, spit out, and then crushed will have a wonderful magical effect. Finally, a young man can pick the most beautiful "apple of love" from his garden, core it, and slip a piece of paper into the center on which he has written his name and that of his beloved, and then tie it with six strands of hair. Placed under a woman's bed, this apple doesn't shrivel until love has won the person over.

In order to attract a person you love, stick two pins into a candle, and then light the candle—when the flame reaches the pins, the loved one will knock on the door.

Once love has been conquered, it must be protected from sorcery, as well as from the impulsive instincts of certain people.

In general, a benumbed little finger or sudden palpitations of the heart inform you of a spell that a loved one is preparing for you. In order to maintain love, the best thing to do is to sniff marrow from a wolf's left foot from time to time. Also you must carry with you half of the laurel leaf that your beloved gave to you. In Germany, girls light three candles on the wrong end and recite three Our Fathers. Finally, it is inadvisable to take embers out of a fire. For a long time it was believed that lovers should not have their picture taken if they wanted to protect their feelings for each other.

All talismans of love must be placed under the sign of Venus and offered on a Friday. Love letters must always be written in ink, a bloodlike substance. If your hand shakes while you are writing, it is a sign of mutual love. The best sign is an ink blot because it indicates that the other person is thinking of you. In a letter you must not ask for a postcard, because it will cast a shadow over the love. Also, if a letter arrives damaged or improperly stamped, it announces an approaching misfortune. In Scotland, letters are not mailed on Christmas, February 29, or September 1. In general, letters should not be mailed on Sundays. In addition, it is ill-advised to burn love letters. A person who dares to commit such an act, however, can foretell his future: If the flame is high and light in color, the love will remain ardent: if it is weak and blue, the love will die out quickly.

It is said that love strikes those whom it chooses like a bolt of lightning. And everyone knows that a loving heart is instantly broken by Cupid's arrows.

In general, it is believed that men who have large hands and feet and women who have large mouths have sex organs that are larger than average. Due to the sun's influence, Latins are supposed to have a particular virile energy. It is also affirmed that too much sex tires the heart and makes a person go blind.

FIDELITY

A betrayal usually appears to be linked to a spell and it is necessary to drive it away.

A person is informed of infidelity by certain signs: a sudden blow to the heart, a numbing of the little finger on the left hand, or even by excessive wins in gambling. Certain potions allow a person assurance of his beloved's fidelity. The beloved can be made to eat wolf's marrow or wolf's eyelashes and whiskers can be burned, reduced to a powder, and then mixed into the beloved's food.

Engraving from the 19th c. illustrating an English custom relative to wives who deceived their husbands.

Also, before going on a trip a man must make love to his wife and smear himself with honey mixed with her hair. Upon returning, in order to regain his wife's love, he must perform the ritual again with his own hair and a little chive.

Marriage

This religious sacrament or civil ceremony has put the ancestral tradition of abduction of a woman by a man into ritual form. A clan or group steals the wealth of another by seizing one of its women. This practice is explained by the forbidding of marriage within one's family.

Marriage plays such an important role in social life that young people are anxious to know if they have any chance of reaching it. In

Brittany, a girl asks the first cuckoo she sees in the year how long it will be before she will marry. The number of cries from the bird corresponds to the number of years of waiting. She can question a fountain while letting her pitcher fall into it. The number of air bubbles that comes to the surface equal the number of years left to wait. The number of leaves that fall from a salad bowl when a girl tosses a salad or the number of seeds that remain on a dandelion after she has blown on it have the same significance. The most common practice consists of her putting a mirror under her pillow; if she dreams about a coffin, it is a sign of celibacy, but she can also dream about her future husband. At night, from nine to midnight, the girl can set herself in front of three lights and stare at them without stopping, so that the mirror will be effective. She can open her window on the night of the last day of February and the first day of March and say, "Hello, March. How are you, March? When I go to sleep, let me see the husband of my life." A girl who eats an apple in front of a mirror with her eyes closed will, after the apple is eaten, see the face of her future husband over her shoulder. On New Year's Eve, she can dip a mirror in a spring and the mirror will reflect the man who is promised to her. If, on the eve of the Epiphany, she slips three laurel leaves or her garters under her pillow; if, on the night of Saint John, she calls upon the stars; or if, seven nights in a row while the moon is still in its first quarter, she calls upon the moon; she will dream of her future husband that night.

At night, this girl can also go to a pond, walk around it three times tossing a coin in each time, go back home walking backwards, and go to bed. She will see her future husband in a dream. She can also take an apple and peel it so that there is only one peel, and then throw it over her shoulder. If the peel breaks, she will marry a nobleman who has as many titles of nobility as there are pieces.

It is also possible to meet one's future husband or wife in the flesh. Seven Sundays in a row, a girl can throw a hawthorn berry on the ground and when the moment of consecration is sounded during a Mass. On the last Sunday, a boy will present her with some holy water—and he will be her husband. If a girl catches sight of one hundred white horses in a day, the last will be ridden by her future husband. In general, a boy has fewer means of foreseeing his conjugal future. However, just as he is getting up in the morning, he can hold a mirror in his left hand—the first face that is reflected there will be that of his future wife. A girl who clips her nails nine Fridays in a row will meet the man destined for her on the Sunday that follows the ninth Friday.

Some signs determine the imminence of marriage. On New Year's Day, a bachelor should toss his right shoe into the air—if it falls back to the ground right side up, he will marry within the year. Whoever succeeds in blowing all the seeds off a dandelion, whoever finds a four-leaf clover without having looked for it, or whoever unintentionally finishes a bottle of wine during a feast can be assured of marrying within the year. A girl can fling a pin at the gown of a statue of the Virgin Mary in a church. If the pin stays stuck to a fold in the gown, the girl will marry before the New Year. If the pin falls, she must begin the operation again—each failure delays her marriage one year. In Brittany, a girl can toss nine peas from a peapod into a fountain. If they all disappear, her wedding is near. In central Europe, a blindfolded girl should pick a branch from two plants in the garden and tie them together with a ribbon. If she chose two branches from different species, she can hope to marry soon.

A marriage proposal, lithography from 1820.

If you really want to get married, it is necessary to assist destiny by jumping over nine different fires on the night of Saint John. Parisian lovers pick a few box leaves that grow on the grave of Abélard and Héloise in the Père-Lachaise cemetery.

A wedding will not take place at the scheduled hour if the fiancée tears her dress in a bramble bush or boils the water that was meant for doing the dishes. A fiancée who cleans a saucepan with a piece of bread will have a bad marriage.

An adolescent girl who sings from the moment she wakes up will not find happiness in marriage except with a crazy man. She who likes cats will marry a handsome man. A boy with clammy hands will find a young and pretty wife; if his hands are dry and cold, he will marry an ugly creature.

LUCKY AND UNLUCKY PERIODS

Certain periods are inadvisable, even forbidden, for celebrating a wedding. Times that are particularly unlucky are Lent and fasting days—they are taboo. Getting married must be avoided during a waning moon or during the three days that follow a new moon. Likewise, getting married after sunset must be avoided because the couple will be unhappy and their children will be stillborn. Either one of the spouse's birthdays is also not recommended.

Certain months prove to be more favorable than others for celebrating this ceremony:

- In January, the bride risks becoming a widow very early on.
- If married in February, the two parties will deceive each other.
- March couples will both be lonely.
- May is the last month a person should get married in because it is named after the goddess Maia, Vulcan's wife and protector of elderly people. At this time, Romans offered gifts to the dead and the Church has made it the month of the Virgin Mary.
- June, on the contrary, is the ideal month; it is, in fact, placed under the sign of Juno, Jupiter's wife, who presides over the happiness of married couples.
- Those who marry in July risk having some regrets.
- But in August, your spouse will live surrounded by loyal friends.
- A September couple will have a tranquil and serene life.
- An October couple will have financial problems.
- In November, on the contrary, the spouses also marry fortune.
- A December couple will love each other a little more every day.

The days of the week can also determine the future of the marriage. Mondays and Tuesdays are by far the best days—one brings fortune, the other health. Thursdays, on the other hand, are completely covered with shame because it is believed that a man married on this day has every chance of being a cuckold. Since a Wednesday wedding night ends on a Thursday, the third day of the week is also not very appreciated. Neither Sunday nor Saturday is lucky, even though most weddings take place on Saturday. In Alsace, however, unlucky days for weddings are considered to be Mondays, Wednesdays, and Fridays.

A person must not get married on a martyr's feast day, because the union will break apart very quickly. The birthday of a widow in the family must be avoided—one of the two spouses will die very quickly. In contrast, certain dates during the year have a reputation for favoring the future of newlyweds: January 2, 4, 11, 19, and 21; February 1, 3, 10, 19, and 21; March 3, 5, 13, 20, and 23; April 2, 4, 12, 20, and 22; May 2, 4, 12, 20, and 23; June 1, 3, 11, 19, and 21; July 1, 3, 12, 19, 21, and 31; August 2, 11, 18, 20, and 30; September 1, 9, 16, 18, and 28; October 1, 8, 15, 17, 27, and 28; November 5, 11. 13, 22, and 25; and December 1, 8, 10, 19, 23, and 29.

The weather conditions on a wedding day also influence the couple's life. Rain announces either wealth or a sad future. Wind is a sign of misunderstanding. A cloudy, heavy sky is full of innuendos: The husband will be cunning, the wife frivolous. The number of snowflakes indicates the number of coins and future children. Finally, if there is good weather, there is no cloud on the horizon!

The wedding ceremony immunizes the couple against venereal diseases.

Two sisters must not marry two brothers, because fortune cannot favor both couples at the same time. A woman who changes her name but keeps the same initials after marrying will regret her childhood once she is married. In addition, jasmine must not be offered to a woman who is getting married, because she will be sick or die within the year.

THE PREPARATIONS

The groom wears new clothes that he saves to wear in his coffin. He puts three grains of salt or three coins in his left pocket. It is he who must offer the bride her shoes into which he will have slipped a coin.

A bride must not make her wedding gown herself. Brides have been dressed in white since the beginning of the century. Red is strictly forbidden, and the slightest spot of this color on a gown is an omen of terrible misfortune. Green is a sign of jealousy.

The gown must be made of silk because satin brings misfortune and velvet is an omen of poverty. Also, prints, birds, or floral patterns are a bad omen.

The bride's mother's gown remains the most capable of bringing her happiness and fertility.

The garments must be brought by the tailor or seamstress before sunrise. If a string hangs out, it must be burned with a holy candle. In Alsace, if the seamstress sticks herself while adjusting the wedding dress, it is said that the bloodstain must be left because it promises eternal happiness. The dress must not be shown to spinsters who could have the evil eye. The fiance does not have the right to see his fiancée in her wedding dress before the day of the ceremony. The future bride must avoid putting on her wedding dress and she must be even more careful not to look at herself in a mirror when trying it on before that day. In Anglo-Saxon countries, brides traditionally wear "something old, something new, something borrowed, something blue." The "old accessories" are preferably shoes or a handkerchief.

A bride's crown is made of rosemary, myrtle, or, more often, orange blossoms, symbols of purity. A pregnant woman has the right to only a straw crown.

A veil protects a bride from evil spirits who are attracted by her beauty. Its purpose, therefore, is to hide her features.

The ribbons that surround a bride's bouquet symbolize the wishes of happiness formulated by her friends.

On the eve of the wedding, the fiance breaks some plates in front of his future wife's door. This gesture is linked to both an ancient destruction rite that brought happiness and to a symbolic loss of virginity.

The bride cries before leaving for the church and crushes an egg with her left foot when leaving her father's house. In going to the church, you should never take detours or shortcuts. The procession begins to advance on the third toll of the bells. If the bride loses a heel or someone steps on her train, the couple's unity risks being compromised. The marriage is in danger if the procession encounters a policeman, priest, doctor, lawyer, or a blind man. If the procession comes across a funeral, the sex of the deceased indicates which of the two spouses will die first. The worst sign is a groom who loses his hat.

THE CEREMONY

Once inside the church, the big question is to know which of the two spouses will die first and who will wear the pants in the family. If a candle goes out during the sacrament, the spouse who is closest to it will die within the year. The first one to rise up after the priest's benediction will be the first to die. A man who wants to assure himself of the direction of his family must step on his wife's train or, better still, on her foot! If the

"A Republican Marriage," engraving from the revolutionary period by Legrand (Musée Carnavalet).

wedding ring does not go past the second knuckle, the woman will wear the pants in the family.

The ring, a symbol of eternity, is put on the fourth finger of the left hand because it was long believed that a vein ran directly from the ring finger to the heart. Breaking or losing this wedding band is an omen of death for one of the spouses. If it falls during the service or at the justice of the peace, only the priest or civil servant can pick it up in order to exorcize the misfortune. When the groom raises the bride's veil to kiss her, she must burst into tears so she won't cry for the rest of her life. During the ceremony, a joker who wants to know which of the two spouses is more jealous tosses nuts at their backs or sticks them from behind. The first one to turn around is certain to be the most possessive.

AFTER THE CEREMONY

The procession must enter and leave by the same door. In coming out of the church, someone runs ahead to inform the dead of the event so that they do not come and complain for not having been invited. Rice is thrown on the newlyweds as a sign of fertility; confetti can be thrown, but it must not touch them. If the wedding party encounters a funeral or a pig in its path, it is an omen of misfortune. But a black cat, a chimney-sweep, or an elephant are excellent signs for the couple's future.

During the wedding dinner, it is advisable to break as many dishes

"The Young Bride," imagery by Épinal, beginning of the 19th c. (Musée Carnavalet)

as possible in order to attract happiness. Young bachelors present at the meal must steal the bride's garter and one of her shoes that will be put up for auction and make excellent talismans. Likewise, the veil must be torn up and distributed among those present.

A fiancée never participates in the making or decorating of the cake and avoids tasting it before the wedding dinner or else she will lose the love of her future husband. Being a symbol of fertility and good luck, this cake was popular with the Romans, who crumbled it up over the couple. In certain countries, the eating of cake is in itself a marriage ceremony. In England, all the guests bring a cookie that is then crushed on the floor of the reception hall. If the newlyweds succeed in kissing while standing over the crumbs but not touching them, the marriage will be happy. In China, a piece of cake is always saved for those absent. It brings misfortune to refuse them a piece. The bride must not forget to eat a piece if she wants her husband to remain faithful. Some young girls put a piece of wedding cake under their pillows in order to dream about their future husbands.

Wedding presents themselves have a significance. If a vase or other object is broken on this occasion, the couple will have a serious quarrel. If plants wither, the marriage runs the risk of not lasting long.

BRIDESMAIDS

Originally bridesmaids protected the bride when the despoiled clan attempted to take back their property. A bridesmaid's dress is preferably blue, pink, or yellow. When the bride tosses her bouquet into the air, a bridesmaid hopes to catch it because it is a sign that she also will get married. But, if she trips in walking up to the alter, it is more probable that she will remain single.

In addition, it brings misfortune to be a bridesmaid three times, but it is possible to be one four times without any problem.

ALONE AT LAST!

Before entering the house, the husband throws an egg over the roof. If the egg breaks on the tiles, the wife will be head of the household. In memory of a time when a woman, taken away against her will, tried to flee, it is customary for the husband to carry his new wife over the threshold when the couple enters their house for the first time. A handful of mistletoe is hung from the door in order to assure them a happy life. In Austria, a new bride immediately throws three of her hairs in the fireplace. It is the husband who must shut the front door before going to bed or a quarrel will break out during the night.

Formerly, tradition had it that young newlyweds not consummate the marriage for three days in order to save a soul from Purgatory. The first day was consecrated to God, the second to Mary, and the third to Joseph. On the wedding night, the first one to put out the candle or fall asleep will be the first to die.

Military Service

Being obligatory in numerous countries, this stage of life is known as an initiating period that makes a man out of a boy.

Less than a century ago the most important phase of military service consisted of drawing numbers to find out who would not be sent too far away from his people! In France, on the day of the drawing, many young men had a Mass said, placed a talisman in their left shoes, or carried a human bone in their pockets. It was necessary to avoid walking backward or to clamber up a stairway two steps at a time. Today, those who seek to be exempt continue the tradition.

In general, it is believed that a soldier who is leaving for the army must not turn his head back to salute his village, because he will not see it again in his life.

Nursing

For a long time, particularly in towns, this task was entrusted to a wet nurse who watched the child for a few years. Today, it is preferable for the mother to nurse her child so that he or she will be normal.

If some milk trickles from a child's chest, it is said that a devil came to suckle him or her during the night. Likewise, a child who refuses to suck the mother's breast is said to be bewitched; in this case, an exorcist must be called and all openings to the house must be protected against possible evil spirits.

In order to promote the coming of maternal milk, women are advised to drink beer, eat a mixture of fennel and honey, or make themselves a cataplasm of parsley.

A wet nurse must take various precautions so that her milk does not dry up: She should never respond to calls from outside, burn wood in the fireplace, or hold a needle by its point. She must also spit on those who stare at her when she is out walking her suckling. Weaning is a period that is almost as decisive as birth, because it corresponds to the moment when a child is really separated from the mother. A baby who has been weaned must never be put to the mother's breast again, or the child will become an accomplished liar. A child weaned in the spring will turn gray earlier than others. In addition, a child must never be weaned on a Good Friday or he or she will not eat again.

Old Age

Old age must be accepted without reserve because to ignore it is a sacrilegious act that only the Count of Saint-Germain and Cagliostro can commit. But today people still dream about a fountain of youth. Duplicating the water from such a fountain was one of the goals of alchemy that researched drinkable gold and elixirs of long life. This beverage was supposed to darken white hair, make teeth grow back where others had fallen out, and transform dull-witted old man into a young man full of desires.

In Brittany, elderly people awaited their death omen; this omen took the form of a granddaughter or great-granddaughter called a "grave-digger."

Pregnancy

It is believed that a pregnant woman is attended by diabolical spirits—her touch alone brings misfortune. It is dangerous to touch her, and she should be separated from the food and life in a house. In a certain way, a pregnant woman, like a menstruating woman, is taboo.

Legends have always been invented in order to answer children's questions about the origin of babies. It is often said that little boys are born in cabbage patches and little girls in rose bushes. It is sometimes a cat but usually a stork that delivers a baby to the mother or midwife; sometimes the latter goes and picks him from a tree or looks for him near a sacred rock. A very ancient belief was that of wells for children, often consecrated to the Virgin Mary. Every night she descended to earth and transformed well water into milk and nourished the orphans and abandoned children. As a general rule, it is a doctor or midwife who goes to look for a baby in a place or even a store where all babies wait to be chosen.

A pregnant woman must not spin yarn, sew, or knit, because she risks strangling her child with the umbilical cord. She also risks harming her baby if she sees a priest putting on his garb, especially just at the moment when he is putting on the belt of his alb. She must not bow down two times in a row, pass under a table or clothesline, wash windows, or cross her legs. Her child will die if she looks at herself in a mirror or even weighs herself. She must not walk on a grave or approach death in any form—her child will die immediately. If she enters a dying person's chamber, her child will have a white spot called a "bier" over his or her nose. A false witness on the mother's part will have the same effect. She cannot be a godmother, must avoid approaching the alter, and must especially fear a glance from sorcerers. In Germany, it is said that in order for her to avoid a premature birth, it is a good idea for the future mother to carry one of her husband's socks.

A pregnant woman spoils food: If she touches milk, it goes sour; wine turns into vinegar when she enters a cellar.

A pregnant woman is subject to many troubles; in the Middle Ages it was believed that her uterus came out on some nights to go bathe itself. In order to protect herself from illnesses and evil influences, she must be made to wear a talisman on which there is an outline of a toad. In a general way, this animal that symbolizes the womb favors pregnancy. So that a woman has an easy delivery, she must wear a blessed belt or a little birthing sachet of Saint Marguerite.

The most widespread superstition is that everything that a woman does, thinks, sees, hears, and dreams will have repercussions on the baby's spirit and body. A future mother must not look at a monster or anything ugly, because the child will be in the image of what she saw. If she comes across a hunchback, her baby will be deformed. If she touches a rabbit, her child will have a harelip; if she touches a cow, the child will have hair on his or her forehead and the nape of his or her neck; a cat, the child will have the head of a feline; and an albino animal, the child will have red eyes. A woman who drinks from a cracked cup will have a child made ugly by having a harelip; if she steps on a cat, the child will be a hermaphrodite. Should she mount a horse, her child will have one cheek larger than the other. A future mother frightened by an animal or insect avoids touching her face: her baby will have a facial mark. If she scratches herself, her child will have birthmarks. When a woman is frequently nauseated, it is said that her baby has an abundant head of hair and that it is tickling her stomach.

If a woman swallows an octopus egg while swimming, she will give birth to an octopus.

A woman who steals something will give birth to a thief; if she stares at an empty sack, her child will be hungry all its life. In order to have an intelligent baby, a mother must read a lot of books or eat almonds during her pregnancy.

In order to have handsome children, a future mother must look at handsome images on old French gold coins, eat a lot of fruit, and in Alsace especially, drink a glass of brandy every day. If she puts too many spices on her food, her newborn will be ugly.

Innumerable superstitions allow a baby's sex to be determined in advance. In general, a boy is associated with the right side and a girl with the left. If a baby kicks on the right side of its mother's stomach, it is certainly a boy. If a woman always moves her right foot first or has a heavier step on that side, her baby will be of the masculine sex. She can also slip a coin between her breasts: If it falls to the left, the baby will be a girl; to the right, it will be a boy. If a mother's right breast is larger than her left, it is a sign that she is expecting a boy. Finally, if she has more pain on her left side, the baby will be a girl.

"Giovanni Arnolfini and His Bride," by Van Eyck (London, British Museum).

A boy, being stronger and more solid, draws more strength from a mother, but a girl, being less welcome, is detrimental to her—she has the "mask of pregnancy" on her face.

A woman's skin, the shape of her belly, and the quality of her milk are also useful in determining the baby's sex—spots and freckles on the face foretell a boy. If her belly is pointed or round and big on the right side, it is a boy; if it is round on the left, it is a girl. If the mother's milk is thick, she is expecting a boy. A little drop of milk or blood can be drawn from the mother's right side and dropped into water from a fountain: If it sinks immediately, it is a boy. If salt placed on her nipples does not dissolve, it is also a boy.

If a mother drops a pair of scissors, she will have a girl; if it is a knife, she will have a boy. In certain regions, each one of these instruments is hidden under a cushion in a room. Then the mother is asked to come in. If she sits down on the cushion that hides the scissors, the newborn will be a girl. If during the month that precedes the delivery, a mother finds a needle, she will have a girl; if she finds a pin, the child will be a boy. When a black cat sets itself on the knees of a pregnant woman and closes its eyes three times, it is a sign that the woman is expecting a boy. When a pregnant woman unintentionally finishes a bottle of wine, she can be assured that she will have a girl. In Brittany, the mother puts a girl's and a boy's shirt on top of the water in a fountain—the shirt that sinks first indicates the sex of the future child. A mother can also walk around a church three times, then strike the earth by the cemetery very hard with her heel—if the trace is not erased after three days, by all evidence her child will be a boy. In Wales, in order to know a child's sex before it is born, a sheep's shoulderbone is burned in the fireplace. Then the father makes a hole in it with his finger and hangs it with a little string over the back door of the house. The first person who is a stranger to the family to cross the threshold indicates the sex of the child. If, during childbirth, flies are buzzing around the room, they announce the coming of a little girl.

A future mother who wants to have a boy wears blue clothes and puts a few poppyseeds on her windowsill; if she prefers a girl, she dresses in pink and replaces the poppyseeds with sugar.

You must never mention something that a pregnant woman might desire in vain in front of her. Her unsatisfied desires are in fact very detrimental to her child. When she cannot satisfy a craving for cherries or strawberries, her child will have a strawberry mark at birth. Formerly, pregnant women were given the right to steal three fruits or vegetables—two for her and one for her child.

A future mother who finds a twinned hazelnut or almond knows that she will have twins.

School

At school, problems particularly concern results obtained on exams.

A person can try, by as many ways as there are people, to foretell the subject of an exam, the person who will be designated to give it, or his or her chances of passing. It is popular to make bets with yourself: Walk on a sidewalk without stepping on the cracks, cross a street without touching any nails or the yellow stripes, count to ten and wait for your choice of a bearded man, blond woman, baby, and so forth.

Before an exam, the ritual is just as complex—all talismans and good-luck gestures are welcome. In any case, it is recommended that you take an exam with a pen you have been using all year.

Distribution of the general examination prizes at the Sorbonne, end of the 19th c. (Bib. des Arts Déco)

Let's not forget either that professors have eyes behind their heads and you must not stare at them or you might risk being interrogated. In addition, a schoolboy who drops his books on the way to school will make a mistake in his lessons.

Solemn Communion

"For young Christians, this religious ceremony replaced the Romans' taking of the virile robe."
(Francois-Rene de Chateaubriand, Memoirs from Beyond the Grave*)*

This ceremony that concerns boys and girls of about twelve years of age brings to mind initiation rites practiced by adolescents in antiquity as much as in traditional civilizations. Like baptism, which for a long time it used to follow quite closely, communion implies an explicit renunciation of Satan and a definitive introduction into adult society. Beginning on this day, a boy often has the right to wear long pants and a girl dons her future wedding gown for the first time. The ritual gifts—a wristwatch, pen, or bicycle—are symbols of a newly acquired autonomy.

291

A solemn communion in the 19th c.

Widowhood

Superstitious people are especially anxious about marrying a widowed person without vexing the deceased. During a second wedding, those gathered must make as much noise as possible, yell, whistle, or bang on pans, in order to ward off the deceased who might seek revenge in order to show their disapproval. This latter emerges if the marriage is too hasty or if their is too much of an age difference between the new spouses. A widow always wears a glove when receiving her new wedding band.

Widowers who wish to dream of their new spouses mix coral with magnet dust and blood from a dove. They wear this mixture around their neck in a little piece of blue cloth. Widows with the same aim tie a branch from a poplar tree to the stockings or socks, then put it under their pillow. Also, before going to sleep, they rub their temples with a few drops of blood.

Objects,
the House, Clothing

The material universe has never appeared to be a neutral domain to the superstitious. Objects or clothing are tainted with one or more meanings linked to their useful value or their intrinsic qualities. So, according to its shape, color, or symbolism, an object takes on a significance of its own. A ladder forms a sacred triangle with the wall against which it is learning; it also allows the heavens to be touched from a distance. A chalice or axe are sexed articles. The use of these popular objects often results in an identification between the means and the end, the thing itself and that for which it is used. A hat signifies headgear as well as the head. This world sometimes comes alive, on its own, to warn man of some event; sometimes the world is under the influence of evil forces that use it as a tool. In a sense, therefore, a material object actually becomes what it symbolizes, like a cork or a stone becomes a dog or a car for a child.

Barn

Like a grain loft, a barn shelters a farmer's wealth that must be protected against demons, natural elements such as lightning, and thieves.

A new barn must be blessed with salt and water, and small sacred statues are often incorporated into its foundation. This rite, inspired by Christianity, is completed with a series of much less "orthodox" practices that are supposed to ward off witches and their sorcery. Finally, in order

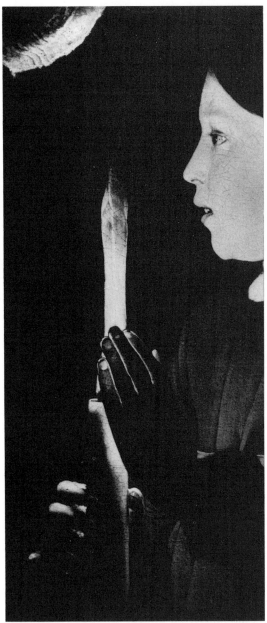

"Saint Joseph the Carpenter" (detail), by Georges de La Tour (Musée du Louvre).

to protect the barn loft from rats, sprinkle three corners of it with holy water on the first Sunday of Lent—the rodents will flee by the fourth corner.

294

Basket

It was to a wicker basket that Moses owed his life. As a general rule, baskets are favorable on the condition that they are never left empty, because a devil will make his home there. Therefore, it is necessary to leave a stone, fruit, or some other object in the bottom of the baskets that are not being used.

Bed

Linked to the essential stages of life, birth, love, dreams, suffering, and death, a bed must be protected against the mischievous influences of devils who seek to affect it. Specific rites determine its place in a room and how it is made.

It is preferable that a bed be placed in an east-west direction like that of the sun, but it is essential that a person sleeping is not touched by moonlight and that his bed does not form a cross with the ceiling beams.

A guest's bed must not be made until at least an hour after he has left; otherwise, you risk receiving an unwanted visit. There must never be more than two for carrying out this task: If three people take turns in making one bed, death will soon strike the house. If one person does not make a bed all at once, she will meet with hinderances all day long. A bed that is left turned down during the day risks serving as a refuge for demons. Turning a mattress over on a Friday leads a guest to dream about the witches' Sabbath.

Putting a hat on a bed is to wish the death of its occupant.

During the day, a container of spring water must be left by a bed in order to protect it, but whoever uses water that has been boiled will provoke Satan's vengeance and anger. Straws tied in a cross and placed at the four corners of a bed ward off nightmares.

Upon awakening, it is essential to get up on your right foot. Whoever forgets this rule will see his or her day spoiled. Some affirm that a bed must be gotten in and out of on the same side—preferably the right; changing sides involuntarily announces a surprise in the day.

Bell

This essential element of Christian rites played a large role in Celtic cults. This metal, therefore lucky, object wards off evil spirits when it rings. A bell also has the ability to chase away mice, and snakes, cure fevers and illnesses, and protect the earth from serious bad weather, storms, hail, or fog. A witch in flight falls when the Angelus sounds.

Bell carriers. Wooden statue, 17th c. (Paris, Musée Guimet)

The Church has made it a living being that is baptized and that makes a pilgrimage to Rome every year to be purified. On Easter Day it brings back eggs that it distributes to children. A bell is the voice of God and of religion: It announces hours, services, deaths, births, and weddings, thus expressing daily power and the permanence of religion. When it sounds, it wards off evil forces and, like a cock's crow, at regular intervals proclaims the victory of what is sacred over Satan's sorcery.

A bell that sounds without human intervention is always a sinister omen. It can announce a catastrophe or else salute death that just went by. Some, however, see it as a sign that a soul has ended its time in Purgatory and is asking for entry into Heaven. Hearing two bells sound at the same time tells you that someone is going to leave the house.

When you are far from the shoreline, bells you hear while at sea are those from the city of Is, which was formerly swallowed up. On the day when Is is brought back to life, the first man to see a bell surface or hear its ring will be king of the country.

Handbells, like larger bells, ward off spirits. They are found in most Western as well as Oriental religious rites.

Whoever wants to call upon the dead must take a handbell made of an alloy of the seven metals: mercury, lead, silver, gold, tin, copper, and iron. On the outside he ingraves the sacred word *tetragrammaton*, then the names of the spirits that govern the seven planets. At the top of the bell he inscribes *adonai* and on the ring *Jesus*. He must then keep it wrapped in green taffeta at the bottom of a freshly-dug grave for seven days.

Belt

Like necklaces and bracelets, a belt wraps around the body and protects it from sorcery. It must never be thrown away, because a witch could get hold of it and hold you at her mercy. Wearing a blessed belt facilitates difficult childbirths.

Bible

Besides the sacred character of its contents, this book has always had an intrinsic power. When it is open, its simple presence in a room wards off evil spirits. The "Bible" was used in ordeals of the Middle Ages: Whoever did not uphold an oath sworn on this sacred book supposedly perished on the spot. A key tied to a Bible reputedly twirled on its own when the name of a person guilty of a crime was uttered.

For many superstitious Christians, *The Bible* is a book of divination. Whoever has a problem to be resolved should open *The Bible* to a random place, then with his eyes closed, put his finger on a word—this word will give the answer. On New Year's Day, in order to know whether the year will be unhappy or serene, it is sufficient to randomly put your finger on a page.

The "Song of Songs" attributed to Solomon directs a girl who wishes to get married—she must place her house key on this passage and let the keyring hang over the page. She closes the book and ties it up with a stocking or stocking suspender. Then two people hold the book and put a finger through the ring. The girl must recite one of the verses from the Song. If the book turns or falls at that moment, the girl is assured that she will be married. A young man can know the qualities of his future wife by reading the first Psalm. The verse that corresponds to his loved one's age will reveal her underlying nature.

Boat

Both a means of transport and a house, a ship is a place where all are interdependent, passengers and sailors. Any unfortunate gesture can displease the sea gods whom, on the contrary, it is necessary to conciliate. The eyes painted on the bows of ships in the Orient are there to frighten evil spirits; sirens or other female figureheads on the prow of a ship have the same function.

Like a child, a boat has no real existence until it has been baptized. If the person doing the christening is pregnant, the vessel will be wrecked

297

on its first voyage. The bottle of champagne that she hits against the boat's hull must break on the first blow—doing this a second time is a very bad omen. Formerly, this offering to the sea gods was the ritual sacrifice of an animal whose throat was slit. In the south of France, it was also the custom to nail a toad to the hull. It is inadvisable to give a boat a name that ends in "a." Once a ship is baptized, its name must not be changed—it will provoke the gods.

In order to protect a vessel from evil spells, it is a good idea to hide an empty brandy bottle in its prow. But when a spell persists against it, it is a good idea to spit, to steal an object from another boat and burn the object once it is on board, or even to make the hull pass through a ring formed by all the ropes put end to end.

If a vessel is transporting a dead body, eggs, or rabbits, winds will be adverse. A woman or a priest among the passengers is also a bad omen. A child's presence, on the other hand, calms the waves. One black cat on board is frightening, but two bring luck. The words "rope," "rabbit," "priest," and "pig" are prohibited—uttered on board they attract misfortune. A person must never whistle on a boat unless there is a perfect calm, because this action risks making the wind rise up. If the mop or bucket goes overboard, the vessel will be wrecked. Whoever does not cross himself when he sees a phantom ship will soon join the crew of the damned.

Tradition has it that the passengers give each other presents whenever the equator is crossed. If they forget to offer fruits or meat, the gods will take revenge.

Bolt

A widow who does not bolt her door at night before going to bed will never love again.

Sterile women must polish the bolts of churches in order to have children.

Bottle

According to numerous legends, a bottle, no matter what its contents, represents the course of human life that flows drop by drop until the dregs. It often encloses mysterious knowledge, magical powers, or devils and genies.

When little rings form inside the neck of a bottle that has just been used, it is a sign of a visit, letter, or news within the week. If you served with the right hand, these messages will be pleasant; if the bottle was held with the left hand, they will surely bring disagreements.

Whoever drinks the last drop in a bottle, preferably under a beam, will have a wife within the year if he is single, or if he is married, will have a child. If it is a pregnant woman who drinks the last drop, she will have a girl; if it is an old man, he is assured of living long enough to drink a new bottle! He who finishes three bottles in the course of a feast will die in the year.

Breaking a bottle of oil presages a terrible misfortune.

A christener who does not succeed in breaking a bottle of champagne with the first blow when baptizing a boat attracts the evil forces of the sea to the boat. In general, the noise of the cork popping frightens evil powers.

Bridge

Like a house, a bridge calls for many foundation rites destined to protect it against the evil eye. Sometimes a few drops of wine are put in the mortar that holds the keystone. Others mix a coin or iron object into the masonry.

Whoever is first to walk on a newly-made bridge is destined to damnation (a black cat is usually made to go first).

You must never take leave of a friend on a bridge, because you risk never seeing him or her again.

If a coffin is taken over a bridge, the rest of the procession must take a detour, otherwise the bridge will collapse. Soldiers never march in time on a bridge, because it is believed that the vibrations made by the regular rhythm risk making the bridge fall from under their feet.

In order to destroy a bridge, simply put a finger on a specific, but undetermined, point of the masonry.

Passing under a bridge when a train is rolling over it brings misfortune.

Broom

Originally, a broom was a sacred instrument of monks who alone had the power to eliminate impurities. Its utilization was reserved for priests and initiates. But in Germanic legends, witches ride on their brooms backwards when they go to the Sabbath. It is known that irritable women prefer to use this instrument for beating their husbands.

You must never sweep after sunset because it will chase away the happiness in the house or hurt a wondering soul. It is also necessary to avoid cleaning the floor on Good Friday or New Year's Day. A broom is not used when there is a dead person in the house.

A woman must never use a new broom to sweep outside the house; she must first clean the inside, otherwise her luck will leave with the dust. She can sweep the dust balls into the middle of a room; they will protect against bad luck.

Walking on a broom brings misfortune; for a woman it is a sign that she will have a child before being married. A broom that falls across your path is a bad omen.

Departure for the Sabbath, engraving from Goya's "Caprices" series (Bibl. Nat.).

A broom must not be borrowed or lent out, cut into pieces, or burned.

It is inadvisable to bring an old broom into a new house—this would be moving in misfortune. In contrast, a new broom, some bread, and salt assure a happy life in a new house.

If a child takes a broom and begins to sweep the floor, he or she announces unexpected visitors.

If a person is suspected of being a witch, simply place a broom across a doorway—she will not dare step over it for fear that it will come alive and take her off to the Sabbath.

In order to protect a newborn, turn a broom upside down on each side of his or her bedroom door or the door to the house and put three grains of salt on each one. In general, people who fear witches turn their brooms upside down. A broom must never be left outside on a Saturday, because it will go join the other brooms at the Sabbath.

Soaking a broom in water brings on rain.

In Africa, when a man is struck by a broom, he must grab hold of it and hit the broomstick seven times in order to escape the impotence that is lying in wait for him.

Button

Whoever makes a mistake in buttoning an article of clothing must take it off immediately and start all over again, because this error is not pardonable and brings misfortune.

In order to know her future husband's profession, a girl counts the buttons on her blouse from top to bottom, saying, "Doctor, lawyer, businessman, statesman, richman, poorman, beggarman, thief." Finding a button announces a new friend.

Candle

A very ancient form of divination by wax existed whereby melted wax was poured into water. When it hardened, the forms it took on were interpreted by keromancians.

Girls of marrying age perpetuate this custom—the wax represents the tool of their future husband's trade. When there is a serious illness, women who do not know which saint to devote themselves to light a candle in honor of all the healing saints. The candle that goes out first designates the saint who should be called upon. Still today, three candles are lit one after another and put by a sick person's bedside. If the third candle goes out first, the person will die; if it's the second, the illness will be long; the first candle announces a quick recovery. This method is also valid for knowing the future of projects or trials. If a candle refuses to light, it heralds a storm; if the flame flutters, it is a sign of coming bad weather; and if the flame has a blue tinge it presages either a freeze or an approaching death. In addition, the streams of wax that flow down the side of a candle are signs of death in the family. The wick of a lit candle leans in the direction of where a visitor will come from.

In general, candles are lit at births, weddings, and burials, because these little tongues of flame frighten evil spirits. But it is inadvisable to bring three candles together in a room, because their presence becomes confused with the group of the three Fates, divinities that weave man's destiny. In the case of absolute necessity, the last two candles must be lit with the wick from the first. Whoever lights a candle from a fire in a fireplace will never be rich. It brings misfortune to let a flame go out on its own. But putting a candle out unintentionally presages marriage. In any case, only a virgin can revive the flame of a candle that is smouldering.

When a candle is set on a table and spits out a little spark, it indicates, to the person facing it, the arrival of a letter or a visit from a stranger.

In northern England, two pins are stuck into a lit candle; when the wick comes to their level, love is near.

During Christmas feasts, families put candles in their windows in order to direct the Holy Family toward Bethlehem.

A blessed candle from a Candlemas service has the virtue of conjuring sorcery, especially storms. But whoever uses it frivolously bears the mark of damnation and will hold it in his or her hand eternally.

In certain regions, in Brittany and Alsace in particular, during a wedding ceremony a candle is lit in front of both the bride and the groom; the candle that goes out first indicates which one of the two people will die first.

Car

Like all dangerous means of transportation, a car gives rise to a series of benefits that attempt to guide destiny.

You must especially not speak of accidents nor boast of your good luck before undertaking any trip in a car. When a driver is satisfied with a certain make of car, it is in his best interest to get that make for the rest of his life. Certain cars are marked with the evil eye—they can be repaired or overhauled, but they always break down, especially if they were bought on a Friday the 13th. It is said, however, that if a car is not totalled after an accident, you must get back in it as quickly as possible— otherwise you will not dare to drive again.

Whoever has a small accident in a new car will never have big problems on the road. Two flat tires are always followed by a third. A driver whose new car goes perfectly for three, six, or nine days will never have an accident at the wheel of that make of car.

Most motorists used to hang a Saint Christopher medal on their rearview mirrors because the saint protected travellers and vagabonds, even though he probably never existed.

If you catch sight of a green car, cross your fingers and make a wish, because it will come true.

Cards

Tarot cards are a very ancient system of divination playing on a complex symbolism. More recently playing cards have been used by diviners and charlatans. Still today, a fortuneteller plays a large role in social life. Many people consult one. Above all, cards are attached to the image of gamblers; this is why they are condemned by religions. Just their presence on a ship is considered to be unlucky by some. Since they are linked to vice and demons, a soldier had to throw them as far away as possible when his life was threatened.

Cartomancy does not belong to the subject of our study, but some use it to answer questions regarding daily life. They shuffle a deck of cards and cut it with their left hands. The suit of the "cut" card gives destiny's

The ace of spades, caricature from the beginning of the century.

answer: A heart is favorable; a club announces a success along professional lines or a gain of money; a diamond is more neutral, more or less a sign of news or travel; and a spade is frightening, symbolizing illness, misfortunes, and even death. An ace of hearts is a sign of joy; a king, a powerful protector; a queen, a woman ready to help you; and a jack, a favorable young man. A ten announces a pleasant surprise; a nine, friendship; an eight, children; and a seven, marriage. An ace of clubs foretells a sizeable receipt of money; a king, a useful friend; a queen, a disappointed friend; a jack, marriage; a ten, financial success; a nine, success in love; an eight, joy; and a seven, a small gift. An ace of diamonds indicates that an important letter is slowed up; a king lets you know that a man is getting ready to betray you; a queen, that a woman is getting ready to betray you; a jack announces bad news; a ten, a short trip; a nine, a delay in the arrival of some money; an eight, a project in the making that has some chance of turning out; and a seven, a small gain. An ace of spades is a sign of mourning or catastrophe; a king announces a conflict with the law; a

303

queen is a tormented, elderly woman; a jack is a young man who wants to do you wrong; a ten is unlucky; a nine indicates a delay; an eight, bad news; and a seven, worries. This list has innumerable variations.

Miners and sailors never take playing cards to work—the cards will bring them misfortune. It is said that thieves, for the same reason, do not take cards from a house that they are robbing.

Usually card players are the most superstitious. Cards must never be played on a polished surface or in the presence of a dog. It is a good sign to come across a hunchback, but encountering a man who squints brings bad luck. Before sitting down, a card player either walks around the table or his chair three times, then sits astride his chair but never with his legs crossed. If he wants to have a good hand, he can touch a good card with his index finger before shuffling the cards. Whoever wants to have a good game blows on the cards. In general, a player cuts with his left hand and picks up tricks with his right hand—neglecting to do this goes against destiny. It is a good idea to sit on a handkerchief and to stick a pin in your pants or dress. A person who whistles or sings during a card party attracts bad luck. A card that falls, especially a spade or club, is a very bad omen.

Certain cards have a very bad reputation—a nine of diamonds is reputed to bring bad luck. A succession of black cards, spades in particular, is a bad omen. Whoever has the four of clubs on the first hand will not have any luck for the entire party. In poker, two pairs, an ace, and an eight bring bad luck.

Whoever does not have mascots or talismans is not a good card player.

Chain

It represents a link in all its forms: open, it is the image of a group and continuity, like in a farandole (Provencal dance); closed, it is both a children's round and a shackle that tortures a prisoner. Worn around the neck, a gold chain symbolizes a union of the earth and sky. When you are faced with temptation or in the presence of evil forces, it is a good idea to pull lightly on the chain around your neck in order to get nearer to God.

Before beginning work, blacksmiths, sons of Vulcan, traditionally hammer on their anvils three times in order to tighten the chain that is holding Satan prisoner.

Chair

This object has a sacred value by the very material it is made of, wood, and by its function, being sat on. A king's throne or a patriarch's chair are insignias of the power that it is sacrilegious to insult.

You must never forget to place as many chairs around a table as there are guests. Forgetting one is an omen of approaching death. In leaving a house, whoever puts his or her chair back against a wall will never come back to that house.

As a general rule, tipping over a chair brings misfortune; in order to conjure the spell, you must cross yourself five times. A fiancée that tips over a chair will have an unfaithful husband; in order to save her marriage, she must give the chair to the parish priest. Whoever spins a chair around will soon have a quarrel with relatives or go through a trial. Three chairs placed side by side announce a death in the family. Whoever tips over a chair in getting up from a meal is a liar.

In order to attact luck, many gamblers spit under their chairs or else walk around them three times.

Whoever turns over the cushion on a praying stool in sitting down will have twenty bad Sundays.

Chimney

It incarnates the household and the sacred reunion of people, but it also plays the role of a door by which more or less beneficent powers can enter, such as Santa Claus, witches, and little house genies. A hearth is still confused with the fire that is lit there and whose smoke symbolically links the earth and sky. Although respected, a chimney is also feared, and you must ward off all the evil forces that could take advantage of this gap in order to get into a house.

A chimney must never be used for the first time on Friday, the day of Christ's death and of the witches' Sabbath, or on the feast day of a martyr who died by fire, such as Joan of Arc or Saint Lawrence.

In general, before lighting a fire in a fireplace, make a Solomon's seal or three signs of the cross in the air and throw three grains of salt in the fireplace. In case of a chimney fire, three signs of the cross are also effective.

At the time of a birth or death, salt or holy water is thrown into the fire and the sign of the cross is made again. Then the brooms and the fire tongs that are placed on the right of the hearth are turned upside down. The aim of these practices is to ward off witches who are always interested in moments of human weakness.

Being the seat of a fire, a fireplace deserves respect and care—it is not to be spit in nor pointed at with a finger. A stranger does not have the right to poke the fire. A hearth must be cleaned before going to bed.

Certain precautions are taken in order to conciliate a fire, this dangerous element. Logs are spit on before they are burned, and they are put in the fireplace smallest end first. Holding a log by the smallest end exposes you to seven years of poverty. In addition, it is advisable to spit on the bundle of kindling where a witch could be hidden, and to always place the firepoker on the right-hand side of the hearth.

If a pair of damaged bellows is repaired, the master of the house will die from suffocation.

If a snake or a clump of soot falls from a chimney, it presages a catastrophe.

A chimney sweep is a beneficent person who brings good luck, especially to those he kisses. If a young couple encounters one when returning from their wedding ceremony, they will have serene and permanent happiness.

Cigarette

Tobacco, a rare and hallucinogenic plant introduced in Europe rather late, was long considered with respect and sacrificed to gods of the home. In fact, tobacco was put in the foundations of some houses.

An insomniac who wishes to have twenty-four hours of rest must smoke a cigarette made from bones from a toad. In addition, tobacco wards off snakes and protects a baby's cradle from evil spirits.

CIGAR

A young woman who draws the last puff of a cigar will marry the first man she meets immediately afterward.

PIPE

Reserved for old sages, it represents the experience and wisdom of these men with whom it is identified. Its heavy, brown smoke undoubtedly links it to the world of spirits. Passing around a pipe is, like exchanging blood, a sign of friendship.

A man must never light a pipe from a candle—his wife will become a shrew and deceive him. In order to make wild boars run away, old broken pipes are buried in the fields. If some lit tobacco drops out of a pipe on its own, it is a sign of rain.

Clock

The tick-tock of a clock and the continuous cycle of its hands illustrate the relentless passing of time. All changes in the rhythm of a watch, clock, or alarm clock indicate a break in the harmony of the world. A sudden acceleration, stop, and an alarm going off unexpectedly are also unlucky omens. They announce that death is approaching or going to strike. A person's favorite watch stops when he dies; and no one will be able to wind the watch any longer—little by little the watch had come to identify itself with its owner's heart. Clocks must be treated with respect. Making a clock sound thirteen times summons the Devil.

When someone dies, all the clocks in the house must be stopped immediately; you must not wind your watch again until after the burial. The stopping of clocks at the time of a death signifies to the soul that it has entered into eternity; without this it could not leave the body.

Hearing an alarm clock sound or a clock strike the hour when the ringing of church bells can be heard outside is always a bad omen. If clocks are heard while a death bell is tolling, it will toll again very soon. In Wales, when a church bell and the clock on a public building sound at the same time, it is said that a fire will soon break out.

The sound made by worms and larvae that are gnawing on the beams and furniture is called a "death clock." Whoever hears this noise knows that his death is near.

Clothes

Despite the well-known affirmation "A cowl doesn't make a monk," the garment is usually identified not only with the physical character of whoever wears it, but also with his moral traits and social activity. There is no need to call up the fascination people who are greedy for glory and honor have for uniforms or the simplicity of dress of those who are modest or moralists. An old garment steeped in an entire human life is a valuable good-luck charm; a poor man's tattered clothes are kept as talismans, and people are instinctively attached to old coats or shirts.

In England, it is said that whoever puts on a new garment must ask a neighbor to pinch his or her arm—this is undoubtedly in order to ward off the evil eye. When a dress or coat is worn for the first time, it is advisable to slip a few coins into one of the pockets; fortune will smile on you for as long as this garment is useful to you.

A woman who on Easter Day dresses herself with three new articles of clothing will be happy for all the coming season. But putting a jacket on inside out, putting in your left arm before your right, or buttoning it wrong are all unlucky oversights.

A mother dresses a fragile child in white until he or she is seven years old, in order to put the child under the protection of the Holy Virgin.

You must never darn a jacket—you expose yourself to always lacking money. If a woman sticks herself or breaks a needle in mending a garment, she will have every chance of receiving a kiss on the day she wears the garment. But, whoever burns his or her pants or dress can be certain that someone is telling a lie about him or her. Many people refuse to give their old clothes to elderly or sick persons. They are afraid that when these people die, they will transmit the same fate to the former owners by means of the clothes.

In Russia, it is affirmed that if a robber enters your house and forgets some article of clothing, simply hit it with a stick and the guilty man will fall ill and reveal himself.

Some people put their jackets on inside out to go looking for snails; this precaution guarantees them good results!

It is still affirmed that women seen dressed in tatters on the edge of a wood in the evening are witches.

Coffin

A carpenter is always mysteriously warned in advance that he must make a coffin for the next death.

A living person must not sleep in a coffin nor put an article of clothing there. This is the reason many people hesitate to give their old clothes to elderly or sick persons.

Ordinary objects must be placed in a coffin; if the dead person is a child, a marble is placed in his or her hand. The deceased must be dressed in his wedding shirt that washes him of all his sins. In Brittany, it is said that his left arm must never be placed under his body or he will come back and haunt. It is also affirmed that the Turks let the dead person's leg hang out of the coffin so he will be able to kneel on Judgment Day. In Brittany, it is a good idea to kiss the deceased before he is put in his coffin, so that he will not cross your path afterwards.

A coffin must always be taken out of a house head first so that the soul can take flight.

A child's coffin must be taken out of a house by a window, in order to protect future mothers who enter the house by the door.

If there is a problem in getting a coffin into a grave, it is a sign that the dead person's soul is struggling to take flight or else that it is waging a final battle against evil spirits. If a coffin does not go into the grave at all, it is a very bad omen for the entire gathering. No animal must approach a coffin at this time because it could take hold of the dead person's soul.

Coffin nails stuck into a bedroom door ward off nightmares.

In addition, it is known that only vampires have the power to open their coffins.

Coins

Being made of metal, usually silver or iron, a coin conjures evil spells and allows sorcery to be combatted. When carried on you, a coin helps to ward off illness.

The Devil cannot bewitch metal, so a coin can be used in questioning without fear of evil intervention. Certain coins are excellent good luck charms, particularly those that bear the date of your birth or pierced coins that were put in a bride's pocket before the ceremony. You must, however be careful of them because some sorcerers offer you a coin with a hole in it in order to cast a spell on you. A coin found during a storm is reputed to have fallen from the sky and is enchanted.

Custom has it that if you want to see one of your wishes come true, toss a coin in a spring or fountain. Only the poor have the privilege of being able to pick up these coins.

When you hear a cuckoo for the first time in the year or try a garment on for the first time, having a few coins on you signifies that you will have money all year long. Whoever receives a pair of scissors or a knife for a gift must give a coin in exchange if he or she doesn't want these objects to cut the friendship.

There is a tradition that says that a silver or gold coin should be put in a dead person's mouth so that he can pay for his passage into the beyond. Others place a coin on each eye. A person who drinks wine in which these coins have soaked becomes blind to the infidelities of his or her spouse.

A curious belief, still found today in eastern France, is that a tree grows wherever a coin is buried.

Comb

A simple, useful object in Western countries, a comb is also a decorative accessory that sometimes has the value of a talisman in the Orient. Its qualities rest in the living matter from which it is made: ivory, which brings a tooth to mind; horn, which is also the matter of hair and nails; and shell, which protects certain animals.

Tortoise-shell combs calm nervous people and refine their intelligence.

You must never use a comb that was used on a dead person, because it will bring death.

If a hair remains on a comb or brush, you must not throw it away because a witch could get hold of it and use it to cast a spell on you or make you bald.

If a tooth breaks while you are using a comb, it is a bad omen. A mother must not comb her child's hair until he has all his teeth or else each time the comb loses a tooth, so will the child!

A comb is not to be lent, especially not to a person with a different color of hair than yours.

Dice

The six sides of these little cubes and the six dots of the side with the highest value symbolize the constitutive elements of the universe joining six realms: mineral, plant, animal, human, psychic, and divine. Of course, dice interest primarily gamblers, who never miss blowing on them before tossing them. Most also cross their fingers for even more certainty. Others rub them on the head of a redhaired person!

In general, whoever carries dice will never lack money.

The black dots inscribed on the sides of dice have a prophetic value in terms of their number:

One dot: An important letter could come your way.

Two dots: You will make a successful trip.

Three dots: You will be taken by surprise.

Four dots: Problems are on their way.

Five dots: There will be changes in your family.

Six dots: An unexpected sum of money will increase your savings.

Door

Like the mouth of a human being, the door is the place in a house that must be protected the most because it is by a door that demons can enter most easily.

It is a good idea to pound some nails in the center of a door in such a way that they represent a cross and to hang a horseshoe on the lintel to attract happiness to the house. For the same purpose, St. John's wort is hung on the inner side of the front door. In order to protect barns and stables, it used to be recommended that a screech owl, bat, wolf's head, or owl be nailed to the door.

A person entering a house must cross the threshold with the right foot first. If the left foot goes first, it introduces bad luck into the house. A visitor must leave through the same doorway he entered, or else he will take the luck of the house away with him. In contrast, when returning from a baptism or funeral, you must enter the house by a door other than the one you used in leaving; if there isn't another door, it is then preferable to come in through a window. Slamming a door in a house where there has been a recent death is sacrilegious and risks attracting misfortune because this gesture can hurt the soul of the deceased.

Two doors to the outside must never be left open at the same time nor should the front door be open when all the doors on the inside of a house are open.

A door that opens on its own announces an unpleasant visit near at hand.

Fountain and Spring

Divinities of running water were long the object of worship—a spring whose water pours forth pure and virginal incarnates life itself (springs are still revered in Alsace and Brittany, for example). In order to regulate this adoration, the Church gives names of saints to most of these springs.

On New Year's Day wishes of happiness and gifts of flowers and fruits are presented to fountains. Water from a fountain, which has the same value as holy water and therefore wards off demons, must not be spilled. It bubbles on Trinity Sunday during the high Mass. In order to unveil witches who hide themselves under the guise of a human or animal, two knives must be crossed on the edge of a fountain on Christmas Day during midnight Mass or a four-leaf clover must be placed there.

Being an image of life, running water is perceived as a fecundating power—an egg is placed near a fountain so that its hatching is successful. In order to bring on rain, the foot of a cross is soaked in fountain water or some of this water is sprinkled on a slab of stone.

A fountain sometimes answers man's pressing questions. Whoever does not know which saint to devote himself to, writes the names of all the saints on ivy leaves and tosses them in a fountain. The first leaf to float away indicates the path to follow. Whoever wants to see the face of her future husband places a mirror in the water of a fountain at midnight. Others use a pitcher—the number of bubbles that come to the surface indicate the number of years of waiting before the wedding. The shirt of a newborn or sick child is put in a fountain; if it floats, it is a sign of luck or recovery. If a pure, virgin girl places a pin on the surface of a fountain, it will not sink! Worried wives of sailors put a piece of bread in a fountain; if it sinks, it is a sign of a shipwreck, but if it floats, the man is still alive. In order to uncover a robber or a liar, some, on a Monday and on an empty stomach, toss a series of pieces of bread into a fountain, calling out with each toss the name of a suspect—the piece that sinks designates the guilty person.

When a silver or gold coin is thrown into a fountain or spring, a wish must be made, but this action must be carried out in a specific way: The coin must be tossed over your left shoulder, with your back to the fountain and your eyes closed. Some choose heads or tails and if the coin lands on the correct side, the wish will come true. Whoever carries out this rite at the Trevi Fountain in Rome is assured of returning to the eternal city again some day.

Fountain water is celebrated for its curative virtues. A person can swim in it, sprinkle himself with it, or drink it. In Alsace, when children swim in a spring, one of them throws a straw on the water, and the last child to get out must pick the straw out of the water with his teeth; if he fails, illness could strike a member of his family. In Lorrain there is a "day of fountains": Everyone drinks from as many fountains as possible to be assured of good health during the year. Every spring placed under the patronage of a saint conceals the saint's same virtues: One cures bellyaches and rheumatisms; another is more favorable for women who have just given birth. In Wales, water drawn from a fountain at midnight on a saint's feast day is said to protect against all illnesses. Some put on their eyes water taken from a fountain on the night of Saint John in order to guard against vision troubles for one year.

A sorcerer, often the seventh son in a family, uncovers underground waters with the help of a hazelwood stick. A horse that stamps its hoof on the ground three times indicates the presence of a source of water.

Furniture

If a piece of furniture rocks or tips over on its own, it is an omen of death in the family. A picture that falls from a wall is particularly unlucky.

In Scotland, furniture is believed to crack like rheumatic joints when the weather changes.

It is always preferable to place furniture parallel to the lines of a room or house; in this way the formation of unwanted crosses is avoided.

At night, a dead soul becomes detached from the closet mirror in a bedroom, but during the day it remains enclosed and invisible.

Garter

This accessory that is of little use today is still the object of many superstitions linked especially to its color and the material it is made of.

A woman who wishes to have children must wear a garter of straw or shell, preferably on the eve of her wedding. If its fibers come from wheat, a boy will come into the world; if they are from oats, a girl will be born. But this garter is effective only if the young woman is still a virgin. A garter made from pieces of cork protects against bellyaches.

During a wedding dinner, single men always try to steal the bride's garter, because it is regarded as a talisman of happiness and luck. A young girl slips a garter under her pillow in order to dream about her future husband.

A woman who tries to attach her garter three times and fails will have a good day.

It is still affirmed that red garters relieve rheumatisms.

A "traveller's garter" allows a traveller to move faster than a horse. It is made with a hareskin and dried artemisia. Another recipe proposes writing a magic formula with your blood on a wolfskin on a Wednesday in spring. It is also possible to braid the hair of a hanged man and attach these strands to a colt's legs; the colt must then walk backward twenty steps, then run free for a few hours.

A girl who loses her garter during the Procession of the Virgin will have a child within the year whether she is married or not.

Glass

It was not without reason that the object from which we drink took the name of glass, a transparent and fragile substance. Linked both to water and mirrors, a glass has certain divinitory powers—a simple glass of water can be used instead of a crystal ball.

Breaking a glass by accident brings happiness as long as the glass was white or crystal; colored glasses lose the magical force that is due, above all, to purity. However, another person must never be looked at through a piece of broken glass—you will soon have a quarrel with whomever you were observing. The Russian custom of breaking your vodka glass at the end of a meal by throwing it over your shoulder is not due so much to the beneficent power of broken glass as to ancient destruction or "potlatch" rites that were an offering or sacrifice made to the gods.

You must never hold a glass out to another person. It is preferable to set it beside the person and let him take hold of it himself. Not following this rule risks making a quarrel break out between you and the other person.

Whoever drinks from another person's glass, especially if he or she drinks the last drop, will know that person's thoughts.

In Brittany, some people believe that a glass that rings for no reason announces the death of a sailor.

"Family of Country People" (detail), by Mathieu Le Nain (Musée du Louvre).

In order to speed the recovery of certain afflictions, a bedridden person was made to drink a glass of water "in a cross" (from the four "corners" of the glass). A glass of water drunk with your head bent forward and your upper lip on the far side of the glass gets rid of hiccups.

Gloves

A synonym of authority and nobility, gloves are worn today at grand occasions such as weddings and burials. For a long time their use was reserved for the upper classes of society who came to identify gloves with their honor: To take them off was a sign of allegiance; to throw them down was a sign of defiance. The white gloves of people of the church, like those of a bride, illustrate physical purity. A woman's glove can be enough to represent her entirely. A man who picks up a young lady's glove that has fallen on the ground can, therefore, hope to see his passion shared. In general, it is best to let someone else pick up your glove on the ground—picking it up yourself brings misfortune. At a wedding, during the exchanging of rings, the bride takes off her gloves as a sign of consent, but a widow who is marrying a second man must leave her gloves on. A fiancée must never look at herself in a mirror with her bridal gown on unless she is wearing a glove, or else she risks becoming entranced.

Wearing gloves on a Wednesday brings misfortune. Losing your gloves is a bad omen, but to find a pair, especially on a Sunday, brings luck for the entire week.

314

Whoever forgets his gloves at a friend's house must observe a very strict ritual in order to not be excluded from further invitations: He must return to where he was, sit down before claiming his gloves, and not put them on until he is about to leave. Putting on gloves is a gesture that indicates that a person is getting ready to leave, so it can be insulting to do this just after arriving!

A superstition anchored in common rules of social politeness forbids shaking a stranger's hand without taking off your glove. This would indicate to the stranger that you do not wish to maintain a genuine relationship.

Hammer

A hammer is placed on a dying person's forehead so that his soul can reach Paradise without striking a blow. This is why the forehead of a dead Pope is tapped with an ivory hammer before his burial.

A new husband who wants to be sure of directing his household must buy a hammer before anything else.

Handkerchief

Being an intimate object, a handkerchief, like a glove, can be a means of seduction, a sign, or a message that a person lets fall to the ground. It can also be an object of contamination in the magical sense of the term, and it is advisable to beware of it.

Two lovers or a married couple must avoid exchanging their handkerchiefs or even offering them to each other—it could cause a quarrel or even a break-up.

The knot that is tied in a handkerchief is a conjuration against the Devil who could play a trick on you to make you forget.

Hat

A hat draws its symbolic power from the thought it supposedly covers up. A person who "talks through his hat" changes his mind every time he changes his hat. A symbol of power, a hat is an important part of a uniform. A beret, helmet, and a military cap are at once the crown and tiara of the little potentates of daily life. As a general rule, it brings happiness to touch these hats. Lightly touching the red pompon on a sailor's beret with your left index finger is enough to make you lucky. Touching a bishop's mitre also brings happiness.

Whoever doesn't take his hat off when a funeral is passing lacks respect for the dead and risks finding himself in the dead person's place.

Setting a hat on a table or bed brings misfortune into a house. Whoever leaves his hat on someone's bed wants to make him die soon.

Putting a hat on backwards brings misfortune; if it is a cap, this act announces that you will soon have dealings with the law, or if you are already involved in a trial, that you will lose.

A hat or cap is used in drawing lots because it is in part linked to destiny.

A fiance who forgets his hat on his wedding day risks being an unfaithful husband. A woman who puts on a man's hat would like to be kissed.

Holy Water Basin

Holy water sprinkled in the form of a cross is the most certain of exorcisms for Christians. Holy water repulses witches and demons and allows their presence to be revealed.

If a black cat struggles when it is put in a holy water basin, it is a sign that the cat served as a disguise for a witch. Sprinkling a field with holy water in the direction of the four cardinal points chases evil spirits away. If holy water is sprinkled in three corners of a bedroom or loft, the rats will escape by the fourth corner.

Holy water from Easter Sunday chases away sorcerers; holy water from Palm Sunday has the power to ward off storms. Demons have a habit of hiding their treasures in the form of stones and plants: Whoever wets these treasures down with holy water will see them appear in their true form.

On Christmas Eve, the water contained in all holy water basins changes into wine between eleven o'clock and midnight.

Washing your hands in a holy water basin keeps away perspiration in the future. To get rid of warts, dip your hands in a holy water basin— the person who takes some holy water after you will take on the warts. A child who is held high above a holy water basin will grow quickly.

Horseshoe

Along with a four-leaf clover, lizard's tail, and rabbit's foot, a horseshoe is one of the most popular good luck charms. Its name in French, "fer," (iron) confuses it with a sacred and conjuratory metal. In English, the term links it to the lucky symbolism of a shoe. Some see the celestial canopy in its form; Catholics read it as Christ's initial.

The placing of red hot iron on a horse's hoof has a magical and mysterious aspect that has long fascinated imaginations.

The shoeingsmith, anonymous from the 16th c. (Bibl. Nat)

In order for a horseshoe to be a good talisman, it must be found accidentally on a sunken road, its two ends must be directed toward the person who finds it, and its nails must be directed toward the ground. Finding a horseshoe with seven nails still driven into it is ideal.

The horseshoe is hung on the lintel of the front door of a house in order to bring luck and ward off evil spirits. Hung on the mast of a ship, it calms the furor of the elements. Some wear a nail from a horseshoe in jewelry or carry it as a trinket—it is an excellent talisman.

House

Being a sacred enclosure, a house lends itself to all practices aimed at protecting a household from outside, hostile influences. For centuries people have believed that anyone who crosses the threshold of a new house for the first time—and who therefore enters a space that has not been purified—is destined to death and damnation. Formerly, new residents conducted a ritual sacrifice, usually on a human. A man or child was walled-in alive during the construction of a house. The house is sprinkled

"Door Leaf," etching by Bracquemond, 1865 (Bibl. des Arts Décoratifs).

with fresh blood before anyone crosses the threshold. Today, burying a commemorative object and laying of a cornerstone have replaced the practice of immuring. In addition, an animal is sacrificed instead of a human.

In general, these foundation rites preceded a family's installation in a new house. Some rites still deal with a bloody sacrifice. Some people pour he-goat's blood on the threshold before entering a new house. But usually, a rooster's throat is slit and its blood is sprinkled on the front doorstep, then the rooster is eaten. Others throw it outside after plucking it. Still others throw the rooster's head over the roof of the house or rub the outside walls with its blood. In general, red wine replaces a rooster's blood—in Brittany, the ground is wet down with some wine, a little hole dug, and a few drops poured into it. These effusions of blood correspond to a tribute that family members must make in order not to perish in crossing the threshold.

Other rites seek to assure the security of a new house. Three pieces of paper on which the name of God has been written are buried in iron boxes, preferably in the cellar. The boxes must be placed at three corners of the cellar—demons will flee by the fourth corner. Others hide pots and pitchers under the threshold of a house. A pitcher that contains a virgin girl's blouse protects against fires. Sometimes money or animals' bones

318

are incorporated into the walls in order to guarantee prosperity in the house.

The laying of the cornerstone of a house, as we have seen, has a very great importance for the future of the inhabitants. In some regions, the eldest son takes on this task, then taps the stone three times; in other regions, it is the eldest daughter who gives the taps, then kisses the workers.

In the Auvergne region, as soon as a house is completed, people throw a bouquet of flowers on the roof that has also been covered with a few protective tiles decorated with symbolic signs. A tree decorated with ribbons is also set up on the upper part of the roof. Others throw dried fruit or money from the roof to the people gathered below. Sometimes a carpenter throws a glass against a wall: if the glass breaks, it is a sign of happiness in the household. In addition, the head of the family walks so that his shadow is cast across the outside of the house or else he throws tobacco on the ground. Often a family uses the earth from the first hole dug to plant a tree that will grow in the image of the household.

Spell casting object (private coll.).

Once in a new dwelling, you must make the rounds of all the rooms carrying a loaf of bread and a plate of salt to show the evil spirits that you do not fear them. It is advisable, all the same, to ward them off by hanging a cross on the chimney and a horseshoe on the lintels of all outer doors. The first night, farmers put a little holy water or salt in the milk cans to keep witches from souring the milk. In general, weasels and crickets are welcome around a house, but magpies, ravens, and toads bring misfortune.

The evil eye will lurk in a house if one of the construction workers dies during the house's construction. But in any case, it is recommended that you always enter your house with the right foot first. Also, when visiting someone, it is necessary to enter and leave by the same door; whoever neglects this rule takes the proprietor's luck with him when he leaves.

A door that opens on its own announces an undesirable visitor.

If the plants that grow on the roof of a house bear flowers, they will maintain happiness in the household. But lichen have an evil influence. Houseleeks that grow from between the tiles on a roof protect the family from illness, but in England they attract lightning.

A person who has forgotten his keys and finds himself at the door to his house must enter by a window, open the door from inside, go back out through the window, and then enter his house normally.

In order to protect a roof from lightning, light three Candlemas candles or put three coals from a yule log in the fireplace. In order to ward off hail, throw three grains of salt on the threshold.

Abandoned houses are known to shelter phantoms.

Ink

For a long time a form of divination existed based on the shapes and sizes of inkblots that were interpreted in terms of rather simple principles—specialists compared the contours of the blots to forms in nature, animals, or vegetables. Rorschach's psychological test renewed this ancient belief in part.

In any case, making an inkblot while writing a letter is an excellent omen. If you are writing a love letter, it is a sign that the person who will receive it is thinking of you.

Jewelry

Like tattoos and masks, jewelry protects against evil influences. When pierced and worn around the neck, sharks' teeth, pieces of shell, bones, pebbles, and flint formerly played a conjuratory role. Rings worn in the ears, nose, or mouth protected these very sensitive orifices from the actions of demons.

Most jewelry is in the shape of a circle, the symbol of completeness and communion with the universe.

Jewelry influences whoever wears it according to the time it was made, offered, and used. It is linked to the plants, perfumes, seasons, and parts of the body. In China, a boy was covered with necklaces and rings in order to persuade the spirits that he was a girl and therefore not an important prey. In addition, the clinking noise of charms or even little bells chases away forces of Evil. A pregnant woman must remove all her jewelry during childbirth. It brings misfortune to make a copy of a piece of jewelry without following the original exactly.

When worn, pierced earrings cure vision defects. Sailors wear gold rings in their left ears to protect themselves against drowning.

"The Trickster" (detail), by Georges de La Tour (private coll.).

Like all circular jewelry, a necklace suggests a possession. A woman who does not like a man must not accept a necklace as a gift from him.

An open copper bracelet cures rheumatisms. An open bracelet made from a single piece of silver wards off sorcerers and demons.

Endowed with a magical power, a metal ring is an emblem of power received from God or one that is to be delegated to a relative. It signifies an alliance between two clans; an engagement ring precedes a conjugal ring. It is a bad omen to lose or break a wedding ring.

The most well-known magic ring is Solomon's, to which innumerous virtues are attributed, but whose secret remains unknown. A traveller's ring was sold in the Middle Ages—it rivaled seven-league boots. The ring that Gyges wore to conquer the queen of Lydia and kill the king without being seen can still be reconstituted today. Its making is placed under the sign of Mercury, god of thieves, merchants, and travellers, who especially presides over the third day of the week. Therefore, on a Wednesday in spring, a stone found in a hoopoe's nest must be set in a metal ring and the ring engraved: "Jesus, passing through the middle of the water, vanished." Then this ring is placed in a bowl of mercury and wrapped in a colored cloth. Then it is put in a hoopoe's nest for nine days. The ring will make you invisible if the setting is turned toward the outside of your hand and visible if it is turned toward the inside. Another formula recommends braiding hairs from a hyena's head in such a way as to make a ring, then putting this ring in a hoopoe's nest for nine days. But in order to become visible again, this ring must be completely wrapped up. In addition, it is possible to make a ring that counters the effects of this sorcery. A weasel's eye must be set in a lead ring and the ring engraved with "Apparuit Dominus Simoni." This operation must be executed on a Saturday, the day dedicated to Saturn, Mercury's enemy. This counter ring is then wrapped in a funeral shroud and buried in a cemetery for nine days.

A dogfish tooth or malachite that is set in silver and then called a "toad's eye" wards off sorcery.

The value of a ring is linked to the materials used. Some have the function of chasing away spirits, particularly ivory, silver or gold rings, and diamond, coralline, or coral settings. Others are sometimes unlucky. An opal for instance, brings misfortune except to people born in October.

Knights value rings for the seals engraved on them. Solomon's seal, representing the seven elements, and a pentagram, a five pointed star that is divided into six elements, are among the most highly prized figures.

Key

Its double usage for opening and closing, fastening and unfastening, has made the key an emblem of initiation. It is also a sign of power and prosperity—whoever possesses knowledge or wealth, has, in a ring of keys, a key that allows these things to be offered or protected.

Jingling a ring of keys on a Wednesday makes you go crazy: In effect, Wednesday is Mercury's day and he, being both a merchant and a thief, knows the double usage of keys. If, despite all cares taken, a ring of keys insists on rusting, it announces that you are soon going to inherit something.

A key has always been a divinatory object. In the Middle Ages, a key attached to a *Bible* open to the first page of the Gospel of Saint John twirled on its own when the name of a person guilty of a crime was uttered. Still today, a person who loses his way stops at a crossroads, closes his eyes, and tosses his key ring over his left shoulder—the longest key indicates the direction that should be taken.

Illustration by Gustave Doré for Charles Perrault's "Bluebeard" (detail).

This metal object is an excellent talisman; it is always a good idea to carry a key and grab hold of it whenever you come across a phantom, sorcerer, devil, or priest. Touching a key is touching iron! It allows all bewitched objects to be exorcized and returns a werewolf to human form when the werewolf is beaten with it until he bleeds. Slipped under a child's pillow, a key protects him from sorcery.

A small gold key worn crosswise is an excellent talisman. A key of Paradise or key of dreams is very useful when there is a difficult or dangerous choice to be made.

Knife

A traditional instrument of sacrifice, this cold steel menaces and protects according to its characteristics: The tip and the entire knife in a crossed position attract all sorcery, but the metal and sometimes the handle ward off evil powers.

Two knives crossed on a table bring misfortune, due to the accidental forming of a cross, and they are also a sign of hostile intention, because of the customary usage of a knife. In addition, if you offer a knife to a friend, you should also give him a small coin in order to avoid the evil eye or the breaking up of the friendship. Whoever knocks a knife off of a table risks breaking up his current love affair or receiving an undesirable visit. If a knife falls during a meal, it must not be picked up until the meal is over.

Some people consider dust stirred up by tempests to be nothing other than sorcerers; if a well-sharpened knife is tossed into the air, it has every chance of falling back to the ground bloody after having wounded a sorcerer. You must never rest a knife on a table with its cutting edge turned up, because you could wound a wandering soul.

Even though the sign of the cross is made on a loaf of bread before it is broken, it is still unlucky to slice it or stick it with a knife; the same is true for a table.

On the other hand, this iron instrument protects against demons. It can be put under your pillow at night to keep fairies from taking advantage of you by seizing your soul while you are sleeping. Hidden under a window, it keeps the Devil away from a house.

If someone surrounded by friends spins a knife on top of a table, the tip of the knife will designate the person who will die before the others. In some cases, it can indicate a murderer in a gathering of people.

A man who forgets his knife must go get it in person if he doesn't want to attract misfortune to himself.

Whoever gives a dog the first piece of bread cut with a new knife is assured of never losing the knife.

Finally, it is affirmed that a person who has colic will get well quickly if for a few days he eats using a knife with a white handle.

Knot

The expression "to be tied up" brings to mind the idea of conflict that a person cannot seem to manage. Untying is to free yourself from yourself or occult forces. Tying or untying can be positive or negative depending on whether it is a matter of favorable or hostile forces. A hanged man's rope is a universal talisman that bears a slip knot. Tying knots is one of the popular practices of sorcerers who want to cast an evil spell. They knot a groom's codpiece to keep a couple fron consummating their union.

A knot can, however, be a protection: During a tempest, a sailor ties a knot in his clothes; a gambler who wants to attract luck ties a knot in his shirt. Knots are tied in a girl's hair with ribbons or in the form of braids, and a horse's tail and mane are twisted to ward off evil spirits. A lock of a sick person's hair is knotted to aid in his recovery. Before a harvest, it is a good idea to tie a few stalks of wheat together along the edge of the field so that the crop will not be destroyed by bad weather.

A groom goes to the alter with one shoe untied to keep from having an evil spell cast on him. In Russia, a bride's belt bears many knots in order to combat the evil eye. A belt that comes undone is generally a bad omen, but if, during a wedding ceremony, that of the officiating priest comes undone, it foretells that the marriage will be fruitful and that the wife will soon have a child.

During childbirth, anyone who approaches the future mother must undo his or her shoelaces and any other knots that are a part of the clothing. This gesture facilitates delivery. In a coffin the deceased must not have his shoelaces tied. If his shoelaces were tied, his soul would not be able to leave the earth—attached to the terrestrial envelope, the soul would find no peace and would bother the living until it was liberated.

A knot also symbolizes the link between a couple's marriage and fidelity. In certain Mediterranean countries, a husband who must be away from home ties two branches together from two trees near his house. If, upon his return, he finds the knot undone, he knows his wife was unfaithful to him.

If a knot is found in a ball of yarn, two people can take hold of the string on each side of the knot, then pull until the yarn breaks. The person who gets the piece with the knot in it will have a wish come true.

Finally, magical knots exist that allow the wind to be changed: When the first knot is untied, it brings light winds; the second brings gusts of wind; and the third brings a tempest. Some sailors of the north say that, having previously tied three knots in their handkerchief, when they untie the first, it brings a steady wind; the second, a tempest; and the third, perfect calm.

Ladder

Due to the form it creates when it is leaned against a wall, a ladder is invested with a meaning that has no real relation to the object itself. A triangle, an alchemical and an esoteric sign, has since antiquity been reputed to be sacred and to misuse it was supposedly sacrilegious. In general, walking under a ladder brings misfortune because it destroys this triangle. A ladder's usage also confers a symbolic significance on it because it illustrates both a link between the earth and sky, and human effort to elevate itself far from the ground. The rungs indicate landmarks or represent hierarchized levels. We hear of ladders of values, virtues, numbers, life, and so forth. A sacred, traditional ladder has twelve rungs that equal the same number of stages in man's initiation to spiritual values in order to reach heaven.

For some, walking under a ladder cancels all chances of marriage within the year; in Holland, you expose yourself to being hung. In any case, this initiative is dangerous. A few strong-minded people say that in fact you risk having a flower pot or tile fall on your head. In "popular" Christianity, walking under a ladder means you lack respect for the Holy Trinity.

In a case where, by accident, you were not able to avoid this ladder, you must cross your fingers until you encounter a dog. Others spit on their shoes and let the saliva dry on its own. Still others recommend making the sign of the cross.

In the United States, it is even affirmed that a person must not climb up a ladder if a black cat is passing under it.

Stepping or passing between the rungs on a ladder (forming a cross) brings misfortune. In Japan, telegraph wires are avoided for the same reason. If you miss one of the rungs on a ladder, a reverse of fortune awaits you.

Ladders with an odd number of rungs must be avoided—for work, an even numbered ladder is best.

Lamp

Here we are referring to a lamp in the sense of an oil burning lamp, paraffin lamp, or lantern—above all, a lamp draws its powers of prediction or conjuration from fire. Electricity made many of these superstitions obsolete.

A person out for a walk at night must always have a lantern in order to ward off evil spirits. For this same reason, a lamp is left lit at the head of a newborn or dying person's bed. It is a good idea to leave lamps lit in the house on the eve of All Souls' Day.

"The Alarm Sounder," drawn and engraved by Schuler, 1861 (Bibl. des Arts Déco)

You must cross yourself if, while standing in the street, you see a lamp glowing at the head of a dying person's bed. This flame must never be put out—it must die on its own after the dying person draws his last breath. If you approach the lantern of someone who is sleeping, you will kill him.

Three lamps lit in the same room announce an approaching death in the house; some see it as a sign of an upcoming marriage. A young woman who wants to get married must make the man she has elected stand immobile between three lamps. It is necessary that she light the lamps herself and that the man not budge for the amount of time it takes to recite a rosary.

A lamp that hisses or flickers lets you know that death is roaming around near by.

Musical Instruments

Music, being of sacred essence, reflects the harmony of the world. Since it is detested by the Devil, it has the ability to ward off evil spirits. A herdsman or shepherd plays a Pan pipe or shepherd's pipe in his solitude to protect himself and his flock. In Germany, a house in which no one plays a musical instrument is said to be inhabited by wicked people.

Hearing music, but not knowing where it is coming from, is a sign of a privileged contract with the world of gods. Hearing music in a dream is a good omen of peace and accord with friends and relatives. But the sound of a fife or flute in the early hours of the day announces a quarrel or turmoil. A flute can even be of diabolical origin: With the sound of his instrument, the Pied Piper of Hamelin saved the town from rats, but when refused payment, he lured the children into the mountains.

Only musicians are allowed to use the word "string" in a theatre, but only under the condition that they use it in an expression, for instance "violin string" or "piano string."

Nail

Like all metal objects, a nail wards off evil forces. It is, however, also linked to suffering—a nail, like a crown of thorns, is one of the emblems of the Crucifixion.

Finding a nail in your path brings good luck, especially if the nail is rusty; you must keep it with you or drive it into your kitchen door. As a general rule, it is good to drive nails into the door of your house in such a

*"The Piper," engraving on copper by
Albrecht Dürer, 1514.*

way that they represent a cross. In order to be protected against telluric, evil forces, some people bury little boxes full of nails under their house.

A nail has a certain curative power: it takes on morbid forces and allows vital forces to be concentrated. Driving a nail into a tree assures the tree of proper growth. The Romans stuck metal nails into trees or walls in order to get rid of an ill.

Whoever wants to cure himself of a toothache must drive a nail into a tree or wall of a house with all his strength. In Alsace, a person's gum is stuck with a nail until the nail is covered with blood. Then the nail is stuck in a place protected from sunlight or moonlight. A few days later the toothache will be gone.

A person who hurts himself with a nail must drive the nail into an oak to keep the wound from festering.

A nail from a crucifix must be placed on an epileptic's arm in order to calm him. Driven into a bedroom door, nails from a coffin ward off nightmares. It is also a good idea to nail one over a newborn's cradle.

Needle

Being very useful to sorcerers who stick it into little figures resembling those they wish to bewitch, a needle harms all it touches. You must stick yourself with it before offering or loaning it to a friend because it has the power to break up relationships.

A tailor, anonymous from the 16th c. (Bibl. Nat.)

Uttering the word "needle" when getting up in the morning brings misfortune. It is a very bad omen to find one in the street, especially if it is stuck into a spool of black thread.

A seamstress who breaks a needle while she is sewing a bridal gown casts a serious shadow of doubt on the happiness of the future couple. In contrast, it is an excellent sign if she sticks herself; the spot of blood left on the cloth is the only impurity tolerated on the virginal gown.

A needle used to sew a shroud is highly sought after for casting evil spells. Placed under a table or plate, it kills the appetite of fellow diners.

This object also has a prophetic value. A pregnant woman who finds a needle on the ground will have a girl; if she finds a pin, she will have a boy. A young woman looking for a husband sticks seven needles into a lit candle and prays to the Holy Virgin until the wick is consumed. She then obtains the love of the man of her dreams or makes him impotent with other women. In order to know when she will marry, she can wipe a needle with her hand, hold it at both ends, and throw it into a fountain. If the needle floats, she will get married soon.

Net

A gladiator's weapon and part of a fisherman's gear, a net stimulates superstitious imagination especially through the surprising treasures and unknown wonders that can be seized between its stitches. Legends about "miraculous catches of fish" are abundant in sacred and popular literature.

A girl who in public mends her future husband's net by herself offends him because it signifies her desire to manage the household.

On All Saints' Day, it is believed that nets can draw in only corpses.

In certain regions of Yorkshire, a small coin is placed in one of the knots in a net to thank the god Neptune for his generous gifts.

Oven

Like a basket, an oven must never remain empty, because the inhabitants of the house risk experiencing famine one day. Many families still today leave an empty plate in an oven when it is not in use.

If an oven for baking bread is to draw well for an entire year, three box branches, blessed during high Mass, must be burned in it on Palm Sunday.

Pin

It defines itself in relation to a needle according to a principle that illustrates a popular superstition very well: A pregnant woman who finds a needle will have a girl; if she finds a pin, she will have a boy.

In general, however, a woman must not pick up a pin by its point if she is pregnant, because her milk will dry up after the birth of her child. It is, however, a good omen to find a pin on the ground; it is even recommended that it be kept as a talisman. If, at the moment it is noticed, it is pointed toward you, it is, on the contrary, a bad omen. But if it is pointed in any other direction, it indicates the road from which fortune will come.

A pin must never be offered or exchanged unless you have stuck yourself with it or obliged the person to whom you are giving it to stick himself or herself with this gift. When you absolutely cannot refuse loaning it, you must turn your back and let the person find it and pick it up by the head.

Whoever steals a pin from a bridal gown is assured of getting married within the year. But a bride must not have a single pin stuck in her dress during the wedding ceremony, or her family will feel the effects of it. Once outside the church, a bent pin, on the contrary, is an excellent talisman for a young, new bride—it will bring her luck and happiness.

A pin used in making a shroud is valued as an amulet against fear. It must be worn on the inside of your jacket collar. But if it is used in other sewing, it brings death.

Pitchfork

This emblem of the Devil (his shoes copy its shape) imprisons a victim between its big teeth. It must, therefore, be stuck in the ground so that the Devil cannot steal it.

Peasants turn pitchforks upside down in a barn in order to keep witches away.

It is advisable to lightly stick one of your fingers with a tooth from a new pitchfork before you use it for the first time.

Plane

Due to its character and dangers, this recent means of transport inspires as many superstitions as ships used to. Although it allows man to realize his ancient dreams to fly, it also frightens him because it mixes him with an unknown and long-time feared element.

A certain number of rites precede boarding a plane, especially among crew members. On the ground, they avoid uttering words such as "crash" or "explosion." Most of them wear various talismans or fetishes and refuse to put flowers, especially if they are red or white, in the plane. Pilots touch wood, but that of a living tree, and not of a table or chair. They cross the seatbelts in the empty seats.

Every accident is followed by two other catastrophes.

When getting out of a plane, the pilot empties his pockets as a sacrificial gift.

Passengers sometimes fear getting on a plane and multiply the gestures for warding off evil spells: They cross their fingers, pick a four-leaf clover, make the sign of the cross, and so forth.

Plate

Breaking plates wards off evil spirits who cannot tolerate the noise. On a wedding day, this act prepares a couple for a radiant future.

Eating off a cracked plate is a good omen, but rotating the plate in front of you on a table brings misfortune.

A plate must never be set on a table upside down, because the person it is meant for will be destined to die soon.

On holidays, an extra plate is left on the table for a passerby or a vagabond so that no revengeful jealousy is created.

On the eve of a funeral, the deceased's family adds a plate to the supper table so that the deceased can build up strength before the long journey.

Plow

This tool participates in the sowing and fecundation of the earth. A plow is protected from evil spells by its metal share, but it is a good idea to have it blessed and to respect it. A plow must never be walked over because all the terrain it works afterward risks becoming infertile. A farmer who abandons his plow in the fields for winter will see his land infested with wolves.

When a baby's navel refuses to heal up, a plowshare must be buried and five Lord's Prayers recited.

Pot

Earthen pots, jars, and pitchers are molds in which liquids and foods are contained or stored. Often being porous, earthenware radiates and transmits the forces that it contains to the surrounding environment.

In order to protect fields from late frosts, a jar containing twelve crayfish in river water can be buried in the middle of them. A jar that contains a frog and a magic formula and is buried in a field protects the seeds from the appetites of birds. When the crops have grown, the jar must be thrown away.

In Central Europe, a woman can break an earthen pot while thinking of the man she loves. She will be happy with him for as many years as there are pieces. A girl who sinks a pitcher in a fountain will marry in as many years as there are bubbles that surface.

Pothook

Hanging a pothook was for a long time an actual practice that concerned a family with the setting up of a caldron in the hearth and that was valued as a foundation rite.

Just as a pothook is being hung, a fire is lit into which seven grains of salt are thrown to keep away sorcerers. Holy water sometimes replaces salt. However, when a fire refuses to catch, salt must be put on the pothook to induce it.

All new animals on a farm—hens, cats, and dogs—are brought before the pothook before actually being accepted into the family.

When it is storming, some prefer to throw the pothook out a window rather than attract lightning.

Ribbon

Like embroidery and jewelry, a ribbon has a conjuratory value in addition to its esthetic function. A ribbon is both a ring, when it is tied around a head, and a knot, when used to tie hair. A headband is, like a turban or crown, a sign of wisdom, distinction, and virtue. For Moslems, a turban can be red or white, but green is prohibited.

A silk ribbon or scarf worn around the neck helps to combat illnesses. Worn around the head, it must be red if it is to bring happiness, but colored ones must never be worn once night has fallen because they attract evil spirits. In order to cure a migraine, you must tie a ribbon

333

around your head; some specify that it must previously have been worn by the man or woman that you love.

A ribbon in your hair protects against evil spells and signifies virginity. In some regions, only girls are allowed to wear them.

Rod

This emblem of power and clairvoyance allowed Moses to make a spring pour forth from a rock. It permits both punishment and knowledge (sorcerers outline magic circles with the end of a rod). Priests use a baton to delineate the portion of the heavens to be consulted. A divining rod directs man or serves as a conduit to its hidden forces. A simple touch from a rod eases pain.

There are two kinds of rods. The first is forked and must be made of wood from a hazel, apple, beech, or alder tree. Some specify that it must be nineteen inches long. You must hold the forked end with both hands and let yourself be led where it directs you. Besides leading you to springs and underground pools, it reveals the presence of ores and buried treasures. It also betrays assassins and thieves.

A straight rod or "magic wand" in the hand of a magician or fairy transforms men into toads and pumpkins into coaches.

A caduceus is a rod intertwined with two snakes. A symbol of power and knowledge, it represents a doctor's scepter. Its touch alone cures the sick. Formerly a king's scepter had the power to cure king's evil or scrofula.

Rope

First of all, a rope evokes ascension toward the celestial world. It is also the image of a link that unites or strangles. These two aspects have made rope a magical object in all civilizations—African sorcerers transformed rope into a snake or a stick at will. In Scandinavian regions, a sorcerer has the power to tie a knot in the wind. He ties three knots in a rope: When he unties the first knot, he liberates the wind from the West; the second, that from the North; untying the third knot unleashes a tempest. A sailor can have the same power, but he only needs his handkerchief.

Usually a rope has a very bad reputation to the point where the use of the word itself is prohibited on board ships and in theatres. (The first stagehands were often former sailors.) The origin of this taboo can perhaps be found in the practice of death by hanging that, in the West at least, was

The hanging of Judas (Notre Dame-des-Fontaines, La Brigue).

the infamous punishment reserved for criminals. Let us note that hanging also evokes suicide and this act has always been considered to be of diabolical nature by religious minds. By a curious reversal, although the word "rope" is prohibited, the object is sought after as one of the most precious talismans: Provided it actually brought on death, a hanged man's rope brings happiness and luck to whoever possesses it. Put in contact with a sore tooth, it promotes recovery.

Saucepan

Caldrons and kettles are the accessories of devils and sorcerers. Saucepans are their pale substitutes. Some people do, however, attribute them with powers of divination.

Whoever wishes to know the fate of a dead person's soul can shut a black cat up in a copper saucepan for one day. If the cat is alive the next morning, you can be assured that the soul is in Heaven or Purgatory; if the cat is dead, the soul is damned. A girl who wipes the bottom of a saucepan with a piece of bread will never find a husband. She who leaves a tea kettle on the fire with the spout turned toward the wall will meet with the same fate.

Scale

This instrument of justice allows sins to be weighed.

A virgin can sit down on one side of a scale without unbalancing it.

A woman who weighs more than a *Bible* will be burned like a witch!

An accused man whose weight increases between the beginning and end of his trial is guilty.

A sick person is put on one side of a scale and his weight in rye or wheat on the other. When the scale begins to tip toward the side of the grain, the doctor can leave, because the illness has changed sides.

A newborn must not be weighed—it is not proper to measure God's gifts.

Scissors

By their form (a cross), their matter (cold metal), their configuration (sharpened edges), and the primitive usage that they suggest (castration), scissors belong to an essentially negative register.

In Africa, whoever opens and closes a pair of scissors during a wedding ceremony makes the groom impotent.

Just as for a needle or a knife, you must stick yourself with a pair of scissors before giving them to a friend; it is preferable to sell or exchange them because they have the power to cut actual bonds.

It is inadvisable to close a pair of scissors immediately after using them, but they must not be left open on a table because it is a sign of hate or vengeance. Whoever drops a pair of scissors on the ground cannot pick them up himself without exposing himself to misfortune. The person who risks picking them up in his place does so with caution and rubs them to make them warm before using them again. In addition, if these scissors fall and the tips stick into the ground, they presage an approaching death. If they fall open, they announce a catastrophe or great worries.

A child's nails are never cut with scissors. The mother must bite them off, otherwise her baby will become a thief.

Scythe

Blind and irrevocable, a scythe is the image of the equality of all in the face of death. It was not until the 15th century that it became a tool of Death. Any scythe found abandoned in a field is a mark of death. It is preferable to make the sign of the cross and then get away from it.

A sickle, curved and crescent-shaped, is linked to the idea of fertility and harvesting. It is a ritual instrument—the Druids used a gold sickle to gather mistletoe from sacred oaks.

The first time you use a sickle, you must cut yourself with it lightly and draw a drop of blood if it is to be an effective and not wound again. Also, the first tuft of grass cut with a sickle must be offered to a cow or ox.

A sickle stuck in a roof protects a house from lightning. Two crossed sickles placed at the foot of a cradle protect the newborn.

Shirt

Being both a garment and undergarment, a shirt sticks to the skin— changing your shirt is like changing your skin. It was, like shoes, one of the first goods on earth. A poor man doesn't even have a shirt, and a saint gives his to the unfortunate.

Wearing another person's shirt means you assume his sins or take on his powers. A father's shirt put on his child protects the child from evil spirits and sustains his growth. On the day of a baptism, which corresponds to a purification ceremony, the godfather must always wear a clean, if not new, shirt to church. This clean garment is, in addition, a mark of respect.

After a child is born, his or her shirt is thrown into a fountain: If it floats, the child will be in good health; if it sinks, the contrary is feared. The same signs are used to find out the evolution of a child's illness. Finally, a pregnant woman can place a girl's shirt and a boy's shirt in a spring—the first shirt to sink announces the sex of the child she is expecting.

Like all clothing, it is a good omen to accidentally put a shirt on backwards, but a bad omen to put it on inside out or button it wrong. It is

*"The Little Laundress," by Pierre Bonnard,
Lithography, 1896.*

recommended that you cross yourself when you change your shirt and
that you avoid taking this hygenic measure on a Friday. If this rule proves
to be inapplicable, it is best to choose a blue shirt and not a white one. But
in any case, if this article of clothing is sewn on a Friday, it attracts lice.

Shoe

Like many everyday garments, a shoe is identified with the part of the
body to which it corresponds. In the case of the foot, this link confers a
quasi-magical significance on a boot or slipper for instance. Walking on
and plowing the earth are ways of appropriating the ground; a shoe, from
then on, becomes a symbol of explicit property. This possession can concern anything that is linked to the shoe itself and not just to the foot.
Formerly, a shoe was believed to serve in concluding contracts or pacts in
the same way as a written or oral promise. For a long time a shoe was
identified with a man's liberty: Slaves walked barefooted as a sign of
humiliation, because, by definition, they possessed nothing, and only a
well-shod traveller could allow himself to experience the world. From
this constraint, which has disappeared, was undoubtedly born the myth of
the seven league boots, which with one step covered an enormous
amount of ground. The legend of Cinderella's glass slipper illustrates very
well the identity established between a foot's owner and its shoe: The

young girl was only recognized or unveiled by her second shoe. Finally, the virtues with which old shoes are adorned seem to lead to the same conclusion—it is believed that a man's experience is communicated to the used article of clothing.

Tradition demands that an old shoe be tied to the back of a newlywed couple's car. This custom perpetuates an older tradition: A father must toss an old shoe on the couple to signify to the groom that his daughter has become the groom's property. In this way a bride was passed from her parents' authority to that of her husband. In order to assure himself of keeping his bride, the groom placed one of her shoes at the foot of their bed on their wedding night. A young bride who, on the contrary, wished to wear the pants in the family arranged to take off her husband's shoes on their wedding night.

An old shoe is also adorned with magical virtues. In Scotland, an old sandal is tossed behind a person suspected of sorcery. Camel drivers protect their beasts by hanging an old shoe called "Hussein's shoe" on their camels.

Some people affirm that shoes must never be offered to a friend, but others say that whoever has not given this gift at least once in his life will wander in Purgatory barefooted. A child's first shoes must be made of wolfskin in order to protect him or her against chilblains and evil spells. In Great Britain, if a new pair of shoes squeak too much, it is believed that their owner didn't pay for them.

In the morning, it is advisable to always put the right shoe on first in order to finish with the left, which brings happiness. But putting a shoe on the wrong foot or walking with only one shoe on attracts misfortune. In Jewish tradition, whoever hobbles around with one shoe on brings death to one of his relatives.

Shoes must not be left turned upside down on the ground—a quarrel might break out in the house. Likewise, it is a bad omen to leave them crossed one on top of the other. Anyone who sneezes while putting shoes on in the morning must spit immediately to chase away the demons. Some even spit directly into their right shoe, then warm it up again before putting it on.

If, on New Year's Day, you toss your shoe into the air and it falls to the floor right side up pointed to one side, it announces engagement within the year. If it is pointed toward you, it presages marriage, but if it is pointed toward the door, there will be a few extra months of waiting. In order to keep death away from a house, a shoe must be turned upside down on the threshold of the front door.

Some burn on old shoe in their fireplaces in order to guard their houses against epidemics. Lovers avoid giving each other shoes—this gift will bring them unhappiness. In addition, a pair of shoes on a table presages either a hanging (death in general) or a family dispute.

Before tossing a bouquet, a bride threw one of her shoes in the air for her bridesmaids; the one who caught it was assured of getting married within the year. Formerly, in Russia, a groom's napkin from the wedding dinner was folded into the shape of a shoe and the bride's napkin was folded into the shape of a swan.

In Japan, it is affirmed that new sandals must never be worn for the first time at five o'clock in the afternoon.

In Alsace, the village priest can toss his shoe into the air in order to divert hail away from the region.

A dead person should never wear clogs, because he will hurt himself in entering Paradise. But if a person is too long in dying, his clogs are filled with dirt.

SHOELACE

Whoever forgets to tie his or her shoelaces will have a good day. In contrast, not fastening your left shoe brings misfortune, whereas this same negligence on the right side brings luck. It is a good sign to find a knot in your shoelaces. If you notice that your left shoelace is undone, it means that someone is speaking ill of you. In the case of the right shoelace, on the contrary, someone is praising you.

When lacing someone else's shoes, make a wish—it has every chance of being granted.

You must never wear one shoe with a brown shoelace, color of the earth in the cemetery, and one with a black shoelace, the color of death.

Shroud

Like a coffin, a shroud serves to protect the deceased as much as the living. Being pure white, it wards off deadly powers; when it is well sewn, it keeps the deceased's soul from coming back to trouble the living. Being the deceased's ultimate garment, it covers his skeleton or nudity when he reappears in the form of a phantom.

A dead person must never be put in his shroud on a table in his room—there will soon be another death in the family. A shroud must be well sewn without leaving any gaps through which the deceased's soul can escape; after this operation, it is a good idea to close up the end of the shroud with a pin.

A needle that was used to sew or hem a shroud must be saved. When worn, it wards off fear, but if a sorcerer gets hold of it, he can use it for his sorcery. Placed under a plate, it keeps a guest from eating; placed under a table, it kills the appetites of all fellow diners. When pinning a shroud, if you stick yourself and you bleed, it means that the deceased held a grudge that he was not able to gratify. It is a good idea to have a Mass said for his peace.

The hem of a shroud must be torn, never cut—it then has great therapeutic virtues. Worn around the arm or neck, it cures a fever; tied around the waist, it calms stomachaches.

Silverware

The custom of setting a table by placing the knife and the fork on either side of a plate—the sides vary according to societies—seems to be especially linked to the symbolism of a knife. Formerly, a person would hold his knife in his hand while eating, but in order not to look like he was threatening his neighbor or after him for some reason, he placed this piece of silverware alongside his plate. It is a bad omen to put a knife in the middle of a table. Likewise, crossing a knife and fork on a plate is of no consequence, but on the table, this negligence brings misfortune. Whoever drops a piece of silverware can expect company during the day.

In England, some believe that when a knife drops, a man is calling for help; when a fork drops, a woman is calling; and when a spoon drops, a child is babbling somewhere.

Smoke

Being a link between the earth and sky, smoke carries the scent of the perfumes or sacrifices that are burned to honor the gods. Smoke never directs itself toward a place without reason—it precedes fate. Smoke also serves as a language for the American Indians: It permitted communication both near and far and was used in concluding peace treaties.

When a man dies, his mattress is burned at a crossroads: If the smoke goes straight up, you can be assured that the deceased's soul is in Paradise; after that the smoke directs itself toward the house where the next death will take place.

So that a fireplace doesn't make a room all smoky, you must take the precaution of spitting on the log before putting it in the fireplace. If, during the day, a stranger was ill-received in a house, a sharp and malodorous smoke that will be impossible to dissipate will shoot out of the hearth.

When a smoker accidentally makes a ring with the smoke he

Sorcerers in Corrèze, engraving from the end of the 19th c. (Bibl. des Arts Déco.)

exhales, it is a good omen for him and those around him; others see it as the halo of a new saint in Heaven. In England, it is sometimes said that in a gathering of people, smoke follows beauty.

Snare

Poachers are, like all hunters, very superstitious people. Whoever sets a snare must follow very specific rites; otherwise, the snare will catch no game. A snare is usually made of iron wire, a beneficent matter, but it also has a slip knot, a death object that evokes hanging.

A good hunter never loans his snares because they will lose their power. He also blows on them before setting them.

Snares meant for capturing birds must not be left near a fire or they will catch nothing but toads. Snares must never be set while the Angelus is tolling, or on Christmas night you risk imprisoning a devil. The night of Saint John, on the contrary, is very favorable for setting snares.

Spade

No one should bring a spade into a house over his shoulder—this signifies that a grave is being dug for one of the inhabitants.

You must never use a gravedigger's spade in your own garden.

Greeting someone with a spade in your hand attracts death to the person unless he or she responds by tossing a few dirt clods in the gardener's direction.

Spoon

Stirring a spoon in a cup with your left hand takes seven years off of your life. Two spoons in the same pot or plate announce a marriage in the family. In Scotland, the hand that a baby uses for grabbing onto a spoon for the first time is said to be an indication of the future: Good fortune awaits him or her if the right hand is used, misfortune awaits if the left hand is used.

If a spoon falls from a cup and lands upside down, you can expect a surprise; if it lands right side up, it foretells disappointments.

Stairway

Its symbolism is close to that of a ladder, but being less aerial, a stairway can also lead to an alchemist's lab. A stairway is generally felt to be a place of danger.

As a general rule, it is not good to pass another person on a stairway. It is preferable to wait on the landing or until the other person is at your level and cross your fingers. If you want to avoid any risk of falling, cross yourself before using a stairway. Tripping on a stairway is traditionally considered a bad omen. Some optimists prefer to see it as the announcement of an approaching marriage in the house.

Stocking

A woman who puts on a stocking inside out in the morning will experience a quarrel during the day, but it is also said to be a good omen. She who puts on both stockings inside out will quarrel with her lover three days in a row. Wearing two socks or stockings of different colors protects against sorcery. This formula is especially effective if the stockings are old. It is a good omen to put the left stocking on first. If your toes go into the heel by accident, a letter awaits you.

When socks or stockings fall down on your legs for no reason, someone is thinking of you.

It brings misfortune to finish putting a stocking on one leg before starting the other.

"Alfred! Alfred!" (detail), lithography by Maurin (Bibl. Nat.).

If two holes or runs appear in a stocking at the same time, you can expect a gift within the week.

A nylon stocking taken from a girl's leg and wrapped around your neck cures anginas.

Your stockings or socks must be hung at the foot of your bed if you fear nightmares.

If stockings twist in drying, it is a sign of happiness or love.

String

Most talismans are attached by a new string whose color varies in terms of an amulet's symbolism. In addition, a string is often seen as a link: in the Far East, the image of marriage is illustrated by a genie who ties two red silk threads together, joining the destinies of the two spouses in a single element. Also, a bride and groom's wrists are joined together with a white cotton string.

If a thread knots when you are mending a garment, it is a sign of a dispute. If it wraps around the needle, it foretells health and fortune for the seamstress. Whoever breaks her thread three times in a row while sewing must abandon her work. Finally, dark thread must not be used to mend a light-colored garment.

Certain strings have curative virtues, particularly against warts. In order to get rid of this scourge, all that is necessary is to wrap a red string around your finger three times, then throw the string on the ground; whoever picks it up "catches" the illness. Some people prefer to use a black string and wrap it, in the same way, around the wart, then throw it in a grave during a burial—when the string rots, the wart disappears. A red string also stops a bloody nose if the string is tied around the little finger on the hand that corresponds to the bleeding nostril.

You risk experiencing a year of poverty if you cut a string for no reason.

Fairies weave gossamer (in French, "Threads of the Virgin") between tree trunks along paths. When a person out walking touches this thread, he or she must give a sign to signify sadness.

Sweater

Formerly, garlic merchants of Paris marketplaces wore only this woolen garment.

Whoever puts his arms in the sleeves of a sweater or pullover before putting his head through the neck is assured of never dying by drowning. It is a good omen to accidentally put a sweater on backwards. A hole in a sweater brings happiness, but you must be careful not to mend a light colored pullover with dark thread—it attracts evil spells.

Table

A dining room table remains a sacred place around which a family unites like the twelve apostles at the Last Supper. Those gathered must always number more or less than thirteen people; otherwise, one of the fellow diners will be destined to die soon.

Undoubtedly in reference to this moment in Christ's life, it is recommended that a person always keep the same place at the table once one has been assigned. A young girl seated at the corner of a table will never marry. She who sits down to the table while talking to her fiance will never marry him.

A child must never crawl under a table, because he or she will not live; in order to conjure this spell, the child must be made to crawl under it again in the other direction.

A stranger who leans his hip against the family dining table must excuse himself immediately because this person is being irreverent toward the spirit of the household.

Telephone

This apparatus has taken on such importance in modern life that it often replaces visits. We might well have added the following phrase to all omens of news or visits: ". . . or else announce a phone call shortly!" Its ring has often taken the place of the chime of a clock and can give rise to the same interpretations.

Some people and animals are reputed to have a presentiment of phone calls and are never wrong.

When the telephone rings and there is no one on the other end, it could be death looking for you. Practical jokes must never be played with this apparatus.

Towel

In general, a towel or napkin is not to be loaned. If two lovers dry themselves with the same piece of cloth, they have every chance of separating in the coming days, and two friends will have an argument.

When a napkin or towel is dropped, it is a sign that a visitor is going to arrive. In order to conjure this fate, you must walk over the cloth backward.

In returning from a burial, all the guests wash their hands. The last person to wipe his or her hands on the towel puts it on the windowsill—when the wind carries it off, it is a sign that the deceased's soul has arrived in Heaven.

Trivet (or Three-Legged Stool)

Less stable than a chair or a footstool, a three-legged stool is a sacred piece of furniture. It was from a trivet that Pythia of Delphi delivered her oracles.

More commonplace, a farmer milks his cows seated on a trivet. It allows him to remain insensitive to sorcery that otherwise might be cast on him.

If a metal trivet on a fire has nothing on top of it, an old belief says that the horses on the farm will quickly turn white. This is undoubtedly due to the sacrilegious character of the act that shows respect for neither the number three nor fire.

Alchemists often set their retorts on trivets—here you also find a connection between the number three and fire.

Umbrella

Like the parasol of tropical or temperate regions, an umbrella remains associated with the sun and with royalty, who for a long time had a monopoly on umbrellas. It is perhaps for this reason that it is particularly dangerous to open an umbrella between the four walls of a room that already screen sunlight. Opening an umbrella outside when the weather is nice brings on rain.

Whoever accidentally drops an umbrella must not pick it up. This especially applies to young women—they will never marry.

Undergarments

More than a coat or dress, undergarments identify with the body they touch directly. This proximity also explains why they are sometimes the object of rather lewd superstitions.

When a girl's petticoat or slip hangs below her dress, it is said to be a sign that her father loves her more than he loves her mother. In addition, if one of her undergarments creeps up for no reason, it is proof that she is dreaming about her lover. In the case of a married woman, this incident foretells problems in her marriage. In contrast, if a pregnant woman's pregnancy belt slips down around her knees, it presages a painless and easy childbirth.

It is not advisable to mend undergarments without taking them off first—lazy people will be punished during the day. Whoever obtains an article of lingerie from a recently married woman will be at the alter within the year.

A girl must place a few valerian leaves in her bra or panties in order to attract men.

In Portugal, women wear seven petticoats in order to ward off the evil eye. A new bride puts on three petticoats on the evening of her wedding: She takes the first one off that night, the second on the day after, and the third on the day after that when the marriage is actually consummated. This practice of abstinence allows a dead soul to be saved from Purgatory. A girl must put one of her petticoats under her pillow in order to dream of her future husband.

Formerly, custom obligated a husband to pay any debts acquired by his wife before the wedding. For this reason, undoubtedly, it is affirmed that a woman who goes to the alter wearing nothing but her dress will be happy all her life.

Walking Stick

It is made according to an ancestral formula that protects a traveller against highwaymen, ferocious or poisonous beasts, and rabid dogs. An elder branch forms the body of the stick and must be collected on All Souls' Day. Then, it is hollowed out and a powder or wolf's eye, a dog's tongue and heart, three green lizards, and three swallows' hearts are put in it. Seven vervain leaves gathered on the eve of Saint John and a stone from a hoopoe's nest are also added. This stick, corked with a box tree cone, immunizes men who use it to help support their weight while walking.

Hung on the door of a house, a walking stick guarantees good luck. Sometimes it is made of glass and filled with sand, white seeds, or hair. It then fascinates any evil spirits that have come into a house so much that they forget their plans.

Weapons

Since the most distant time, weapons have been, more than tools of war, sacred objects. A knife is used to slit the throat of a human being or animal that is being offered to the gods. A shield is as protective by its shape as by the signs and designs drawn on it; the designs have the value of talismans. Likewise, the blades of swords are engraved with formulas that guarantee the death of an adversary. A weapon is an emblem of power, like a scepter or a ring. An archbishop gives a king a blessed sword at the time of the king's coronation. King Arthur's sword, Excalibur, was equal to the greatest sacred symbols. Making a sword was more than just hammering it out—it was giving it a soul. It shares the privilege with bells and boats of having a Christian name. Let us also note that a sword is baptized by the blood that it spills—in a sense it is deflowered. Arms makers used to be magicians.

A simple touch of a sword that had cut off a head and was then dipped in wine cured and protected against fevers. Brandished about a pregnant woman's belly, it facilitates childbirth. Sailors often placed a naked sword at the top of a ship's mast in order to avoid the risk of shipwreck.

An oath taken on a sword cannot be broken; the hilt, in effect, forms a cross with the handle.

A rifle with poor aim was reputed to be bewitched. In order to conjure the spell, the barrel was cleaned with an artemisia liqueur made on May 5. Blessed bullets were shot into the air in order to conjure storms and kill the sorcerer who brought them on.

Sorcery by a bow, engraving on wood taken from a work from 1489 (Bibl. de l'Ancienne Faculté de Médecine de Paris).

Arrows were shot into the air during lunar eclipses in order to destroy the monsters that were attempting to devour the moon. In certain regions, an arrow that had already been used to kill was shot into the roof of a house to assist a dying person's soul in escaping.

An axe is more complex because it is both an executioner's weapon and a work instrument of honest woodcutters. Woodcutters had their axes placed beside them in their coffins so that they could defend themselves in the beyond. No axe should be brought into a house—it risks bringing in death. A tradition had it that flocks should be made to cross over an axe to protect them from epidemics.

349

Well

Unlike spring water, well water gushes up secretly. A well that links three elements—air, earth, and water—can however, reach infernal regions. Because it is a source of life and knowledge, you cannot hide from it. It is proper to both fear and respect it.

In order to keep a well from drying up, you must make an offering of a piece of bread every New Year's Day.

It is always possible to confide a very confidential secret to a very deep well. It is necessary to act by moonlight and to speak to your own reflection. But, if surrounding willows or reeds hear, they will repeat it in all directions.

A person who suffers from a toothache can draw water from a very deep well at dawn—his pain will be soothed.

Window

Placed under the sign of the cross, windows, by letting purifying sunlight penetrate, stop evil spirits. Still, werewolves and vampires take advantage of this opening for getting out of a house.

Windows in a dying person's room are opened because the deceased's soul can also use this passageway.

Certain rites for conjuring fevers demand that the sick person leave the house at dawn through an open window—if a door is used, the fever will penetrate into the house again. A stillborn child's coffin is taken out of the house through a window—if it went through a doorway, it might contaminate the next pregnant woman to pass over the threshold.

A funeral that is passing by must never be watched through a window, or you will take the place of the deceased.

The cords that draw curtains over a window should have an acorn on the end of them to protect the house from storms (an oak, being a sacred tree, cannot, in effect, be struck by lightning).

Shutters that slam shut with a single blow for no reason are, in general, considered to be bad omens.

INDEX